One by one

by / por
Edward R. Rosset

Written by / Escrito por:
Edward R. Rosset
Member of the Bachelor of Arts Association
of Euskadi.
Miembro del Colegio de Licenciados de Filosofía y
Letras de Euskadi

Published by / Editado por:
Editorial Stanley

Layout / Diseño y Maquetación:
Angela Gómez Martín

Front page design / Diseño portada:
Diseño Irunés S.L.

© *Editorial Stanley*
Apdo. 207 - 20302 IRUN - SPAIN
Telf. (943) 64 04 12 - Fax. (943) 64 38 63

ISBN: 84-7873-327-2
Dep. Leg. BI-2129-04

First edition / Primera edición 1996
Reprinted / Reimpresión 1998
Reprinted / Reimpresión 2000
Reprinted / Reimpresión 2001
Reprinted / Reimpresión 2004

Printers / Imprime:
Imprenta Berekintza

Introducción

English Verbs one by one es un libro para los estudiantes de inglés que quieran tener una referencia a la hora de conjugar un verbo en ese idioma.

En este libro se les muestra la construcción de un verbo, tiempo por tiempo, y en sus cuatro formas posibles: afirmativa, interrogativa, negativa e interrogativa-negativa.

Aquí el estudiante encontrará cincuenta y tres verbos, conjugados en su totalidad, que sirven de modelo para todos los demás. Sólo hay que mirar el número de referencia y ver el modelo que corresponde.

Este libro es también apropiado para los profesores que quieran explicar a los alumnos la conjugación de los verbos de una forma sencilla.

TEMAS:

El libro se divide en varios apartados. En el primero están todos los verbos auxiliares o defectivos; diferencias entre el **MAKE** y el **DO**; el **SAY** y el **TELL**; la diferencia entre el **GOING TO form** y el **WILL**; diferencias en la escritura de algunas formas verbales entre el inglés británico y el americano; la explicación y uso de todos y cada uno de los tiempos.

En la segunda parte están conjugados tanto en forma afirmativa como negativa e interrogativa los 53 verbos que sirven de modelo a todos los demás. También se pone la primera persona de cada tiempo en español. Hay un verbo modelo en forma continua; otro en voz pasiva.

Así mismo, se conjugan los defectivos **Can-could, Must, May-Might** y el verbo **There to be.**

La tercera parte corresponde a las listas de verbos irregulares, y todos los verbos regulares.

El índice muestra dónde encontrar cada una de estas secciones.

No hemos incluido un apartado de verbos compuestos (PHRASAL VERBS) debido a su extensión y particular temática. Para el que quiera profundizar en esos verbos aconsejamos el libro GUIDE TO PHRASAL VERBS, de esta misma editorial.

El autor.

Index · Índice general

Part one
Primera Parte

To be

1. El verbo to be se usa:

Para la formación de los tiempos continuos en activa.

* She **is** singing.

y en pasiva.

* The bread **is eaten** by the dog.

En la forma progresiva o '**going to**' form.

* They **are going to** play football.

2. Usamos el be...

... en tiempos progresivos para hablar sobre las actividades y comportamientos de la gente.

* We **are** being very careful.
* She **is** being very stupid.

También para expresar una condición física o mental.

* I **am** happy.
* You **are** angry.
* He **is** furious.
* We **are** ill.
* They **are** cold.

3. Be + infinitive (I am to... etc.)

Es una estructura que se usa para hablar sobre arreglos que se han planeado para el futuro.

* The President **is to** visit Europe next year.
* They **are to get married** in November.

También se puede usar en el pasado.

* She felt nervous because she **was to fly** for the first time.

A veces usamos este tipo de frases para 'cosas del destino'.

* We said goodbye, but we **were to meet** again years later.

Be + infinitive se puede usar para dar órdenes.

* You **are to be** on guard all night.
* She **is to wait** here.

4. El infinitivo pasivo es muy corriente para dar noticias o instrucciones.

* This form is **to be filled in** and returned within a week.
* Medicines **are to be kept** out of reach of children.

5. Nótese el uso especial de los infinitivos pasivos de **see, find** y **congratulate.**

* She **is** nowhere **to be seen.**
* They **are** nowhere **to be found.**
* You **are** all **to be congratulated.**

6. Usamos **to be** para expresar la fecha y la hora.

* What time **is** it? - It **is** half past ten.
* What **is** the date? - It **is** April 13.

7. Para hablar del tiempo atmosférico.

* **Is** it hot? - Yes, it **is** very hot.
* **Was** it cold? - Yes, it **was** very cold.
* **Is** it windy? - Yes, it **is** very windy.
* **Is** the weather good? - Yes, it **is** very good weather.

8. También expresamos la edad con el verbo **be.**

* How old **are** you? - I **am** twenty (years old).
* How old **is** that castle? - It **is** nine hundred years old.

9. Para expresar el precio de una cosa.

* How much **is** it? - It **is** ten pounds.
* **Is** it expensive? - No, it **is** only twenty dollars.

10. Para expresar distancia.

* How far **is** it? - It **is** ten miles away.
* Paris **is** not very far.

11. Para expresar tamaño y peso.

* How heavy **is** he? - He **is** nearly two hundred pounds.
* How tall **are** you? - I **am** five feet ten inches.

To have

I. Básicamente have indica posesión.

Cuando éste es el caso, se suele añadir **got**, sin que esto altere para nada el sentido de la frase.

    * I **have** a dog = I **have got** a dog = I**'ve got** a dog.

La forma negativa se suele expresar de dos maneras.

    * I **haven't got** a dog   * I **don't have** a dog.

La interrogativa también puede ser de dos formas.

    * **Have you got** a dog?   * **Do you have** a dog?

La primera forma es muy usual en G.B. mientras que en USA es más corriente la segunda.

2. Como verbo auxiliar:

Como verbo auxiliar **have** se usa para formar los tiempos compuestos.

Present Perfect:	I have loved
Past Perfect:	I had loved
Future Perfect:	I will have loved
Conditional Perfect:	I would have loved

3. Have + object: actions (tomar, celebrar, etc.)

El verbo **have** seguido de un objeto se puede referir a muchas actividades diferentes. **Have** puede reemplazar a: **eat, drink.** También a: **receive, spend, take, go for,** etc.

        Tomar: **have** breakfast/lunch/tea/dinner/a meal/coffee/a beer.
        Tomar: **have** a bath/ a shower/ a shave/ a wash/ a rest.
        Tener: **have** a talk/ a chat/ a conversation/ an agreement.
    Celebrar: **have** a party.
Tropezarse: **have** difficulties.
  Divertirse: **have** a good time.
        Coger: **have** a holiday/ vacation/ a day off/ a nice evening.

Nota: Cuando el verbo **have** se usa de esta manera, sigue la regla de los verbos ordinarios:

    a) no se le añade **got.**
    b) no se contrae.
    c) las formas interrogativas y negativas se forman con **do, does, did**
    d) se puede usar en tiempos continuos (I'm **having** a look)

---

4. Uso causativo del verbo have

En este tiempo de oraciones, el sujeto no realiza la acción, sino que emplea u ordena a otra persona que la realice.

* I **had** my car repaired. (hice que me arreglaran...)
* He **had** his hair cut. (le cortaron el pelo)
* We **had** our house decorated. (nos decoraron...)

Esta misma construcción se puede hacer con el verbo **get**.

* I **got** my car repaired.

etc.

La misma construcción se puede usar coloquialmente para sustituir a un verbo en voz pasiva, sobre todo cuando hablamos de un robo o desgracia.

* I **had** my car stolen this moning. (me robaron...)

Shall

Shall es un verbo auxiliar 'modal''. Se suele contraer en **'ll**; la contracción de la negación es **shan't**. Como los demás verbos modales auxiliares, el **shall** va seguido del infinitivo sin el **to**. Hoy en día, **shall** se usa mayormente en las primeras personas del futuro.

> ❈ I **shall** ring you up tomorrow morning. (I'll ring...)
> ❈ Where **shall** we be next week?

Aunque gramaticalmente esto es así, la tendencia es a usar **will** en todas las personas.

> ❈ I **will** ring you up tomorrow.
> ❈ Where **will** we be next week?

Sin embargo, sí hay algunos casos en los que siempre se usa **shall**. Por ejemplo, para ofertas, sugerencias y petición de instrucciones.

> ❈ **Shall** I open the window for you?
> ❈ **Shall** we go to the beach, boys?
> ❈ What **shall** we do?

En inglés antiguo, era corriente usar **shall** en la segunda y tercera persona, cuando se quería mostrar una gran emoción (amenazas, promesas, etc.)

> ❈ You **shall** pay for what you've done!
> ❈ They **shall** suffer for this, I swear it!

Hoy en día esta forma, prácticamente, no existe.

Should

1. Como verbo auxiliar modal puede ser considerado el pasado de **shall**. Esto sucede, por ejemplo, en habla indirecta.

* I **shall be** there before nine.
* I said I **should be** there before nine.

> **Should** también es posible en una construcción de 'futuro en el pasado'.
>
> * so this was the place where I **should work** for the next six months

2. Should no sólo se refiere al pasado, también se puede usar como unas formas de **shall**, que se refieran al presente o al futuro. Por ejemplo en las primeras personas del condicional.

* I **should be** perfectly happy lying on the beach. (I **would be**...)

Se puede usar en ofertas, sugerencias y petición de instrucciones.

* **Should** I help you with the washing-up?
* What do you think we **should** do now?

3. Should se usa después de **if** y **in case** para sugerir una posibilidad menos clara.

* If you **should** see Mary, give her my regards.

También se puede usar después de **so that** y **in order that**.

* I did it **so that** you **should** be happy.

A menudo invertimos el orden de estas frases.

* **Should** you see Mary...

4. Should se usa (en Gran Bretaña) en ciertas oraciones subordinadas que expresan reacciones personales o acontecimientos.

* I was astonished **that he should do** such a terrible thing.
* She was anxious **that everyone should have** a good time.

> Aunque should se puede usar perfectamente, como hemos dicho, para formar las primeras personas del condicional, en práctica se prefiere usar el **would** en todas las personas para evitar confusiones con el **should** como verbo defectivo.

Will

Will es un verbo auxiliar que se usa para formar el futuro. No se traduce. Como hemos visto, gramaticalmente se usa en las segundas y terceras personas, aunque en práctica también se usa con las primeras.

La forma negativa es **won't.** (will not).

A menudo usamos **will you?** como equivalente al español ¿**quieres?**

* Shut the door, **will you?**
* Children, come here, **will you?**
* You'll come with me, **won't you?**

Would

1. Would es un verbo auxiliar que se usa para formar el condicional. No se traduce. Lo mismo que el **will**, gramaticalmente se usa para formar las segundas y terceras personas, aunque en la práctica, las primeras también se forman con **would**.

* **I would** come (vendría)

2. Would se emplea para expresar una petición cortésmente.

* **Would** you come with me, please? (Tendrían la amabilidad de venir...)

3. La palabra **would** a veces se usa para indicar un hábito en el pasado. Tiene el mismo significado que **used to** (solía).

* He **would** go for a walk down the river. (solía ir...)
* She **would** get up early and light the fire. (solía levantarse...)

4. En frases condicionales expresa mucha amabilidad.

* If you **would** sign this... (si tuviera la amabilidad de firmar...)

5. Would se puede usar detrás de **I wish/if only.** (ya podía...)

* I wish it **would** stop raining. (ya podía dejar...)
* I wish he **would** come earlier. (ya podía venir...)

Used to

Used to se puede considerar como una especie de auxiliar, ya que el uso de **do** es opcional.

Used to expresa una costumbre en el pasado.

* My father **used to** smoke a lot. (solía fumar...)
* My father **didn't use** to smoke very much. (no solía...)
* My father **used not** to smoke. (no solía...)

Algunas veces equivale al pretérito imperfecto castellano.

* Did she **use to** know him? (¿Le conocía...?)
* **Used she to** know him? (¿Le conocía...?)

La primera forma es mucho más corriente.

Need

Need tiene dos formas: las de un verbo auxiliar modal, y las de un verbo ordinario.

> ❀ **Need** you go?   ❀ Do you **need** to go?

1. Cuando **need** se usa como verbo auxiliar no añade 's' la tercera persona. Tampoco admite el **to** ni delante, ni detrás. Para preguntar se invierte el orden de verbo-sujeto. La contracción de la negación es **needn't**.

> ❀ **Need** you speak like that?
> ❀ You **needn't** speak like that.

2. Cuando **need** es usado como verbo normal, añade **s** la tercera persona del singular y admite el **do** y el **to** como los demás verbos.

> ❀ **Do** you **need** to go? - You **don't need** to go.
> ❀ **Does** he **need** to do that? - She **doesn't need** to do that.

3. El uso de **need** en frases afirmativas sólo se hace cuando éstas llevan adverbios con implicaciones negativas: **never, hardly, scarcely.**

> ❀ I **hardly need** say that.

4. Con **needn't** expresamos una falta de obligación.

> ❀ You can buy today, but you **needn't** pay yet. (no tienes que...)
> ❀ You **needn't** tell him. (no hace falta que...)

5. **Needn't + have + participio** se usa para expresar una acción que no hacía falta que se llevara a cabo, pero que se hizo.

> ❀ You **needn't have paid** yet. (no tenías por qué haber pagado...)

Dare

1. Dos formas

Al igual que el verbo **need, dare** tiene dos formas, como verbo auxiliar y como verbo normal.

a) Como verbo auxiliar no añade 's' la tercera persona del singular. Tampoco admite las particulas **to** ni **do** ni delante, ni detrás.

* **How dare she** tell you... (cómo se atreve a...)
* She **daren't** tell you what she knows. (no se atreve...)

b) Como un verbo ordinario con 's', **do** y **to**.

* If he **dares** to tell... (si se atreve a...)
* How **dare** you...? (¿cómo te atreves...?)

2. Expresiones con dare.

a) **I dare you**, se usa como desafío.

* **I dare you** to ride the bike between those two trees. (te desafío...)

b) Las expresiones **you dare! don't you dare!** se usan (por ejemplo por las madres) para que los niños no hagan algo.

* 'Mum, I'll walk on top of the wall.' **'Don't you dare!'**

c) Usamos **How dare you**, como una exclamación de una persona indignada.

* **How dare you!** Take your hands off me!

d) **I dare say** quiere decir 'probablemente'.

* **I dare say** it will rain tomorrow. (yo diría que...)

Usos de Can - Could

1. La palabra **can** sólo se conjuga en Presente de Indicativo.

   ❀ We **can** play football today.

2. **Could** sólo se conjuga en **Pasado** y **Condicional**.

   ❀ I **could** smell something burning. (podía oler...)
   ❀ I **could** do it for you. (yo podría hacerlo...)

Usamos **could** sobre todo con los verbos: **see, hear, taste, remember, understand, smell, feel.**

3. Para los demás tiempos se usa la locución **be able**.

   ❀ We **will be able** to meet on Sunday. (podremos vernos...)
   ❀ She **hasn't been able** to go. (no ha podido...)

4. **Can** no añade 's' en la tercera persona del singular.

   ❀ He **can** go tonight.

5. Ni **can** ni **could** admiten la particula **to** ni delante, ni detrás. Mientras que **be able** sí la admite.

   ❀ We **can** play tennis.
   ❀ I **could** remember very well.
   ❀ She **will be able to** go tonight.

6. Ni **can** ni **could** admiten las partículas **do, does, did** para la forma interrogativa y negativa.

   ❀ **Can** you go today? I cannot (can't) speak.
   ❀ **Could** you understand him? I could not (couldn't) understand him.

7. **Can, could** se usan para expresar habilidad, capacidad o facultad de llevar a cabo algo, o saber hacerlo.

   ❀ **Can** you speak English? (sabe usted...?
   ❀ I **can** swim. (yo sé...
   ❀ She **could** play the piano when she was six. (ella sabía...)

8. Usamos el **was/were able** en vez de **could** cuando queremos decir que alguien consiguió hacer algo en una situación en particular.

   ❀ The building was on fire but everyone **was able** to escape.
   ❀ He didn't want to come but I **was able** to persuade him.

En las formas negativas usamos **couldn't** en todas las ocasiones.

   ❀ He **couldn't** swim.
   ❀ I **couldn't** persuade him to come.

Usos de May - Might

1. Este verbo se usa para solicitar permiso o para concederlo.

 ❀ **May** I smoke in this room?
 ❀ **May** I come in, Mr Brown?

May tiene un sentido más cortés pero también más dubitativo.

 ❀ **Might** I call your attention for a moment?

2. También usamos **MAY - MIGHT** para expresar una posibilidad o duda.

 ❀ We **may** finish today. (Puede que terminemos hoy)
 ❀ He **may** come tonight. (Puede que venga esta noche)

Might tiene un sentido mucho más ambiguo y lejano. Indica una posibilidad muy remota.

 ❀ He **might** come tomorrow, but I'm not sure.
 ❀ It **might** be true, but I don't really know.

3. **May** + *have* + *participio* indica duda en el momento de hablar sobre algo que ha pasado. (puede que haya...)

 ❀ 'He hasn't come.' 'He **may have missed** the train.'
 ❀ 'They haven't paid.' 'They **may have paid** already.'

El uso de **might** en este tipo de frases indica posibilidad remota.

 ❀ If you had asked him, he **might have lent** you the car.
 (quizá te hubiera prestado...)

4. El verbo **MAY - MIGHT** en frases exclamativas se utiliza para expresar un deseo. Equivale al subjuntivo español.

 ❀ **May** fortune smile at you! ¡que te sonría la fortuna!

5. **May - Might** se pueden usar en oraciones concesivas, con un sentido de¡ *quizá sea/esté...*

 ❀ It **may** be raining but it's not cold.
 ❀ We **may** be poor, but we are honest.

6. **May** seguido de **not** indica prohibición.

 ❀ You **may not** smoke in this area.
 ❀ People **may not** step on the grass.

7. **Might** se utiliza a menudo para reprochar algo. (ya podías...)

 ❀ You **might** come earlier.
 ❀ You **might** listen to me.

Usos de Must y Have to

1. La palabra **must** sólo se usa en presente de indicativo.

   ❋ I **must** go tonight.

2. No añade **s** en la tercera persona.

   ❋ He **must** study more.

3. No admite la partícula **to** ni delante ni detrás.

   ❋ You **must** speak more slowly.

4. No admite la partícula **do** para interrogar ni negar.

   ❋ **Must** you go?   ❋ You **must** not come.

5. Para todos los demás tiempos se usa la locución **have to**.

   ❋ I **had to** go to Paris last week.
   ❋ I will **have to** speak to him.

6. Tanto **must** como **have to** indican obligación. Sin embargo, el sentido no siempre es el mismo.

Must a menudo se usa para hablar de una obligación que depende de la persona que habla o escucha.

   ❋ You **must** go to the doctor.
   ❋ I **must** stop smoking.

Have to o **have got to** se usa para hablar de obligaciones que provienen del exterior; es decir, una obligación impuesta por ley, un acuerdo, etc.

   ❋ Soldiers **have to** wear uniforms.
   ❋ I **have to** go to the dentist. I've got an appointment.

7. Las formas negativas **mustn't** y **don't have to** tienen sentidos muy diferentes.

   ❋ You **mustn't** tell your mother. (no debes decirle a...)
   ❋ You **don't have to** tell your mother. (no tienes por qué contar a...)

8. Usamos **must** para decir que estamos seguros de algo.

   ❋ Jean **must have** a problem. She's always crying.
   ❋ That's the doorbell. It **must** be John.

9. **Must + have + participio** se usa para deducciones en el pasado.

   ❋ That **must have been** very difficult.
   ❋ 'The lights have gone out' 'A fuse **must have blown**.'

Should (deberías..)

1. **Should** es un verbo defectivo que se usa para expresar obligación y deber, para dar consejos, y, en general, para decir lo que creemos que la gente debería hacer.

> ❀ You **should** go to see this film.
> ❀ You **should** have seen her face!
> ❀ People **should** vote even if they don't like the candidates.

2. Usamos **should** cuando damos nuestra opinión subjetiva.

> ❀ You **should** go and see grandmother.

3. El verbo **should** no es tan fuerte como el **must**.

> ❀ You **should** stop smoking. (deberías dejar de ...)

4. A menudo usamos el **should** cuando damos una opinión de algo.

> ❀ I think the government **should do** something about unemployment.
> ❀ I don't think he **should** work so hard.

5. Se usa **should** para decir que algo seguramente sucederá.

> ❀ '¿Will you be late?' 'No; I **should** be home at the usual time.'

6. Usamos **should** para decir que algo no está bien.

> ❀ Those children **shouldn't** be playing. They **should** be at school.

7. Para el pasado usamos **should have** para decir que alguien hizo algo mal. (deberías haber...)

> ❀ You didn't come to the party... You **should have** come. It was great!
> ❀ You **shouldn't have** eaten so much!

Ought to

La forma contracta negativa es **oughtn't to**. Como los demás verbos defectivos, no tiene infinitivo, ni gerundio. Tampoco añade una **s** en la tercera persona singular.

 ❀ He **ought to** understand.

Las preguntas y las negaciones no se forman con **do**.

 ❀ **Ought** we to go now? ❀ That **oughtn't to** take very long.

Sin embargo, **ought** se diferencia de los otros verbos defectivos en que va seguido del infinitivo con **to**.

 ❀ You **ought to** see a doctor.

a) Ought to expresa obligación y entonces tiene el mismo significado que should (debería).

 ❀ He **ought to** know. He wrote the book. (debería saber...)
 ❀ She **oughtn't** even to consider such a thing. (no debería...)

b) También expresamos probabilidad con ought.

 ❀ They **ought to** be half way to New York by now. (deberían...)
 ❀ That money **ought to** be enough. (debería ser...)

c) Ought to puede ir seguido de have + participio para hablar del pasado.

 ❀ She **ought to have** phoned. (debería haber...)
 ❀ They **ought to have** arrived by now. (deberían haber...)

d) Los adverbios como always, never, really suelen ir antes de ought.

 ❀ You always **ought to** carry aspirins with you. (siempre deberías...)

e) En las frases negativas el not se pone antes que el to.

 ❀ You **ought not to** go/You **oughtn't to** go.

Auxiliary verbs

1. do, be y have

Estos tres verbos auxiliares, tienen importantes funciones gramaticales. **Do** se usa para formar las preguntas y las negaciones del presente y del pasado, además de las formas enfáticas. **Be** se usa para las formas progresivas y voz pasiva. **Have** se usa para formar los tiempos compuestos

2. Los verbos defectivos o «modal auxiliaries».

        can - could
        may - might
        will - would
      shall - should
       must - ought to

Verbos que comparten algunas de las características de los verbos defectivos son:

        need, dare, used to

Todos ellos son diferentes del **do, be** y **have** por varias razones. Primero, tienen rasgos gramaticales especiales (no tienen infinitivo, No añaden **s** en la tercera persona singular). En segundo lugar, los verbos defectivos no sólo tienen una función gramatical, sino también un significado: *I can* significa *yo puedo*. **Do, be,** y **have** no tienen significados así, cuando se usan como auxiliares. Cuando el **will** y el **would** se usan para formar el futuro y condicional, desempeñan la misma función que **be** y **have**. Sin embargo, desde el punto de vista gramatical, **will** y **would** pertenecen a los defectivos («modal auxiliaries»)

Por regla general, los verbos defectivos forman las preguntas y las negaciones sin **do**. Cuando van seguidos por un infinitivo, éste no lleva **to**. **Ought to** es la excepción de la regla.

Los verbos defectivos o auxiliares, si van seguidos de infinitivos, indican una posibilidad, permiso, habilidad, obligación, etc.

    ❀ I **can** play the piano. (habilidad)
    ❀ He **may** come tonight. (posibilidad)
    ❀ You **must** come earlier. (obligación)
    ❀ **May** I come in? (permiso)

La conjugación de los verbos auxiliares y defectivos es sencilla.

affirmative	interrogative	negative	interrogative negative
Primero se coloca el sujeto y luego el verbo.	Para formar la interrogación invertimos el orden:	Para formar la negación, colocamos primero el sujeto, después el verbo auxiliar y por último la negación **not**.	En la forma **interrogativa-negativa** colocamos primero el verbo auxiliar, después el sujeto y por último la partícula **not**.
I am you have he can she must	am I? have you? can he? must she?	I am **not** you have **not** he can **not** she must **not**	am I **not?** have you **not?** can he **not?** must she **not?**

Nota: en el índice encontrará la conjugación individual y detallada de todos los verbos auxiliares.

Pronouns

personal	object	possessive	reflexive
I	me	mine	myself
you	you	yours	yourself
he	him	his	himself
she	her	hers	herself
it	it	its	itself
we	us	ours	ourselves
you	you	yours	yourselves
they	them	theirs	themselves

Adjectives

possessive
my
your
his
her
its
our
your
their

To make · To do · Differences

Los dos verbos tienen un significado parecido y a veces es difícil elegir entre los dos.

1. Cuando hablamos de una actividad:

Cuando hablamos de una actividad, sin decir exactamente lo que es, usamos **do**.

- Please, **do** something!
- I don't know what to **do**.
- What are they **doing**?
- They didn't **do** anything.

2. Cuando hablamos de trabajo.

Generalmente usamos **do** cuando hablamos de trabajo.

- He is not **doing** any work.
- I don't like **doing** the homework.
- The maid **does** all the housework.

3. Creación o construcción

Para expresar una idea de creación o construcción usamos **make**.

- I'm **making** a little boat.
- We're going to **make** dinner
- Let's **make** a plan.

Sin embargo, en la inmensa mayoría de los casos no hay reglas claras, y en el caso de no estar seguro, se aconseja mirar en un buen diccionario. A continuación damos una relación de las expresiones más corrientes con ambos verbos.

To make

to make a mistake	cometer una equivocación	to make a plan	hacer un plan
to make an error	cometer un error	to make dinner/ supper/lunch	hacer la comida/cena
to make the beds	hacer las camas	to make bread	hacer pan
to make a hole	hacer un agujero	to make clothes	confeccionar ropa
to make war	hacer la guerra	to make friends	hacer amigos
to make peace	hacer la paz	to make a profit	tener beneficios
to make love	hacer el amor	to make a fortune	amasar una fortuna
to make a noise	hacer ruido	to make a name	hacerse un nombre
to make tea/coffee	hacer té/café	to make a complaint	quejarse
to make money	hacer dinero	to make faces	hacer burla
to make a speech	echar un discurso	to make fire	hacer fuego
to make progress	hacer progresos	to make make fun of	burlarse de
to make a promise	hacer una promesa	to make sail	zarpar
to make an effort	hacer un esfuerzo	to make oneself a reputation	crearse una reputación
to make a decision	tomar una decisión	to make someone happy	hacer a alguien feliz
to make an offer	hacer una oferta	to make someone laugh	hacer reír a alguien
to make a suggestion	hacer una sugerencia	to make merry	regocijarse
to make room	hacer sitio	to make sure of	asegurarse
to make trouble	causar problemas		

To do

to do something	hacer algo
to do nothing	no hacer nada
to do a job	hacer un trabajo
to do work	trabajar
to do the shopping	hacer las compras
to do the ironing	planchar (hacer la plancha)
to do the housework	hacer las tareas de casa
to do the homework	hacer los deberes
to do business	hacer negocios
to do a favo(u)r	hacer un favor
to do justice	hacer justicia
to do the hono(u)r	hacer los honores
to do the trick	servir (para el caso)
to do one's hair	arreglarse el pelo
to do wonders	hacer maravillas
to do well	hacer bien
to do an exercise	hacer un ejercicio
to do badly	hacer algo mal
to do one's duty	cumplir con el deber
to do right	tratar bien
to do good	hacer bien
to do time	cumplir condena
to do harm	hacer mal
to do one's best	hacer lo mejor posible

Aparte de estos usos más corrientes de **do** y **make** existen infinidad de **phrasal verbs** que cambian el significado del verbo al añadir una preposición o adverbio: **make for** (dirigirse), **make up** (maquillarse), **make after** (perseguir), etc.

do for (matar), **do over** (repetir), **do without** (prescindir de).

El estudiante encontrará una recopilación exhaustiva de estos verbos compuestos en el libro PHRASAL VERBS del mismo autor.

To tell · To say. Differences

El significado de ambos verbos es el mismo: **decir.** Sin embargo, usamos **tell** cuando en la frase hay un complemento indirecto, es decir, una persona que recibe la acción del verbo.

Tell

* He **told me** that he's tired.
* I didn't **tell her** anything.
* **Tell Peter** that I want to see him.
* She didn't **tell her mother** what she had seen.
* What did she **tell the children?**

También se usa **tell** en el sentido de contar una historia, narrar un cuento. En esos casos el verbo **tell** puede no llevar complemento indirecto.

* He told a story.   * He told **me** a story.
* Mum, tell a story.   * Mum, tell **us** a story.

Lo mismo ocurre con las palabras **truth** y **lie.**

* He told a lie.   * He told **me** a lie.
* He told the truth.   * He told **you** the truth.

Usamos el **tell** seguido de un infinitivo para dar una orden.

* **Tell** the children **to come** at once.

Usos idiomáticos de **tell.**

* I can't **tell** the difference between those two.
* Can you **tell** me the time, please?
* The gypsy **told** her fortune.
* Will it rain? - I don't know. You can never **tell.**
* You can **tell** from her eyes that she's lying.

Say

Se usa **say** cuando la frase no tiene complemento indirecto, es decir, no hay nadie que reciba la acción del verbo.

* What did you **say?** I didn't **say** anything.
* He **said** that it is going to rain.
* What did Peter **say** last night?
* Don't **say** that!

Say se puede usar tanto en oraciones de estilo directo como indirecto.

❀ He said: 'It's very difficult.'
❀ He said that it was very difficult.

Usos idiomáticos con **say.**

❀ I **say!** Isn't that Henry?
❀ I'm glad to **say** that your life is out of danger.
❀ What do you **say** to a drink?
❀ It is **said** to be worth a fortune.

Recuerda: que en algunos casos **tell** equivale a **say to.**

❀ He **told** me that it was easy. ❀ He **said to** me that it was easy.

A menudo usamos **say to** en el sentido de *informar.*

❀ I **said to** the hotel receptionist that my name was Pérez.

The 'going to' form o Futuro de intención

affirmative	interrogative	negative	interrogative /negative

Futuro de intención

I am going to...	am I going to...?	I am not going to...	am I not going to...?
you are going to...	are you going to...?	you are not going to...	aren't you going to...?
he/she/it is going to...	is he/she/it going to...?	he/she/it is not going to...	isn't he going to...?
we are going to...	are we going to...?	we are not going to...	aren't we going to...?
you are going to...	are you going to...?	you are not going to...	aren't you going to...?
they are going to...	are they going to...?	they are not going to...	aren't they going to...?

Going to se usa:

a) Cuando se tiene intención de hacer algo.

b) para predecir algo.

a). El **going to** expresa la intención del sujeto de llevar a cabo una acción en el futuro. Esta intención es siempre premeditada e indica una cierta preparación; una posibilidad que se lleve a cabo la acción aunque no de una forma tan definitiva como el presente continuo.

  ❀ **I'm meeting** Janet at the station at five.
  ❀ **I'm going to meet** Janet at the station at five.

I'm meeting Janet significa que ya has hecho los arreglos necesarios y has quedado con ella. Mientras que **I'm going to meet** significa que no has hecho ningún arreglo. Quizá Janet se lleve una sorpresa.

Going to se puede usar con expresiones de tiempo:

  ❀ **I'm going to** be a doctor when I grow up.
  ❀ When **are you going to** get married?
  ❀ **I'm going to** think about your proposal.
  ❀ I'm sure she **is going to** like it.

b) El **going to** para predicción.

Podemos expresar un sentimiento de seguridad del que habla.

El tiempo generalmente no se menciona, pero la acción se espera que suceda en el futuro inmediato:

  ❀ I think **it is going to** rain tonight.
  ❀ We **are going to** have a nice trip.
  ❀ I'm afraid she **is going to faint**.
  ❀ He **is going to** fall into that hole!

Si el **futuro de intención** o "**going to**" form hace referencia a una acción en el pasado. Entonces la construcción se realiza con el **Past tense** del verbo **to be**.

- ❀ She **was going to** come yesterday.
- ❀ We **were going to** play a tennis match last Saturday.

Nota:
El futuro de intención no se usa con el verbo **to go**.

- ❀ This afternoon we **are going**.

y no

- ❀ This afternoon we **are going to go**.

Spelling

Duplican la consonante:
A. Los verbos monosílabos que terminan en consonante.

thin:	thinned, thinning
cut:	cutting
hit:	hitting
run:	running
sit:	sitting
put:	putting
shop:	shopped, shopping
stop:	stopped, stopping
knit:	knitted, knitting
drop:	dropped, dropping
dig:	digging
let:	letting
fit:	fitted, fitting

B. Los verbos bisílabos

Los verbos bisílabos que terminan en consonante, duplican la consonante siempre que el acento recaiga sobre la última sílaba.

refer:	referred, referring
prefer:	preferred, preferring
occur:	occurred, ocurring
deter:	deterred, deterring
begin:	beginning
regret:	regretted, regretting
permit:	permitted, permitting

C. Algunos verbos de más de dos sílabas

Algunos verbos de más de dos sílabas también duplican la consonante final en el inglés británico, mientras que en América no lo hacen.

	British English	American English
quarrel:	quarrelled/quarrelling	quarreled/quarreling
model:	modelled/modelling	modeled/modeling
fuel:	fuelled/fuelling	fueled/fueling
kidnap:	kidnapped/kidnapping	kidnaped/kidnaping
signal:	signalled/signalling	signaled/signaling
worshsip:	worshipped/worshipping	worshiped/worshiping
dial:	dialled/dialling	dialed/dialing
travel:	travelled/travelling	traveled/traveling
cancel:	cancelled/cancelling	canceled/canceling

La palabra **handicap** duplica la consonante en ambos lados del Atlántico.

handicap:	handicapped	handicapped

Bias se puede escribir de ambas formas.

bias:	biased - biassed

D. Verbos que terminan en -e (love, like, smoke, etc.)

Si un verbo termina en -e omitimos la -e antes de añadir -ing:
    love -loving   smoke -smoking   hope -hoping   dance -dancing

Excepciones:
    be -being

Verbos terminados en -ee:
    see -seeing   agree -agreeing

Si un verbo termina en -e, añadimos -d para formar el pasado (verbos regulares):
    hope -hoped   love -loved   like -liked   change -changed

E. Los verbos que terminan en s, ss, sh, ch, x y o:

Añaden es en tercera persona del presente, en vez de s.

* I miss, he misses
* I do, he does
* I box, he boxes
* I watch, he watches

F. Los verbos que terminan en:

'y' precedida de consonante, cambian la y por i y añaden -es o -ed excepto en el gerundio: crying

* I cry, he cries/cried/crying
* I try, he tries/tried/trying
* I study, he studies/studied/studying
* I apply, he applies/applied/applying

Sin embargo, los verbos regulares que terminan en y precedida de vocal no cambian, es decir, añaden una s en tercera persona del presente, o -ed en pasado, como los demás verbos.

* I play, he plays/played/playing   * I obey, he obeys/obeyed/obeying

Los irregulares, por supuesto, cambian en el pasado y participio:
* pay, paid   * buy, bought   * say, said

G. Los verbos que terminan en -ie:

Los verbos que terminan en -ie, la -ie cambia por y antes de -ing
* tie, tying   * die, dying   * lie, lying

H. Los verbos terminados en c

Los verbos terminados en c añaden una k antes de -ing o -ed.
    to panic: I panicked/panicking
    to picnic: I picnicked/picnicking
    to traffic: I trafficked/trafficking
    to zinc: I zincked/zincked

Los tiempos del verbo

Infinitive

El infinitivo se forma con la partícula **to**: **to go, to come, to study.** Para formar la negación se pone **not** delante: **not to go, not to study.**

❀ **To** be or **not to** be, that's the question.

Gerund

El gerundio se forma añadiendo **-ing** al infinitivo.

work ❀ working

La forma negativa se forma con **not** delante.

❀ I don't mind **not speaking** to him again.

Sin embargo, los letreros de prohibición se forman así:

No smoking - No spitting

Participle

En los verbos regulares se forma añadiendo **-ed** al infinitivo (o sólo una **d** si el verbo termina en **e**).

wash ❀ washed
change ❀ changed

En caso de que el verbo sea irregular el participio es el que corresponde a la tercera columna de los verbos irregulares.

Infinitive Perfect

Se forma con el infinitivo simple del verbo **have** más el participio del verbo que se esté conjugando: **to have spoken, to have finished.** La negación se forma anteponiendo el **not**:

❀ It was impossible **not to have heard** the explosion.

Past Participle

Se forma con el gerundio del verbo **have** más el participio del verbo que se conjugue.

❀ **Having written** the note, he dropped it in the letterbox.
❀ **Not having worked** for a year you're not entitled to it.

❋ Indicative

Present

La forma afirmativa se forma poniendo primero el sujeto y luego el verbo: **I love, I am.**

Sin embargo para formar la interrogación y negación de los verbos en presente hay que diferenciar si se trata de verbos auxiliares o normales.

affirmative	interrogative	negative

Present

Auxiliary:	Normal:	Auxiliary:	Normal:	Auxiliary:	Normal:
soy/estoy	hablo				
eres/estás etc.	hablas, etc.				
I am	I speak	am I?	do I speak?	I am not	I do not speak
you are	you speak	are you?	do you speak?	you are not	you do not speak
he is	he speaks	is he?	does he speak?	he is not	he does not speak
we are	we speak	are we?	do we speak?	we are not	we do not speak
you are	you speak	are you?	do you speak?	you are not	you do not speak
they are	they speak	are they?	do they speak?	they are not	they do not speak

Como se observará, en un verbo normal, todas las personas son iguales excepto la tercera que añade una **s**. En caso de que el verbo termine en **ss, sh, ch, x, o,** la tercera persona añade **es;** Pero solamente en forma afirmativa!

Para la formación de la forma interrogativa y negativa de un verbo normal usamos las partículas **do/does** seguido del verbo en infinitivo.

No hay que confundir esta partícula o verbo auxiliar, con el verbo **hacer** (to do). (Véase el verbo **to do** conjugado en su totalidad en la unidad 17).

interrogative-negative		interrogative-negative	
Auxiliary:		**Normal:**	
	(Abbrev.)		**(Abbrev.)**
am I not?	------	do I not speak?	don't I speak?
are you not?	aren't you?	do you not speak?	don't you speak?
is he not?	isn't he?	does he not speak?	doesn't he speak?
are we not?	aren't we?	do we not speak?	don't we speak?
are you not?	aren't you?	do you not speak?	don't you speak?
are they not?	aren't they?	do they not speak?	don't they speak?

✿ Indicative

Past tense

El **Past Tense** inglés equivale a dos tiempos españoles: el **imperfec-to** y el **indefinido**. Así pues, el pasado de un verbo inglés se puede traducir de dos formas: **I played** puede significar, **yo jugaba** o **yo jugué**.

En el caso del verbo **to be** se complica más la cosa, pues el verbo **to be** significa **ser** o **estar**. Así que el pasado del verbo **to be: I was** se puede traducir por: **yo era/fui** o **yo estaba/estuve**.

| **affirmative** | | **interrogative** | | **negative** | |

Imperfecto / Indefinido · Past tense

Auxiliary:	Normal:	Auxiliary:	Normal:	Auxiliary:	Normal:
era / fuí	*hablé*				
estaba/estuve	*hablaste, etc.*				
I was	I spoke	was I?	did I speak?	I was not	I did not speak
you were	you spoke	were you?	did you speak?	you were not	you did not speak
he was	he spoke	was he?	did he speak?	he was not	he did not speak
we were	we spoke	were we?	did we speak?	we were not	we did not speak
you were	you spoke	were you?	did you speak?	you were not	you did not speak
they were	they spoke	were they?	did they speak?	they were not	they did not speak

| **interrogative-negative** | | **interrogative-negative** | |

Auxiliary:	(Abbrev.)	Normal:	(Abbrev.)
was I not?	wasn't I?	did I not speak?	didn't I speak?
were you not?	weren't you?	did you not speak?	didn't you speak?
was he not?	wasn't he?	did he not speak?	didn't he speak?
were we not?	weren't we?	did we not speak?	didn't we speak?
were you not?	weren't you?	did you not speak?	didn't you speak?
were they not?	weren't they?	did they not speak?	didn't they speak?

Nota:
En los demás tiempos, tanto simples como compuestos, la formación es la misma para los verbos auxiliares como para los normales: **you will be, you will speak.** Por lo tanto, los ejemplos sólo serán con el verbo **speak**.

❀ Indicative

Futuro imperfecto · Simple future

Hablaré, hablarás, etc.

En inglés, el futuro se forma con las partículas **shall** y **will**. (Para los usos de estos auxiliares véase las páginas 6 y 8)

Shall se usa para las primeras personas **I** y **we**. Aunque solamente en un inglés muy formal. En el lenguaje diario se prefiere usar **will** en todas las personas. Más aún, el futuro se contrae usando **'ll** en todas las personas. Y en forma negativa: **shall not = shan't** y **will not = won't**

El único caso en que se usa el **shall** en la práctica es cuando se hace una pregunta como **oferta** o **sugerencia**.

> ❀ **Shall I** carry the bags?
> ❀ **Shall we** go to the beach?

affirmative	interrogative	negative

Simple future

I shall/will speak	shall/will I speak?	I shall/will not speak
you will speak	will you speak?	you will not speak
he will speak	will he speak?	he will not speak
we shall/will speak	shall/will we speak?	we shall/will not speak
you will speak	will you speak?	you will not speak
they will speak	will they speak?	they will not speak

interrogative-negative	interrogative-negative (Abbrev.)
shall/will I not speak?	shan't/won't I speak?
will you not speak?	won't you speak?
will he not speak?	won't he speak?
shall/will we not speak?	shan't/won't we speak?
will you not speak?	won't you speak?
will they not speak?	won't they speak?

❖ Indicative

Pretérito perfecto · Present Perfect

He hablado, has hablado, etc.

Los tiempos compuestos, tal como ocurre en español, se forman con el auxiliar **have** seguido del participio del verbo que se conjuga.

affirmative	interrogative	negative

Present Perfect

affirmative	interrogative	negative
I have spoken	have I spoken?	I have not spoken
you have spoken	have you spoken?	you have not spoken
he has spoken	has he spoken?	he has not spoken
we have spoken	have we spoken?	we have not spoken
you have spoken	have you spoken?	you have not spoken
they have spoken	have they spoken?	they have not spoken

interrogative-negative	interrogative-negative (Abbrev.)
have I not spoken?	haven't I spoken?
have you not spoken?	haven't you spoken?
has he not spoken?	hasn't he spoken?
have we not spoken?	haven't we spoken?
have you not spoken?	haven't you spoken?
have they not spoken?	haven't they spoken?

❋ Indicative

Pluscuamperfecto / Indefinido · Past Perfect

Había/hube hablado, habías/hubiste hablado, etc.

El **past perfect** inglés equivale al pluscuamperfecto y al anterior, por lo tanto se puede traducir de dos formas diferentes.

affirmative	interrogative	negative

Past Perfect

affirmative	interrogative	negative
I had spoken	had I spoken?	I had not spoken
you had spoken	had you spoken?	you had not spoken
he had spoken	had he spoken?	he had not spoken
we had spoken	had we spoken?	we had not spoken
you had spoken	had you spoken?	you had not spoken
they had spoken	had they spoken?	they had not spoken

interrogative-negative	interrogative-negative (Abbrev.)
had I not spoken?	hadn't I spoken?
had you not spoken?	hadn't you spoken?
had he not spoken?	hadn't he spoken?
had we not spoken?	hadn't we spoken?
had you not spoken?	hadn't you spoken?
had they not spoken?	hadn't they spoken?

⚘ Indicative

Futuro perfecto · Perfect Future

Habré hablado, habrás hablado, habrá hablado, etc.

El futuro perfecto se forma con las particulas **shall** y **will** más el auxiliar **have,** seguido del participio del verbo que se conjuga.

affirmative	interrogative	negative

Perfect Future

I shall/will have spoken	shall/will I have spoken?	I shall/will not have spoken
you will have spoken	will you have spoken?	you will not have spoken
he will have spoken	will he have spoken?	he will not have spoken
we shall/will have spoken	shall/will we have spoken?	we shall/will not have spoken
you will have spoken	will you have spoken?	you will not have spoken
they will have spoken	will they have spoken?	they will not have spoken

interrogative-negative	interrogative-negative (Abbrev.)
shall/will I have not spoken?	shan't/won't I have spoken?
will you not have spoken?	won't you have spoken?
will he not have spoken?	won't he have spoken?
shall/will we not have spoken?	shant/won't we have spoken?
will you not have spoken?	won't you have spoken?
will they not have spoken?	won't they have spoken?

❀ Condicional

Presente · Present

Hablaría, hablarías, etc.

El condicional se forma con las partículas o auxiliares **should** y **would**. La contracción de ambas es **'d**. La negación es **wouldn't** y **shouldn't**.

Tal como ocurre en el futuro, la partícula **should** sólo se usa en un inglés muy formal. En el lenguaje cotidiano se usa siempre **would** en todas las personas. Más todavía; se contrae a **'d**.

affirmative	interrogative	negative

Present

affirmative	interrogative	negative
I should/would speak	should/would I speak?	I should/would not speak
you would speak	would you speak?	you would not speak
he would speak	would he speak?	he would not speak
we should/would speak	would/should we speak?	we should/would not speak
you would speak	would you speak?	you would not speak
they would speak	would they speak?	they would not speak

interrogative-negative	interrogative-negative (Abbrev.)
should/would I not speak?	shouldn't/wouldn't I speak?
would you not speak?	wouldn't you speak?
would he not speak?	wouldn't he speak?
should/would we not speak?	shouldn't/wouldn't we speak?
would you not speak?	wouldn't you speak?
would they not speak?	wouldn't they speak?

✿ Condicional

Compuesto · Perfect

yo habría hablado, tú habrías hablado, él habría hablado, etc.

igual que el condicional simple, se forma con los auxiliares **should** y **would**. Va seguido de **have** más el participio del verbo que se conjuga.

affirmative	interrogative	negative

Compuesto · Perfect

I should/would have spoken	should/would I have spoken?	I should/would not have spoken
you would have spoken	would you have spoken?	you would not have spoken
he would have spoken	would he have spoken?	he would not have spoken
we should/would have spoken	would/should we have spoken?	we should/would not have spoken
you would have spoken	would you have spoken?	you would not have spoken
they would have spoken	would they have spoken?	they would not have spoken

interrogative-negative	interrogative-negative (Abbrev.)
should/would I not have spoken?	shouldn't/wouldn't I have spoken?
would you not have spoken?	wouldn't you have spoken?
would he not have spoken?	wouldn't he have spoken?
should/would we not have spoken?	shouldn't/wouldn't we have spoken?
would you not have spoken?	wouldn't you have spoken?
would they not have spoken?	wouldn't they have spoken?

❈ Modo Imperativo

El imperativo es una orden. La segunda persona bien sea del singular como del plural se forma con el infinitivo sin el **to**.

> ¡habla! speak!
> ¡hablad! speak!

Como **tú** y **usted** no se diferencian en inglés. El imperativo se puede traducir por: habla (tú), o hable (usted). También, hablad (vosotros/as) o hablen (ustedes)

Las demás personas de imperativo se forman con **let**.

En español no existe la primera persona del imperativo; sin embargo, en inglés sí existe: **let me speak.** La traducción de esta frase habrá que hacerla literalmente, **déjame hablar.**

La forma negativa del imperativo se forma poniendo delante de todas las personas **do not (don't).**

La primera persona del plural tiene dos formas para construir la negación; **don't let us** o **let's not.**

singular		plural	
Afirmative			
let me speak	*déjame hablar*	let us speak	*hablemos*
speak	*habla*	speak	*hablad*
let him/her/it speak	*que hable él/ella/ello*	let them speak	*que hablen ellos/ellas*
Negative			
do not let me speak	no *me dejes hablar*	do not let us (let's not) speak	*no hablemos*
do not speak	*no hables*	do not speak	*no habléis*
do not let him/her/it speak	*que no hable él/ella*	do not let them speak	*que no hablen*

✿ Modo Subjuntivo

Presente · Present

Yo hable, tú hables, él hable, etc.

El presente de subjuntivo apenas se usa en inglés. Se prefiere usar el indicativo, así:

    when he speaks   *cuando él hable*

Solamente se usa en exclamaciones como:

    Bless you, my son!   God **save** the King!

Imperfecto

Yo hablara o hablase, tú hablaras o hablases, etc.

El único verbo que sí se usa en este tiempo es el verbo **to be**

affirmative	interrogative	negative

Imperfecto

if I were	*si yo fuera*	La forma interrogativa	La forma negativa es como el en
if you were	*si tú fueras*	no existe en	Past tense de indicativo:
if he were	*si él fuera*	subjuntivo.	If I didn't speak English...
if we were	*si nosotros fuéramos*		*Si **no hablara** inglés...*
if you were	*si vosotros fuerais*		
if they were	*si ellos fueran*		

If I were taller
I'd be a policeman.
    Aunque también se admite:
If I was taller...
    Los demás verbos usan el indicativo.
If he spoke louder...!   *¡si **hablara** más alto...!*

I spoke
you spoke
he spoke
we spoke
you spoke
they spoke

Pretérito perfecto · Present perfect

Yo haya hablado, tú hayas hablado, él haya hablado.

El **pretérito perfecto** de subjuntivo equivale al pretérito perfecto de indicativo.

    I have spoken
    you have spoken
    he has spoken
    we have spoken
    you have spoken
    they have spoken

La forma negativa es igual que la del pretérito perfecto de indicativo. En cuanto a la forma interrogativa no existe en subjuntivo.

Pretérito pluscuamperfecto · Pluscuamperfecto

Yo hubiera o hubiese hablado, tú hubieras o hubieses hablado, etc.

El **Pluscuamperfecto** de subjuntivo es igual que el de indicativo.

    I had spoken
    you had spoken
    he had spoken
    we had spoken
    you had spoken
    they had spoken

If you **had spoken** then...!¡
    *Si **hubieras hablado** entonces...!*

La forma negativa es igual que en el indicativo.

If **you hadn't** spoken...?
    *¡Si no **hubieras** hablado...!*

Part Two
Segunda Parte

1. To be · Ser, estar

affirmative	interrogative	negative

❀ Indicative

Present I am   soy/estoy
you are
he is
we are
you are
they are

am I?
are you?
is he?
are we?
are you?
are they?

I am not
you are not
he is not
we are not
you are not
they are not

Past I was   era/estaba/fui/estuviese
you were
he was
we were
you were
they were

was I?
were you?
was he?
were we?
were you?
were they?

I was not
you were not
he was not
we were not
you were not
they were not

Future I shall/will be   seré/estaré
you will be
he will be
we shall/will be
you will be
they will be

shall/will I be?
will you be?
will he be?
shall/will we be?
will you be?
will they be?

I shall/will not be
you will not be
he will not be
we shall/will not be
you will not be
they will not be

❀ Conditional

Present I should/would be   seria/estaría
you would be
he would be
we should/would be
you would be
they would be

should/would I be?
would you be?
would he be?
should/would we be?
would you be?
would they be?

I should/would not be
you would not be
he would not be
we should/would not be
you would not be
they would not be

❀ Imperative

Singular Let me be   déjame ser/estar
Be   sé/está tú
Let him/her/it be   sea/esté él

* * * * * * * * * *

do not let me be
do not be
do not let him/her/it be

❀ Subjunctive

Present I am   sea/esté
you are
he is
we are
you are
they are

* * * * * * * * * *

I am not
you are not
he is not
we are not
you are not
they are not

Past I were   fuera/estuviera/fuese/estuviese
you were
he were
we were
you were
they were

* * * * * * * * * *

I were not
you were not
he was not
we were not
you were not
they were not

❋ Infinitive	❋ Gerund	❋ Participle
To be	Being	Been

	affirmative	interrogative	negative

Present perfect

affirmative		interrogative	negative
I have been	he sido/estado	have I been?	I have not been
you have been		have you been?	you have not been
he has been		has he been?	he has not been
we have been		have we been?	we have not been
you have been		have you been?	you have not been
they have been		have they been?	they have not been

Past perfect

affirmative		interrogative	negative
I had been	había sido/estado	had I been?	I had not been
you had been		had you been?	you had not been
he had been		had he been?	he had not been
we had been		had we been?	we had not been
you had been		had you been?	you had not been
they had been		had they been?	they had not been

Future perfect

affirmative		interrogative	negative
I shall/will have been	habré sido/estado	shall/will I have been?	I shall/will not have been
you will have been		will you have been?	you will not have been
he will have been		will he have been?	he will not have been
we shall/will have been		shall /will we have been?	we shall/will not have been
you will have been		will you have been?	you will not have been
they will have been		will they have been?	they will not have been

Perfect

affirmative		interrogative	negative
I should/would have been	habría sido/estado	should/would I have been?	I should/would have not been
you would have been		would you have been?	you would have not been
he would have been		would he have been?	he would have not been
we should/would have been		should/would we have been?	we should/would have not been
you would have been		would you have been?	you would have not been
they would have been		would they have been?	they would have not been

Plural

affirmative		interrogative	negative
Let us (let's) be	seamos/estemos	* * * * * * * * *	do not let us (let's not) be
Be	sed/estad		do not be
Let them be	sean/estén		do not let them be

Present perfect

affirmative		interrogative	negative
I have been	haya sido/estado	* * * * * * * * *	I have not been
you have been			you have not been
he has been			he has not been
we have been			we have not been
you have been			you have not been
they have been			they have not been

Past perfect

affirmative		interrogative	negative
I had been	hubiera/hubiese sido/estado	* * * * * * * * *	I had not been
you had been			you had not been
he had been			he had not been
we had been			we had not been
you had been			you had not been
they had been			they had not been

2. To have · Tener, tomar

affirmative	interrogative	negative

✿ Indicative

Present

I have tengo	have I?	I have not
you have	have you?	you have not
he has	has he?	he has not
we have	have we?	we have not
you have	have you?	you have not
they have	have they?	they have not

Past

I had tenía/tuve	had I? (did I have?)	I had not (I didn't have)
you had	had you? (did you have?)	you had not (you didn't have)
he had	had he? (did he have?)	he had not (he didn't have)
we had	had we? (did we have?)	we had not (we didn't have)
you had	had you? (did you have?)	you had not (you didn't have)
they had	had they? (did they have?)	they had not (they didn't have)

Future

I shall/will have tendré	shall/will I have?	I shall/will not have
you will have	will you have?	you will not have
he will have	will he have?	he will not have
we shall/will have	shall/will we have?	we shall/will not have
you will have	will you have?	you will not have
they will have	will they have?	they will not have

✿ Conditional

Present

I should/would have tendría	should/would I have?	I should/would not have
you would have	would you have?	you would not have
he would have	would he have	he would not have
we should/would have	should/would we have	we should/would not have
you would have	would you have?	you would not have
they would have	would they have?	they would not have

✿ Imperative

Singular

Let me have déjame tener		do not let me have
have ten tú	* * * * * * * * * *	do not have
let him/her/it have tenga él/ella		do not let him/her/it have

✿ Subjunctive

Present

I have tenga		I have not
you have		you have not
he has	* * * * * * * * * *	he has not
we have		we have not
you have		you have not
they have		they have not

Past

I had tuviera/tuviese		I had not
you had		you had not
he had	* * * * * * * * * *	he had not
we had		we had not
you had		you had not
they had		they had not

❈ Infinitive	❈ Gerund	❈ Participle
To have	having	had

affirmative	interrogative	negative

Present perfect

I have had he tenido	have I had?	I have not had
You have had	have you had?	you have not had
he has had	has he had?	he has not had
we have had	have we had?	we have not had
you have had	have you had?	you have not had
they have had	have they had?	they have not had

Past perfect

I had had hube tenido	had I had?	I had not had
you had had	had you had?	you had not had
he had had	had he had?	he had not had
we had had	had we had?	we had not had
you had had	had you had?	you had not had
they had had	had they had?	they had not had

Future perfect

I shall/will have had habré tenido	shall/will I have had?	I shall/will not have had
you will have had	will you have had?	you will not have had
he will have had	will he have had?	he will not have had
we shall/will have had	shall/will we have had?	we shall/will not have had
you will have had	will you have had?	you will not have had
they will have had	will they have had?	they will not have had

Perfect

I should/would have had habría tenido	should/would I have had?	I should/would not have had
you would have had	would you have had?	you would not have had
he would have had	would he have had?	he would not have had
we should/would have had	should/would we have had?	we should/would not have had
you would have had	would you have had?	you would not have had
they would have had	would they have had?	they would not have had

Plural

Let us (let's) have tengamos	* * * * * * * * * *	do not let us (let's not) have
have tened vos.		do not have
let them have tengan ellos/ellas		do not let them have

Present perfect

I have had haya tenido	* * * * * * * * * *	I have not had
you has had		you have not had
he have had		he has not had
we have had		we have not had
you have had		you have not had
they have had		they had not had

Past perfect

I had had hubiera/hubiese tenido	* * * * * * * * * *	I had not had
you had had		you had not had
he had had		he had not had
we had had		we had not had
you had had		you had not had
they had had		they had not had

3. To begin · Empezar, comenzar

affirmative	interrogative	negative

❖ Indicative

Present
I begin empiezo	do I begin?	I do not begin
you begin	do you begin?	you do not begin
he begins	does he begin?	he does not begin
we begin	do we begin?	we do not begin
you begin	do you begin?	you do not begin
they begin	do they begin?	they do not begin

Past
I began empezaba/empecé	did I begin?	I did not begin
you began	did you begin?	you did not begin
he began	did he begin?	he did not begin
we began	did we begin?	we did not begin
you began	did you begin?	you did not begin
they began	did they begin?	they did not begin

Future
I shall/will begin empezaré	shall/will I begin?	I shall/will not begin
you will begin	will you begin?	you will not begin
he will begin	will he begin?	he will not begin
we shall/will begin	shall/will we begin?	we shall/will not begin
you will begin	will you begin?	you will not begin
they will begin	will they begin?	they will not begin

❖ Conditional

Present
I should/would begin empezaría	should/would I begin?	I should/would not begin
you would begin	would you begin?	you would not begin
he would begin	would he begin?	he would not begin
we should/would begin	should/would we begin?	we should/would not begin
you would begin	would you begin?	you would not begin
they would begin	would they begin?	they would not begin

❖ Imperative

Singular
let me begin déjame empezar		do not let me begin
begin empieza tú	* * * * * * * * * *	do not begin
let him begin empiece él		do not let him begin

❖ Subjunctive

Present
I begin empiece		I do not begin
you begin		you do not begin
he begins	* * * * * * * * * *	he doesn't begin
we begin		we do not begin
you begin		you do not begin
they begin		they do not begin

Past
I began empezara/empezase		I did not begin
you began		you did not begin
he began	* * * * * * * * * *	he did not begin
we began		we did not begin
you began		you did not begin
they began		they did not begin

✾ Infinitive	✾ Gerund	✾ Participle
To begin	beginning	begun

affirmative	interrogative	negative

	affirmative	interrogative	negative
Present perfect	I have begun he empezado you have begun he has begun we have begun you have begun they have begun	have I begun? have you begun? has he begun? have we begun? have you begun? have they begun?	I have not begun you have not begun he has not begun we have not begun you have not begun they have not begun
Past perfect	I had begun había/hube empezado you had begun he had begun we had begun you had begun they had begun	had I begun? had you begun? had he begun? had we begun? had you begun? had they begun?	I had not begun you had not begun he had not begun we had not begun you had not begun they had not begun
Future perfect	I shall/will have begun habré empezado you will have begun he will have begun we shall/will have begun you will have begun they will have begun	shall/will I have begun? will you have begun? will he have begun? shall/will we have begun? will you have begun? will they have begun?	I shall/will not have begun you will not have begun he will not have begun we shall/will not have begun you will not have begun they will not have begun
Perfect	I should/would have begun habría empezado you would have begun he would have begun we should/would have begun you would have begun they would have begun	should/would I have begun? would you have begun? would he have begun? should/would we have begun? would you have begun? would they have begun?	I should/would not have begun you would not have begun he would have not begun we should/would have not begun you would have not begun they would have not begun
Plural	let us begin empecemos begin empezad let them begin empiecen	* * * * * * * * * *	do not let us (let's not) begin do not begin do not let them begin
Present perfect	I have begun haya empezado you have begun he has begun we have begun you have begun they have begun	* * * * * * * * * *	I have not begun you have not begun he has not begun we have not begun you have not begun they have not begun
Past perfect	I had begun hubiera/hubiese empezado you had begun he had begun we had begun you had begun they had begun	* * * * * * * * * *	I had not begun you had not begun he had not begun we had not begun you had not begun they had not begun

4. Bend · Doblar, torcer, curvar

	affirmative	interrogative	negative
❋ Indicative			
Present	I bend doblo	do I bend?	I do not bend
	you bend	do you bend?	you do not bend
	he bends	does he bend?	he does not bend
	we bend	do we bend?	we do not bend
	you bend	do you bend?	you do not bend
	they bend	do they bend?	they do not bend
Past	I bent doblaba/doblé	did I bend?	I did not bend
	you bent	did you bend?	you did not bend
	he bent	did he bend?	he did not bend
	we bent	did we bend?	we did not bend
	you bent	did you bend?	you did not bend
	they bent	did they bend?	they did not bend
Future	I shall/will bend doblaré	shall/will I bend?	I shall/will not bend
	you will bend	will you bend?	you will not bend
	he will bend	will he bend?	he will not bend
	we shall/will bend	shall/will we bend?	we shall/will not bend
	you will bend	will you bend?	you will not bend
	they will bend	will they bend?	they will not bend
❋ Conditional			
Present	I should/would bend doblaría	should/would I bend?	I should/would not bend
	you would bend	would you bend?	you would not bend
	he would bend	would he bend?	he would not bend
	we should/would bend	should/would we bend?	we should/would not bend
	you would bend	would you bend?	you would not bend
	they would bend	would they bend?	they would not bend
❋ Imperative			
Singular	let me bend déjame doblar		do not let me bend
	bend dobla	* * * * * * * * *	do not bend
	let him/her/it bend doble él		do not let him/her/it bend
❋ Subjunctive			
Present	I bend doble		I do not bend
	you bend		you do not bend
	he bends	* * * * * * * * *	he does not bend
	we bend		we do not bend
	you bend		you do not bend
	they bend		they do not bend
Past	I bent doblara/doblase		I did not bend
	you bent		you did not bend
	he bent	* * * * * * * * *	he did not bend
	we bent		we did not bend
	you bent		you did not bend
	they bent		they did not bend

❋ Infinitive	❋ Gerund	❋ Participle
To bend	bending	bent

affirmative	interrogative	negative

Present perfect

I have bent he doblado	have I bent?	I have not bent
you have bent	have you bent?	you have not bent
he has bent	has he bent?	he has not bent
we have bent	have we bent?	we have not bent
you have bent	have you bent?	you have not bent
they have bent	have they bent?	they have not bent

Past perfect

I had bent había doblado	had I bent?	I had not bent
you had bent	had you bent?	you had not bent
he had bent	had he bent?	he had not bent
we had bent	had we bent?	we had not bent
you had bent	had you bent?	you had not bent
they had bent	had they bent?	they had not bent

Future perfect

I shall/will have bent habré doblado	shall/will I have bent?	I shall/will not have bent
you will have bent	will you have bent?	you will not have bent
he will have bent	will he have bent?	he will not have bent
we shall/will have bent	shall/will we have bent?	we shall/will not have bent
you will have bent	will you have bent?	you will not have bent
they will have bent	will they have bent?	they will not have bent

Perfect

I should/would have bent habría doblado	should/would I have bent?	I should/would not have bent
you would have bent	would you have bent?	you would not have bent
he would have bent	would he have bent?	he would not have bent
we should/would have bent	should/would we have bent?	we should/would not have bent
you would have bent	would you have bent?	you would not have bent
they would have bent	would they have bent?	they would not have bent

Plural

let us bend doblemos	* * * * * * * * *	do not let us (let's not) bend
bend doblad		do not bend
let them bend doblen		do not let them bend

Present perfect

I have bent haya doblado	* * * * * * * * *	I have not bent
you have bent		you have not bent
he has bent		he has not bent
we have bent		we have not bent
you have bent		you have not bent
they have bent		they have not bent

Past perfect

I had bent hubiera/hubiese doblado	* * * * * * * * *	I had not bent
you had bent		you had not bent
he had bent		he had not bent
we had bent		we had not bent
you had bent		you had not bent
they had bent		they had not bent

5. Bet · Apostar

	affirmative	interrogative	negative

❀ Indicative

Present	I bet apuesto	do I bet?	I do not bet
	you bet	do you bet?	you do not bet
	he bets	does he bet?	he does not bet
	we bet	do we bet?	we do not bet
	you bet	do you bet?	you do not bet
	they bet	do they bet?	they do not bet

Past	I bet apostaba/aposté	did I bet?	I did not bet
	you bet	did you bet?	you did not bet
	he bet	did he bet?	he did not bet
	we bet	did we bet?	we did not bet
	you bet	did you bet?	you did not bet
	they bet	did they bet?	they did not bet

Future	I shall/will bet apostaré	shall/will I bet?	I shall/will not bet
	you will bet	will you bet?	you will not bet
	he will bet	will he bet?	he will not bet
	we shall/will bet	shall/will we bet?	we shall/will not bet
	you will bet	will you bet?	you will not bet
	they will bet	will they bet?	they will not bet

❀ Conditional

Present	I should/would bet apostaría	should/would I bet?	I should/would not bet
	you would bet	would you bet?	you would not bet
	he would bet	would he bet?	he would not bet
	we should/would bet	should/would we bet?	we would not bet
	you would bet	would you bet?	you would not bet
	they would bet	would they bet?	they would not bet

❀ Imperative

Singular	let me bet déjame apostar	* * * * * * * * *	do not let me bet
	bet apuesta		do not bet
	let him/her/it bet apueste		do not let him/her/it bet

❀ Subjunctive

Present	I bet apueste	* * * * * * * * *	I do not bet
	you bet		you do not bet
	he bets		he does not bet
	we bet		we do not bet
	you bet		you do not bet
	they bet		they do not bet

Past	I bet apostara/apostase	* * * * * * * * *	I did not bet
	you bet		you did not bet
	he bet		he did not bet
	we bet		we did not bet
	you bet		you did not bet
	they bet		they did not bet

✿ Infinitive	✿ Gerund	✿ Participle
to bet	betting	bet

affirmative	interrogative	negative

Present perfect

I have bet he apostado	have I bet?	I have not bet
you have bet	have you bet?	you have not bet
he has bet	has he bet?	he has not bet
we have bet	have we bet?	we have not bet
you have bet	have you bet?	you have not bet
they have bet	have they bet?	they have not bet

Past perfect

I had bet había/hube apostado	had I bet?	I had not bet
you had bet	had you bet?	you had not bet
he had bet	had he bet?	he had not bet
we had bet	had we bet?	we had not bet
you had bet	had you bet?	you had not bet
they had bet	had they bet?	they had not bet

Future perfect

I shall/will have bet habré apostado	shall/will I have bet?	I shall/will not have bet
you will have bet	will you have bet?	you will not have have bet
he will have bet	will he have bet?	he will not have has bet
we shall/will have bet	shall/will we have bet?	we shall/will not have have bet
you will have bet	will you have bet?	you will not have have bet
they will have bet	will they have bet?	they will not have have bet

Perfect

I should/would have bet habría apostado	should/would I have bet?	I should/would not have bet
you would have bet	would you have bet?	you would not have bet
he would have bet	would he have bet?	he would not have bet
we should/would have bet	should/would we have bet?	we should/would not have bet
you would have bet	would you have bet?	you would not have bet
they would have bet	would they have bet?	they would not have bet

Plural

let us bet apostemos	* * * * * * * * * *	do not le us (let's not) bet
bet apostad		do not bet
let them bet apuesten		do not let them bet

Present perfect

I have bet haya apostado		I have not bet
you have bet	* * * * * * * * * *	you have not bet
he has bet		he has not bet
we have bet		we have not bet
you have bet		you have not bet
they have bet		they have not bet

Past perfect

I had bet hubiera/hubiese apostado		I had not bet
you had bet	* * * * * * * * * *	you had not bet
he had bet		he had not bet
we had bet		we had not bet
you had bet		you had not bet
they had bet		they had not bet

6. Bid · Mandar, ordenar, invitar, dar

	affirmative	interrogative	negative
☼ Indicative			
Present	I bid ordeno	do I bid?	I do not bid
	you bid	do you bid?	you do not bid
	he bids	does he bid?	he does not bid
	we bid	do we bid?	we do not bid
	you bid	do you bid?	you do not bid
	they bid	do they bid?	they do not bid
Past	I bade ordenaba/ordené	did I bid?	I did not bid
	you bade	did you bid?	you did not bid
	he bade	did he bid?	he did not bid
	we bade	did we bid?	we did not bid
	you bade	did you bid?	you did not bid
	they bade	did they bid?	they did not bid
Future	I shall/will bid ordenaré	shall/will I bid?	I shall/will not bid
	you will bid	will you bid?	you will not bid
	he will bid	will he bid?	he will not bid
	we shall/will bid	shall/will we bid?	we shall/will not bid
	you will bid	will you bid?	you will not bid
	they will bid	will they bid?	they will not bid
☼ Conditional			
Present	I should/would bid ordenaría	should/would I bid?	I should/would not bid
	you would bid	would you bid?	you would not bid
	he would bid	would he bid?	he would not bid
	we should/would bid	should/would we bid?	we should/would not bid
	you would bid	would you bid?	you would not bid
	they would bid	would they bid?	they would not bid
☼ Imperative			
Singular	let me bid déjame ordenar		do not let me bid
	bid ordena	* * * * * * * * * *	do not bid
	let him/her/it bid ordene		do not let him/her/it bid
☼ Subjunctive			
Present	I bid ordene		I do not bid
	you bid		you do not bid
	he bids	* * * * * * * * * *	he does not bid
	we bid		we do not bid
	you bid		you do not bid
	they bid		they do not bid
Past	I bade ordenara/ordenase		I did not bid
	you bade		you did not bid
	he bade	* * * * * * * * * *	he did not bid
	we bade		we did not bid
	you bade		you did not bid
	they bade		they did not bid

* Infinitive	* Gerund	* Participle
to bid	bidding	bidden

	affirmative	interrogative	negative

Present Perfect

	affirmative	interrogative	negative
	I have bidden he ordenado	have I bidden?	I have not bidden
	you have bidden	have you bidden?	you have not bidden
	he has bidden	has he bidden?	he has not bidden
	we have bidden	have we bidden?	we have not bidden
	you have bidden	have you bidden?	you have not bidden
	they have bidden	have they bidden?	they have not bidden

Past Perfect

	I had bidden había/hube ordenado	had I bidden?	I had not bidden
	you had bidden	had you bidden?	you had not bidden
	he had bidden	had he bidden?	he had not bidden
	we had bidden	had we bidden?	we had not bidden
	you had bidden	had you bidden?	you had not bidden
	they had bidden	had he bidden?	they had not bidden

Future Perfect

	I shall/will have bidden habré ordenado	shall/will I have bidden?	I shall/will not have bidden
	you will have bidden	will you have bidden?	you will not have bidden
	he will have bidden	will he have bidden?	he will not have bidden
	we shall/will have bidden	shall/will we have bidden?	we shall/will not have bidden
	you will have bidden	will you have bidden?	you will not have bidden
	they will have bidden	will they have bidden?	they will not have bidden

Perfect

	I should/would have bidden habría ordenado	should/would I have bidden?	I should/would not have bidden
	you would have bidden	would you have bidden?	you would not have bidden
	he would have bidden	would he have bidden?	he would not have bidden
	we should/would have bidden	should/would we have bidden?	we should/would not have bidden
	you would have bidden	would you have bidden?	you would not have bidden
	they would have bidden	would they have bidden?	they would not have bidden

Plural

	let us bid ordenemos	* * * * * * * * * *	do not let us (let's not) bid
	bid ordenad		do not bid
	let them bid ordenen		do not let them bid

Present Perfect

	I have bidden haya ordenado	* * * * * * * * * *	I have not bidden
	you have bidden		you have not bidden
	he has bidden		he has not bidden
	we have bidden		we have not bidden
	you have bidden		you have not bidden
	they have bidden		they have not bidden

Past Perfect

	I had bidden hubiera/hubiese ordenado	* * * * * * * * * *	I had not bidden
	you had bidden		you had not bidden
	he had bidden		he had not bidden
	we had bidden		we had not bidden
	you had bidden		you had not bidden
	they had bidden		they had not bidden

7. Find · Encontrar, hallar

	affirmative	interrogative	negative
❀ Indicative			
Present	I find encuentro	do I find?	I do not find
	you find	do you find?	you do not find
	he finds	does he find?	he does not find
	we find	do we find?	we do not find
	you find	do you find?	you do not find
	they find	do they find?	they do not find
Past	I found encontraba/encontré	did I find?	I did not find
	you found	did you find?	you did not find
	he found	did he find?	he did not find
	we found	did we find?	we did not find
	you found	did you find?	you did not find
	they found	did they find?	they did not find
Future	I shall/will find encontraré	shall/will I find?	I shall/will not find
	you will find	will you find?	you will not find
	he will find	will he find?	he will not find
	we shall/will find	shall/will we find?	we shall/will not find
	you will find	will you find?	you will not find
	they will find	will they find?	they will not find
❀ Conditional			
Present	I should/would find encontraría	should/would I find?	I should/would not find
	you would find	would you find?	you would not find
	he would find	would he find?	he would not find
	we should/would find	should/would we find?	we should/would not find
	you would find	would you find?	you would not find
	they would find	would they find?	they would not find
❀ Imperative			
Singular	let me find déjame encontrar	* * * * * * * * * *	do not let me find
	find encuentra		do not find
	let him/her/it find encuentre		do not let him/her/it find
❀ Subjunctive			
Present	I find encuentre	* * * * * * * * * *	I do not find
	you find		you do not find
	he finds		he does not find
	we find		we do not find
	you find		you do not find
	they find		they do not find
Past	I found encontrara/encontrase	* * * * * * * * * *	I did not find
	you found		you did not find
	he found		he did not find
	we found		we did not find
	you found		you did not find
	they found		they did not find

❀ Infinitive	❀ Gerund	❀ Participle
to find	finding	found

	affirmative	interrogative	negative

	affirmative	interrogative	negative
Present Perfect	I have found he encontrado you have found he has found we have found you have found they have found	have I found? have you found? has he found? have we found? have you found? have they found?	I have not found you have not found he has not found we have not found you have not found they have not found
Past Perfect	I had found había encontrado you had found he had found we had found you had found they had found	had I found? had you found? had he found? had we found? had you found? had they found?	I had not found you had not found he had not found we had not found you had not found they had not found
Future Perfect	I shall/will have found habré encontrado you will have found he will have found we shall/will have found you will have found they will have found	shall/will I have found? will you have found? will he have found? shall/will we have found? will you have found? will they have found?	I shall/will not have found you will not have found he will not have found we shall/will not have found you will not have found they will not have found
Perfect	I should/would have found habría encontrado you would have found he would have found we should/would have found you would have found they would have found	should/would I have found? would you have found? would he have found? should/would we have found? would you have found? would they have found?	I should/would not have found you would not have found he would not have found we should/would not have found you would not have found they would not have found
Plural	let us find encontremos find encontrad let them find encuentren	* * * * * * * * * *	do not let us (let's not) find do not find do not let them find
Present Perfect	I have found haya encontrado you have found he has found we have found you have found they have found	* * * * * * * * * *	I have not found you have not found he has not found we have not found you have not found they have not found
Past Perfect	I had found hubiera/hubiese encontrado you had found he had found we had found you had found they had found	* * * * * * * * * *	I had not found you had not found he had not found we had not found you had not found they had not found

8. Bleed · Sangrar, desangrar

	affirmative	interrogative	negative

❁ Indicative

	affirmative	interrogative	negative
Present	I bleed　　sangro	do I bleed?	I do not bleed
	you bleed	do you bleed?	you do not bleed
	he bleeds	does he bleed?	he does not bleed
	we bleed	do we bleed?	we do not bleed
	you bleed	do you bleed?	you do not bleed
	they bleed	do they bleed?	they do not bleed
Past	I bled　　sangraba/sangré	did I bleed?	I did not bleed
	you bled	did you bleed?	you did not bleed
	he bled	did he bleed?	he did not bleed
	we bled	did we bleed?	we did not bleed
	you bled	did you bleed?	you did not bleed
	they bled	did they bleed?	they did not bleed
Future	I shall/will bleed　　sangraré	shall/will I bleed?	I shall/will not bleed
	you will bleed	will you bleed?	you will not bleed
	he will bleed	will he bleed?	he will not bleed
	we shall/will bleed	shall/will we bleed?	we shall/will not bleed
	you will bleed	will you bleed?	you will not bleed
	they will bleed	will they bleed?	they will not bleed

❁ Conditional

	affirmative	interrogative	negative
Present	I should/would bleed　　sangraría	should/would I bleed?	I should/would not bleed
	you would bleed	would you bleed?	you would not bleed
	he would bleed	would he bleed?	he would not bleed
	we should/would bleed	should/would we bleed?	we should/would not bleed
	you would bleed	would you bleed?	you would not bleed
	they would bleed	would they bleed?	they would not bleed

❁ Imperative

	affirmative	interrogative	negative
Singular	let me bleed　　déjame sangrar	* * * * * * * * *	do not let me bleed
	bleed　　sangra		do not bleed
	let him/her/it bleed　sangre		do not let him/her/it bleed

❁ Subjunctive

	affirmative	interrogative	negative
Present	I bleed　　sangre	* * * * * * * * *	I do not bleed
	you bleed		you do not bleed
	he bleeds		he does not bleed
	we bleed		we do not bleed
	you bleed		you do not bleed
	they bleed		they do not bleed
Past	I bled　　sangrara/sangrase	* * * * * * * * *	I did not bleed
	you bled		you did not bleed
	he bled		he did not bleed
	we bled		we did not bleed
	you bled		you did not bleed
	they bled		they did not bleed

❀ Infinitive	❀ Gerund	❀ Participle
to bleed	bleeding	bled

	affirmative	interrogative	negative

	affirmative	interrogative	negative
Present perfect	I have bled he sangrado you have bled he has bled we have bled you have bled they have bled	have I bled? have you bled? has he bled? have we bled? have you bled? have they bled?	I have not bled you have not bled he has not bled we have not bled you have not bled they have not bled
Past perfect	I had bled había sangrado you had bled he had bled we had bled you had bled they had bled	had I bled? had you bled? had he bled? had we bled had you bled? had they bled?	I had not bled you had not bled he had not bled we had not bled you had not bled they had not bled
Future perfect	I shall/will have bled habré sangrado you will have bled he will have bled we shall/will have bled you will have bled they will have bled	shall/will I have bled? will you have bled? will he have bled? shall/will we have bled? will you have bled? will they have bled?	I shall/will not have bled you will not have bled he will not have bled we shall/will not have bled you will not have bled they will not have bled
Perfect	I should/would have bled habría sangrado you would have bled he would have bled we should/would have bled you would have bled they would have bled	should/would I have bled? would you have bled? would he have bled? should/would we have bled? would you have bled? would they have bled?	I should/would not have bled you would not have bled he would not have bled we should/would not have bled you would not have bled they would not have bled
Plural	let us bleed sangremos bleed sangrad let them bleed sangren	* * * * * * * * *	do not let us (let's not) bleed do not bleed do not let them bleed
Present perfect	I have bled hube sangrado you have bled he has bled we have bled you have bled they have bled	* * * * * * * * *	I have not bled you have not bled he has not bled we have not bled you have not bled they have not bled
Past perfect	I had bled hubiera/hubiese sangrado you had bled he had bled we had bled you had bled they had bled	* * * * * * * * *	I had not bled you had not bled he had not bled we had not bled you had not bled they had not bled

9. Blow · Soplar

	affirmative	interrogative	negative
Indicative			
Present	I blow soplo	do I blow?	I do not blow
	you blow	do you blow?	you do not blow
	he blows	does he blow?	he does not blow
	we blow	do we blow?	we do not blow
	you blow	do you blow?	you do not blow
	they blow	do they blow?	they do not blow
Past	I blew soplaba/soplé	did I blow?	I did not blow
	you blew	did you blow?	you did not blow
	he blew	did he blow?	he did not blow
	we blew	did we blow?	we did not blow
	you blew	did you blow?	you did not blow
	they blew	did they blow?	they did not blow
Future	I shall/will blow soplaré	shall/will I blow?	I shall/will not blow
	you will blow	will you blow?	you will not blow
	he will blow	will they blow?	he will not blow
	we shall/will blow	shall/will we blow?	we shall/will not blow
	you will blow	will you blow?	you will not blow
	they will blow	will they blow?	they will not blow
Conditional			
Present	I should/would blow soplaría	should/would I blow?	I should/would not blow
	you would blow	would you blow?	you would not blow
	he would blow	would he blow?	he would not blow
	we would blow	should/would we blow?	we should/would not blow
	you would blow	would you blow?	you would not blow
	they would blow	would they blow?	they would not blow
Imperative			
Singular	let me blow déjame soplar		do not let me blow
	blow sopla	* * * * * * * * * *	do not blow
	let him/her/it blow sople		do not let him/her/it blow
Subjunctive			
Present	I blow sople		I do not blow
	you blow		you do not blow
	he blows	* * * * * * * * * *	he does not blow
	we blow		we do not blow
	you blow		you do not blow
	they blow		they do not blow
Past	I blew soplara/soplase		I did not blow
	you blew		you did not blow
	he blew	* * * * * * * * * *	he did not blow
	we blew		we did not blow
	you blew		you did not blow
	they blew		they did not blow

❀ Infinitive	❀ Gerund	❀ Participle
to blow	blowing	blown

	affirmative	interrogative	negative

	affirmative	interrogative	negative
resent erfect	I have blown he soplado you have blown he has blown we have blown you have blown they have blown	have I blown? have you blown? has he blown? have we blown? have you blown? have they blown?	I have not blown you have not blown he has not blown we have not blown you have not blown they have not blown
ast erfect	I had blown había soplado you had blown he had blown we had blown you had blown they had blown	had I blown? had you blown? had he blown? had we blown? had you blown? had they blown?	I had not blown you had not blown he had not blown we had not blown you had not blown they had not blown
uture erfect	I shall/will have blown habré soplado you will have blown he will have blown we shall/will have blown you will have blown they will have blown	shall/will I have blown? will you have blown? will he have blown? shall/will we have blown? will you have blown? will they have blown?	I shall/will not have blown you will not have blown he will not have blown we shall/will not have blown you will not have blown they will not have blown
erfect	I should/would have blown habría soplado you would have blown he would have blown we should/would have blown you would have blown they would have blown	should/would I have blown? would you have blown? would he have blown? should/would we have blown? would you have blown? would they have blown?	I should/would not have blown you would not have blown he would not have blown we should/would not have blown you would not have blown they would not have blown
lural	let us blow soplemos blow soplad let them blow soplen	* * * * * * * * *	do not let us (let's not) blow do not blow do not let them blow
resent erfect	I have blown haya soplado you have blown he has blown we have blown you have blown they have blown	* * * * * * * * *	I have not blown you have not blown he has not blown we have not blown you have not blown they have not blown
ast erfect	I had blown hubiera/hubiese soplado you had blown he had blown we had blown you had blown they had blown	* * * * * * * * *	I had not blown you had not blown he had not blown we had not blown you had not blown they had not blown

10. Break · Romper

	affirmative	interrogative	negative

✿ Indicative

Present
I break rompo	do I break?	I do not break
you break	do you break?	you do not break
he breaks	does he break?	he does not break
we break	do we break?	we do not break
you break	do you break?	you do not break
they break	do they break?	they do not break

Past
I broke rompía/rompí	did I break?	I did not break
you broke	did you break?	you did not break
he broke	did he break?	he did not break
we broke	did we break?	we did not break
you broke	did you break?	you did not break
they broke	did they break?	they did not break

Future
I shall/will break romperé	shall/will I break?	I shall/will not break
you will break	shall you break?	you will not break
he will break	shall he break?	he will not break
we shall/will break	shall/will we break?	we shall/will not break
you will break	shall you break?	you will not break
they will break	shall they break?	they will not break

✿ Conditional

Present
I should/would break rompería	should/would I break?	I should/would not break
you would break	would you break?	you would not break
he would break	would he break?	he would not break
we should/would break	should/would we break?	we should/would not break
you would break	would you break?	you would not break
they would break	would they break?	they would not break

✿ Imperative

Singular
let me break déjame romper		do not let me break
break rompe	* * * * * * * * * *	do not break
let him/her/it break rompa		do not let him/her/it break

✿ Subjunctive

Present
I break rompa		I do not break
you break		you do not break
he breaks	* * * * * * * * * *	he does not break
we break		we do not break
you break		you do not break
they break		they do not break

Past
I broke rompiera/rompiese		I did not break
you broke		you did not break
he broke	* * * * * * * * * *	he did not break
we broke		we did not break
you broke		you did not break
they broke		they did not break

✿ Infinitive	✿ Gerund	✿ Participle
to break	breaking	broken

affirmative	interrogative	negative

Present perfect

I have broken he roto	have I broken?	I have not broken
you have broken	have you broken?	you have not broken
he has broken	has he broken?	he has not broken
we have broken	have we broken?	we have not broken
you have broken	have you broken?	you have not broken
they have broken	have they broken?	they have not broken

Past perfect

I had broken había roto	had I broken?	I had not broken
you had broken	had you broken?	you had not broken
he had broken	had he broken?	he had not broken
we had broken	had we broken?	we had not broken
you had broken	had you broken?	you had not broken
they had broken	had they broken?	they had not broken

Future perfect

I shall/will have broken habré roto	shall/will I have broken?	I shall/will not have broken
you will have broken	will you have broken?	you will not have broken
he will have broken	will he have broken?	he will not have broken
we shall/will have broken	shall/will we have broken?	we shall/will not have broken
you will have broken	will you have broken?	you will not have broken
they will have broken	will they have broken?	they will not have broken

Perfect

I should/would have broken habría roto	should/would I have broken?	I should/would not have broken
you would have broken	would you have broken?	you would not have broken
he would have broken	would he have broken?	he would not have broken
we should/would have broken	should/would we have broken?	we should/would not have broken
you would have broken	would you have broken?	you would not have broken
they would have broken	would they have broken?	they would not have broken

Plural

let us break rompamos	* * * * * * * * * *	do not let us (let's not) break
break romped		do not break
let them break rompan		do not let them break

Present perfect

I have broken haya roto	* * * * * * * * * *	I have not broken
you have broken		you have not broken
he has broken		he has not broken
we have broken		we have not broken
you have broken		you have not broken
they have broken		they have not broken

Past perfect

I had broken hubiera/hubiese roto	* * * * * * * * * *	I had not broken
you had broken		you had not broken
he had broken		he had not broken
we had broken		we had not broken
you had broken		you had not broken
they had broken		they had not broken

11. Bring · Traer

	affirmative	interrogative	negative

❈ Indicative

Present

affirmative	interrogative	negative
I bring traigo	do I bring?	I do not bring
you bring	do you bring?	you do not bring
he brings	does he bring?	he does not bring
we bring	do we bring?	we do not bring
you bring	do you bring?	you do not bring
they bring	do they bring?	they do not bring

Past

affirmative	interrogative	negative
I brought traía/traje	did I bring?	I did not bring
you brought	did you bring?	you did not bring
he brought	did he bring?	he did not bring
we brought	did we bring?	we did not bring
you brought	did you bring?	you did not bring
they brought	did he bring?	they did not bring

Future

affirmative	interrogative	negative
I shall/will bring traeré	shall/will I bring?	I shall/will not bring
you will bring	will you bring?	you will not bring
he will bring	will he bring?	he will not bring
we shall/will bring	shall/will we bring?	we shall/will not bring
you will bring	will you bring?	you will not bring
they will bring	will they bring?	they will not bring

❈ Conditional

Present

affirmative	interrogative	negative
I should/would bring traería	should/would I bring?	I should/would not bring
you would bring	would you bring?	you would not bring
he would bring	would he bring?	he would not bring
we should/would bring	should/would we bring?	we should/would not bring
you would bring	would you bring?	you would not bring
they would bring	would they bring?	they would not bring

❈ Imperative

Singular

affirmative	interrogative	negative
let me bring déjame traer	* * * * * * * * *	do not let me bring
bring trae		do not bring
let him/her/it bring traiga		do not let him/her/it bring

❈ Subjunctive

Present

affirmative	interrogative	negative
I bring traiga	* * * * * * * * *	I do not bring
you bring		you do not bring
he brings		he does not bring
we bring		we do not bring
you bring		you do not bring
they bring		they do not bring

Past

affirmative	interrogative	negative
I brought trajera/trajese	* * * * * * * * *	I did not bring
you brought		you did not bring
he brought		he did not bring
we brought		we did not bring
you brought		you did not bring
they brought		they did not bring

❋ Infinitive	❋ Gerund	❋ Participle
to bring	bringing	brought

	affirmative	interrogative	negative

	affirmative	interrogative	negative
Present perfect	I have brought he traído you have brought he has brought we have brought you have brought they have brought	have I brought? have you brought? has he brought? have we brought? have you brought? have they brought?	I have not brought you have not brought he has not brought we have not brought you have not brought they have not brought
Past perfect	I had brought había traído you had brought he had brought we had brought you had brought they had brought	had I brought? had you brought? had he brought? had we brought? had you brought? had they brought?	I had not brought you had not brought he had not brought we had not brought you had not brought they had not brought
Future perfect	I shall/will have brought habré traído you will have brought he will have brought we shall/will have brought you will have brought they will have brought	shall/will I have brought? will you have brought? will he have brought? shall/will we have brought? will you have brought? will they have brought?	I shall/will not have brought you will not have brought he will not have brought we shall/will not have brought you will not have brought they will not have brought
Perfect	I should/would have brought habría traído you would have brought he would have brought we should/would have brought you would have brought they would have brought	should/would I have brought? would you have brought? would he have brought? should/would we have brought? would you have brought? would they have brought?	I should/would not have brought you would not have brought he would not have brought we should/would not have brought you would not have brought they would not have brought
Plural	let us bring traigamos bring traed let them bring traigan	* * * * * * * * *	do not let us (let's not) bring do not bring do not let them bring
Present perfect	I have brought haya traído you have brought he has brought we have brought you have brought they have brought	* * * * * * * * *	I have not brought you have not brought he has not brought we have not brought you have not brought they have not brought
Past perfect	I had brought hubiera/hubiese traído you had brought he had brought we had brought you had brought they had brought	* * * * * * * * *	I had not brought you had not brought he had not brought we had not brought you had not brought they had not brought

12. Build · Construir, edificar

	affirmative	interrogative	negative

✻ Indicative

	affirmative	interrogative	negative
Present	I build construyo	do I build?	I do not build
	you build	do you build?	you do not build
	he builds	does he build?	he does not build
	we build	do we build?	we do not build
	you build	do you build?	you do not build
	they build	do they build?	they do not build
Past	I built construía/construí	did I build?	I did not build
	you built	did you build?	you did not build
	he built	did he build?	he did not build
	we built	did we build?	we did not build
	you built	did you build?	you did not build
	they built	did they build?	they did not build
Future	I shall/will build construiré	shall/will I build?	I shall/will not build
	you will build	will you build?	you will not build
	he will build	will he build?	he will not build
	we shall/will build	shall/will we build?	we shall/will not build
	you will build	will you build?	you will not build
	they will build	will they build?	they will not build

✻ Conditional

	affirmative	interrogative	negative
Present	I should/would build construiría	should/would I build?	I should/would not build
	you would build	would you build?	you would not build
	he would build	would he build?	he would not build
	we should/would build	should/would we build?	we should/would not build
	you would build	would you build?	you would not build
	they would build	would they build?	they would not build

✻ Imperative

	affirmative	interrogative	negative
Singular	let me build déjame construir		do not let me build
	build construye	* * * * * * * * * *	do not build
	let him/her/it build construya		do not let him/her/it build

✻ Subjunctive

	affirmative	interrogative	negative
Present	I build construya		I do not build
	you build		you do not build
	he builds	* * * * * * * * * *	he does not build
	we build		we do not build
	you build		you do not build
	they build		they do not build
Past	I built construyera/construyese		I did not build
	you built		you did not build
	he built	* * * * * * * * * *	he did not build
	we built		we did not build
	you built		you did not build
	they built		they did not build

❁ Infinitive	❁ Gerund	❁ Participle
to build	building	built

	affirmative	interrogative	negative
Present perfect	I have built he construido you have built he has built we have built you have built they have built	have I built? have you built? has he built? have we built? have you built? have they built?	I have not built you have not built he has not built we have not built you have not built they have not built
Past perfect	I had built había construido you had built he had built we had built you had built they had built	had I built? had you built? had he built? had we built? had you built? had they built?	I had not built you had not built he had not built we had not built you had not built they had not built
Future perfect	I shall/will have built habré construido you will have built he will have built we shall/will have built you will have built they will have built	shall/will I have built? will you have built? will he have built? shall/will we have built? will you have built? will they have built?	I shall/will not have built you will not have built he will not have built we shall/will not have built you will not have built they will not have built
Perfect	I should/would have built habría construido you would have built he would have built we should/would have built you would have built they would have built	should/would you have built? would you have built? would he have built? should/would we have built? would you have built? would they have built?	I should/would not have built you would not have built he would not have built we should/would not have built you would not have built they would not have built
Plural	let us build construyamos build construid let them build construyan	* * * * * * * * * *	do not let us (let's not) build do not build do not let them build
Present perfect	I have built haya construido you have built he has built we have built you have built they have built	* * * * * * * * * *	I have not built you have not built he has not built we have not built you have not built they have not built
Past perfect	I had built hubiera/hubiese construido you had built he had built we had built you had built they had built	* * * * * * * * * *	I had not built you had not built he had not built we had not built you had not built they had not built

13. Dig · Cavar, excavar

affirmative	interrogative	negative

❀ Indicative

Present			
I dig cavo	do I dig?	I do not dig
you dig	do you dig?	you do not dig
he digs	does he dig?	he does not dig
we dig	do we dig?	we do not dig
you dig	do you dig?	you do not dig
they dig	do they dig?	they do not dig

Past			
I dug cavaba/cavé	did I dig?	I did not dig
you dug	did you dig?	you did not dig
he dug	did he dig?	he did not dig
we dug	did we dig?	we did not dig
you dug	did you dig?	you did not dig
they dug	did they dig?	they did not dig

Future			
I shall/will dig cavaré	shall/will I dig?	I shall/will not dig
you will dig	will you dig?	you will not dig
he will dig	will he dig?	he will not dig
we shall/will dig	shall/will we dig?	we shall/will not dog
you will dig	will you dig?	you will not dig
they will dig	will they dig?	they will not dig

❀ Conditional

Present			
I should/would dig cavaría	should/would I dig?	I should/would not dig
you would dig	would you dig?	you would not dig
he would dig	would he dig?	he would not dig
we should/would dig	should/would we dig?	we should/would not dig
you would dig	would you dig?	you would not dig
they would dig	would they dig?	they would not dig

❀ Imperative

Singular			
let me dig déjame cavar	* * * * * * * * * *	do not let me dig
dig cava		do not dig
let him/her/it dig cave		do not let him/her/it dig

❀ Subjunctive

Present			
I dig cave	* * * * * * * * * *	I do not dig
you dig		you do not dig
he digs		he does not dig
we dig		we do not dig
you dig		you do not dig
they dig		they do not dig

Past			
I dug cavara/cavase	* * * * * * * * * *	I did not dig
you dug		you did not dig
he dug		he did not dig
we dug		we did not dig
you dug		you did not dig
they dug		they did not dig

❖ Infinitive	❖ Gerund	❖ Participle
to dig	digging	dug

affirmative	interrogative	negative

Present perfect

affirmative	interrogative	negative
I have dug he cavado	have I dug?	I have not dug
you have dug	have you dug?	you have not dug
he has dug	has he dug?	he has not dug
we have dug	have we dug?	we have not dug
you have dug	have you dug?	you have not dug
they have dug	have they dug?	they have not dug

Past perfect

affirmative	interrogative	negative
I had dug había cavado	had I dug?	I had not dug
you had dug	had you dug?	you had not dug
he had dug	had he dug?	he had not dug
we had dug	had we dug?	we had not dug
you had dug	had you dug?	you had not dug
they had dug	had they dug?	they had not dug

Future perfect

affirmative	interrogative	negative
I shall/will have dug habré cavado	shall/will I have dug?	I shall/will not have dug
you will have dug	will you have dug?	you will not have dug
he will have dug	will he have dug?	he will not have dug
we shall/will have dug	shall/will we have dug?	we shall/will not have dug
you will have dug	will you have dug?	you will not have dug
they will have dug	will they have dug?	they will not have dug

Perfect

affirmative	interrogative	negative
I should/would have dug habría cavado	should/would I have dug?	I should/would not have dug
you would have dug	would you have dug?	you would not have dug
he would have dug	would he have dug?	he would not have dug
we should/would have dug	should/would we have dug?	we should/would not have dug
you would have dug	would you have dug?	you would not have dug
they would have dug	would they have dug?	they would not have dug

Plural

affirmative	interrogative	negative
let us dig cavemos	* * * * * * * * * *	do not let us (let's not) dig
dig cavad		do not dig
let them dig caven		do not let them dig

Present perfect

affirmative	interrogative	negative
I have dug haya cavado	* * * * * * * * * *	I have not dug
you have dug		you have not dug
he has dug		he has not dug
we have dug		we have not dug
you have dug		you have not dug
they have dug		they have not dug

Past perfect

affirmative	interrogative	negative
I had dug hubiera/hubiese cavado	* * * * * * * * * *	I had not dug
you had dug		you had not dug
he had dug		he had not dug
we had dug		we had not dug
you had dug		you had not dug
they had dug		they had not dug

14. Come · Venir

	affirmative	interrogative	negative

✿ Indicative

Present

affirmative	interrogative	negative
I come vengo	do I come?	I do not come
you come	do you come?	you do not come
he comes	does he come?	he does not come
we come	do we come?	we do not come
you come	do you come?	you do not come
they come	do they come?	they do not come

Past

affirmative	interrogative	negative
I came venía/vine	did I come?	I did not come
you came	did you come?	you did not come
he came	did he come?	he did not come
we came	did we come?	we did not come
you came	did you come?	you did not come
they came	did they come?	they did not come

Future

affirmative	interrogative	negative
I shall/will come vendré	shall/will I come?	I shall/will not come
you will come	will you come?	you will not come
he will come	will he come?	he will not come
we shall/will come	shall/will we come?	we shall/will not come
you will come	will you come?	you will not come
they will come	will they come?	they will not come

✿ Conditional

Present

affirmative	interrogative	negative
I should/would come vendría	should/would I come?	I should/would not come
you would come	would you come?	you would not come
he would come	would he come?	he would not come
we should/would come	should/would we come?	we should/would not come
you would come	would you come?	you would not come
they would come	would they come?	they would not come

✿ Imperative

Singular

affirmative	interrogative	negative
let me come déjame venir		do not let me come
come ven	* * * * * * * * * *	do not come
let him/her/it come venga		do not let him/her/it come

✿ Subjunctive

Present

affirmative	interrogative	negative
I come venga		I do not come
you come		you do not come
he comes	* * * * * * * * * *	he does not come
we come		we do not come
you come		you do not come
they come		they do not come

Past

affirmative	interrogative	negative
I came viniera/viniese		I did not come
you came		you did not come
he came	* * * * * * * * * *	he did not come
we came		we did not come
you came		you did not come
they came		they did not come

❋ **Infinitive**	❋ **Gerund**	❋ **Participle**
to come	coming	come

affirmative	interrogative	negative

	affirmative	interrogative	negative
esent rfect	I have come he venido you have come he has come we have come you have come they have come	have I come? have you come? has he come? have we come? have you come? have they come?	I have not come you have not come he has not come we have not come you have not come they have not come
st rfect	I had come había venido you had come he had come we had come you had come they had come	had I come? had you come? had he come? had we come? had you come? had they come?	I had not come you had not come he had not come we had not come you had not come they had not come
ture rfect	I shall/will have come habré venido you will have come he will have come we shall/will have come you will have come they will have come	shall/will I have come? will you come? will he come? shall/will have we come? will you come? will they come?	I shall/will not have come you will not have come he will not have come we shall/will not have come you will not have come they will not have come
rfect	I should/would have come habría venido you would have come he would have come we should/would have come you would have come they would have come	should/would I have come? would you have come? would he have come? should/would we have come? would you have come? would they have come?	I should/would not have come you would not have come he would not have come we should/would not have come you would not have come they would not have come
ıral	let us come vengamos come venid let them come vengan	* * * * * * * * * *	do not let us (let's not) come do not come do not let them come
esent rfect	I have come haya venido you have come he has come we have come you have come they have come	* * * * * * * * * *	I have not come you have not come he has not come we have not come you have not come they have not come
st rfect	I had come hubiera/hubiese venido you had come he had come we had come you had come they had come	* * * * * * * * * *	I had not come you had not come he had not come we had not come you had not come they had not come

15. Creep · Arrastrarse, deslizarse

	affirmative	interrogative	negative
❀ Indicative			
Present	I creep me deslizo	do I creep?	I do not creep
	you creep	do you creep?	you do not creep
	he creeps	does he creep	he does not creep
	we creep	do we creep?	we do not creep
	you creep	do you creep?	you do not creep
	they preep	do they creep?	they do not creep
Past	I crept me deslizaba/deslicé	did I creep?	I did not creep
	you crept	did you creep?	you did not creep
	he crept	did he creep?	he did not creep
	we crept	did we creep?	we did not creep
	you crept	did you creep?	you did not creep
	they crept	did they creep?	they did not creep
Future	I shall/will creep me deslizaré	shall/will I creep?	I shall/will not creep
	you will creep	will you creep?	you will not creep
	he will creep	will he creep?	he will not creep
	we shall/will creep	shall/will we creep?	we shall/will not creep
	you will creep	will you creep?	you will not creep
	they will creep	will they creep?	they will not creep
❀ Conditional			
Present	I should/would creep me deslizaría	should/would I creep?	I should/would not creep
	you would creep	would you creep?	you would not creep
	he would creep	would he creep?	he would not creep
	we should/would creep	should/would we creep?	we should/would not creep
	you would creep	would you creep?	you would not creep
	they would creep	would they creep?	they would not creep
❀ Imperative			
Singular	let me creep déjame deslizarme	* * * * * * * * * *	do not let me creep
	creep deslízate		do not creep
	let him/her/it creep deslice		do not let him/her/it creep
❀ Subjunctive			
Present	I creep me deslice	* * * * * * * * * *	I do not creep
	you creep		you do not creep
	he creeps		he does not creep
	we creep		we do not creep
	you creep		you do not creep
	they creep		they do not creep
Past	I crept me deslizara/deslizase	* * * * * * * * * *	I did not creep
	you crept		you did not creep
	he crept		he did not creep
	we crept		we did not creep
	you crept		you did not creep
	they crept		they did not creep

❀ **Infinitive**	❀ **Gerund**	❀ **Participle**
to creep	creeping	crept

	affirmative	**interrogative**	**negative**

	affirmative	interrogative	negative
Present Perfect	I have crept me he deslizado you have crept he has crept we have crept you have crept they have crept	have I crept? have you crept? has he crept? have we crept? have you crept? have they crept?	I have not crept you have not crept he has not crept we have not crept you have not crept they have not crept
Past Perfect	I had crept me había/hube deslizado you had crept he had crept we had crept you had crept they had crept	had I crept? had you crept? had he crept? had we crept? had you crept? had they crept?	I had not crept you had not crept he had not crept we had not crept you had not crept they had not crept
Future Perfect	I shall/will have crept habré deslizado you will have crept he will have crept we shall/will have crept you will have crept they will have crept	shall/will I have crept? will you have crept? will he have crept? shall/will we have crept? will you have crept? will they have crept?	I shall/will not have crept you will not have crept he will not have crept we shall/will not have crept you will not have crept they will not have crept
Perfect	I should/would have crept me habría deslizado you would have crept he would have crept we should/would have crept you would have crept they would have crept	should/would I have crept? would you have crept? would he have crept? should/would we have crept? would you have crept? would they have crept?	I should/would not have crept you would not have crept he would not have crept we should/would not have crept you would not have crept they would not have crept
Plural	let us creep deslicémonos creep deslizaos let them creep deslicen	* * * * * * * * *	do not let us (let's not) creep do not creep do not let them creep
Present Perfect	I have crept me haya deslizado you have crept he has crept we have crept you have crept they have crept	* * * * * * * * *	I have not crept you have not crep he has not crept we have not crept you have not crept they have not crept
Past Perfect	I had crept me hubiera/hubiese deslizado you had crept he had crept we had crept you had crept they had crept	* * * * * * * * *	I had not crept you had not crep he had not crept we had not crept you had not crept they had not crept

72

16. Deal · Tratar con, repartir, distribuir, dar (naipes)

affirmative	interrogative	negative

❖ Indicative

Present

I deal trato	do I deal?	I do not deal
you deal	do you deal?	you do not deal
he deals	does he deal?	he does not deal
we deal	do we deal?	we do not deal
you deal	do you deal?	you do not deal
they deal	do they deal?	they do not deal

Past

I dealt trataba/traté	did I deal?	I did not deal
you dealt	did you deal?	you did not deal
he dealt	did he deal?	he did not deal
we dealt	did we deal?	we did not deal
you dealt	did you deal?	you did not deal
they dealt	did they deal?	they did not deal

Future

I shall/will deal trataré	shall/will I deal?	I shall/will not deal
you will deal	will you deal?	you will not deal
he will deal	will he deal?	he will not deal
we shall/will deal	shall/will we deal?	we shall/will not deal
you will deal	will you deal?	you will not deal
they will deal	will they deal?	they will not deal

❖ Conditional

Present

I should/would deal trataría	should/would I deal?	I should/would not deal
you would deal	would you deal?	you would not deal
he would deal	would he deal?	he would not deal
we should/would deal	should/would we deal?	we should/would not deal
you would deal	would you deal?	you would not deal
they would deal	would they deal?	they would not deal

❖ Imperative

Singular

let me deal déjame tratar		do not let me deal
deal trata	* * * * * * * * * *	do not deal
let him/her/it deal trate		do not let him/her/it deal

❖ Subjunctive

Present

I deal trate		I do not deal
you deal		you do not deal
he deals	* * * * * * * * * *	he does not deal
we deal		we do not deal
you deal		you do not deal
they deal		they do not deal

Past

I dealt tratara/tratase		I did not deal
you dealt		you did not deal
he dealt	* * * * * * * * * *	he did not deal
we dealt		we did not deal
you dealt		you did not deal
they dealt		they did not deal

❋ **Infinitive**	❋ **Gerund**	❋ **Participle**
to deal	dealing	dealt

affirmative	interrogative	negative

	affirmative	interrogative	negative
Present perfect	I have dealt he tratado you have dealt he has dealt we have dealt you have dealt they have dealt	have I dealt? have you dealt? has he dealt? have we dealt? have you dealt? have they dealt?	I have not dealt you have not dealt he has not dealt we have not dealt you have not dealt they have not dealt
Past perfect	I had dealt había tratado you had dealt he had dealt we had dealt you had dealt they had dealt	had I dealt? had you dealt? had he dealt? had we dealt? had you dealt? had they dealt?	I had not dealt you had not dealt he had not dealt we had not dealt you had not dealt they had not dealt
Future perfect	I shall/will have dealt habré tratado you will have dealt he will have dealt we shall/will have dealt you will have dealt they will have dealt	shall/will I have dealt? will you have dealt? will he have dealt? shall/will we have dealt? will you have dealt? will they have dealt?	I shall/will not have dealt you will not have dealt he will not have dealt we shall/will not have dealt you will not have dealt they wiil not have dealt
Perfect	I should/would have dealt habría tratado you would have dealt he would have dealt we should/would have dealt you would have dealt they would have dealt	should/would I have dealt? would you have dealt? would he have dealt? should/would we have dealt? would you have dealt? would they have dealt?	I should/would not have dealt you would not have dealt he would not have dealt we should/would not have dealt you would not have dealt they would not have dealt
Plural	let us deal tratemos deal tratad let them deal traten	* * * * * * * * * *	do not let us (let's not) deal do not deal do not let them deal
Present perfect	I have dealt haya tratado you have dealt he has dealt we have dealt you have dealt they have dealt	* * * * * * * * * *	I have not dealt you have not dealt he has not dealt we have not dealt you have not dealt they have not dealt
Past perfect	I had dealt hubiera/hubiese tratado you had dealt he had dealt we had dealt you had dealt they had dealt	* * * * * * * * * *	I had not dealt you had not dealt he had not dealt we had not dealt you had not dealt they had not dealt

74

17. Do · Hacer

affirmative	interrogative	negative

❀ Indicative

Present

I do hago	do I do?	I do not do
you do	do you do?	you do not do
he does	does he do?	he does not do
we do	do we do?	we do not do
you do	do you do?	you do not do
they do	do they do?	they do not do

Past

I did hacía/hice	did I do?	I did not do
you did	did you do?	you did not do
he did	did he do?	he did not do
we did	did we do?	we did not do
you did	did you do?	you did not do
they did	did they do?	they did not do

Future

I shall/will do haré	shall/will I do?	I shall/will not do
you will do	will you do?	you will not do
he will do	will he do?	he will not do
we shall/will do	shall/will we do?	we shall/will not do
you will do	will you do?	you will not do
they will do	will they do?	they will not do

❀ Conditional

Present

I should/would do haría	should/would I do?	I should/would not do
you would do	would you do?	you would not do
he would do	would he do?	he would not do
we should/would do	should/would we do?	we should/would not do
you would do	would you do?	you would not do
they would do	would they do?	they would not do

❀ Imperative

Singular

let me do déjame hacer		do not let me do déjame hacer
do haz	* * * * * * * * *	do not do
let him/her/it do haga		do not let him/her/it do

❀ Subjunctive

Present

I do haga		I do not do
you do		you do not do
he does	* * * * * * * * *	he does not do
we do		we do not do
you do		you do not do
they do		they do not do

Past

I did hiciera/hiciese		I did not do
you did		you did not do
he did	* * * * * * * * *	he did not do
we did		we did not do
you did		you did not do
they did		they did not do

❋ Infinitive	❋ Gerund	❋ Participle
to do	doing	done

	affirmative	interrogative	negative

Present perfect	I have done he hecho you have done he has done we have done you have done they have done	have I done? have you done? has he done? have we done? have you done? have they done?	I have not done you have not done he has not done we have not done you have not done they have not done
Past perfect	I had done había hecho you had done he had done we had done you had done they had done	had I done? had you done? had he done? had we done? had you done? had they done?	I had not done you had not done he had not done we had not done you had not done they had not done
Future perfect	I shall/will have done habré hecho you will have done he will have done we shall/will have done you will have done they will have done	shall/will I have done? will you have done? will he have done? shall/will we have done? will you have done? will they have done?	I shall/will not have done you will not have done he will not have done we shall/will not have done you will not have done they will not have done
Perfect	I should/would have done habría hecho you would have done he would have done we should/would have done you would have done they would have done	should/would I have done? would you have done? would he have done? should/would we have done? would you have done? would they have done?	I should/would not have done you would not have done he would not have done we should/would not have done you would not have done they would not have done
Plural	let us do hagamos do haced let them do hagan	* * * * * * * * * *	do not let us (let's not) do do not do do not let them do
Present perfect	I have done haya hecho you have done he has done we have done you have done they have done	* * * * * * * * * *	I have not done you have not done he has not done we have not done you have not done they have not done
Past perfect	I had done hubiera/hubiese hecho you had done he had done we had done you had done they had done	* * * * * * * * * *	I had not done you had not done he had not done we had not done you had not done they had not done

## 76

18. Draw · Dibujar, trazar, tirar de, sacar, girar (letras)

affirmative	interrogative	negative

❀ Indicative

Present

I draw dibujo	do I draw?	I do not draw
you draw	do you draw?	you do not draw
he draws	does he draw?	he does not draw
we draw	do we draw?	we do not draw
you draw	do you draw?	you do not draw
they draw	do they draw?	they do not draw

Past

I drew dibujaba/dibujé	did I draw?	I did not draw
you drew	did you draw?	you did not draw
he drew	did he draw?	he did not draw
we drew	did we draw?	we did not draw
you drew	did you draw?	you did not draw
they drew	did they draw?	they did not draw

Future

I shall/will draw dibujaré	shall/will I draw?	I shall/will not draw
you will draw	will you draw?	you will not draw
he will draw	will he draw?	he will not draw
we shall/will draw	shall/will we draw?	we shall/will not draw
you will draw	will you draw?	you will not draw
they will draw	will they draw?	they will not draw

❀ Conditional

Present

I should/would draw dibujaría	should/would I draw?	I should/would not draw
you would draw	would you draw?	you would not draw
he would draw	would he draw?	he would not draw
we should/would draw	should/would we draw?	we should/would not draw
you would draw	would you draw?	you would not draw
they would draw	would they draw?	they would not draw

❀ Imperative

Singular

let me draw déjame dibujar		do not let me draw
draw dibuja	* * * * * * * * * *	do not draw
let him/her/it draw dibuje		do not let him/her/it draw

❀ Subjunctive

Present

I draw dibuje		I do not draw
you draw		you do not draw
he draws	* * * * * * * * * *	he does not draw
we draw		we do not draw
you draw		you do not draw
they draw		they do not draw

Past

I drew dibujara/dibujase		I did not draw
you drew		you did not draw
he drew	* * * * * * * * * *	he did not draw
we drew		we did not draw
you drew		you did not draw
they drew		they did not draw

* Infinitive	* Gerund	* Participle
to draw	drawing	drawn

affirmative	interrogative	negative

	affirmative	interrogative	negative
Present perfect	I have drawn he dibujado you have drawn he has drawn we have drawn you have drawn they have drawn	have I drawn? have you drawn? has he drawn? have we drawn? have you drawn? have they drawn?	I have not drawn you have not drawn he has not drawn we have not drawn you have not drawn they have not drawn
Past perfect	I had drawn había dibujado you had drawn he had drawn we had drawn you had drawn they had drawn	had I drawn? had you drawn? had he drawn? had we drawn? had you drawn? had they drawn?	I had not drawn you had not drawn he had not drawn we had not drawn you had not drawn they had not drawn
Future perfect	I shall/will have drawn habré dibujado you will have drawn he will have drawn we shall/will have drawn you will have drawn they will have drawn	shall/will I have drawn? will you have drawn? will he have drawn? shall/will we have drawn? will you have drawn? will they have drawn?	I shall/will not have drawn you will not have drawn he will not have drawn we shall/will not have drawn you will not have drawn they will not have drawn
Perfect	I should/would have drawn habría dibujado you would have drawn he would have drawn we should/would have drawn you would have drawn they would have drawn	should/would I have drawn? would you have drawn? would he have drawn? should/would we have drawn? would you have drawn? would they have drawn?	I should/would not have drawn you would not have drawn he would not have drawn we should/would not have drawn you would not have drawn they would not have drawn
Plural	let us draw dibujemos draw dibujad let them draw dibujen	* * * * * * * * * *	do not let us (let's not) draw do not draw do not let them draw
Present perfect	I have drawn haya dibujado you have drawn he has drawn we have drawn you have drawn they have drawn	* * * * * * * * * *	I have not drawn you have not drawn he has not drawn we have not drawn you have not drawn they have not drawn
Past perfect	I had drawn hubiera/hubiese dibujado you had drawn he had drawn we had drawn you had drawn they had drawn	* * * * * * * * * *	I had not drawn you had not drawn he had not drawn we had not drawn you had not drawn they had not drawn

19. Drink - Beber

	affirmative	interrogative	negative

✿ Indicative

Present
I drink bebo	do I drink?	I do not drink
you drink	do you drink?	you do not drink
he drinks	does he drink?	he does not drink
we drink	do we drink?	we do not drink
you drink	do you drink?	you do not drink
they drink	do they drink?	they do not drink

Past
I drank bebía/bebí	did I drink?	I did not drink
you drank	did you drink?	you did not drink
he drank	did he drink?	he did not drink
we drank	did we drink?	we did not drink
you drank	did you drink?	you did not drink
they drank	did they drink?	they did not drink

Future
I shall/will drink beberé	shall/will I drink?	I shall/will not drink
you will drink	will you drink?	you will not drink
he will drink	will he drink?	he will not drink
we shall/will drink	shall/will we drink?	we shall/will not drink
you will drink	will you drink?	you will not drink
they will drink	will they drink?	they will not drink

✿ Conditional

Present
I should/would drink bebería	should/would I drink?	I should/would not drink
you would drink	would you drink?	you would not drink
he would drink	would he drink?	he would not drink
we should/would drink	should/would we drink?	we should/would not drink
you would drink	would you drink?	you would not drink
they would drink	would they drink?	they would not drink

✿ Imperative

Singular
let me drink déjame beber		do not let me drink
drink bebe	* * * * * * * * * *	do not drink
let him/her/it drink beba		do not let him/her/it drink

✿ Subjunctive

Present
I drink beba		I do not drink
you drink		you do not drink
he drinks	* * * * * * * * * *	he does not drink
we drink		we do not drink
you drink		you do not drink
they drink		they do not drink

Past
I drank bebiera/bebiese		I did not drink
you drank		you did not drink
he drank	* * * * * * * * * *	he did not drink
we drank		we did not drink
you drank		you did not drink
they drank		they did not drink

❀ **Infinitive**	❀ **Gerund**	❀ **Participle**
to drink	drinking	drunk

	affirmative	**interrogative**	**negative**

Present perfect	I have drunk he bebido you have drunk he has drunk we have drunk you have drunk they have drunk	have I drunk? have you drunk? has he drunk? have we drunk? have you drunk? have they drunk?	I have not drunk you have not drunk he has not drunk we have not drunk you have not drunk they have not drunk
Past perfect	I had drunk había bebido you had drunk he had drunk we had drunk you had drunk they had drunk	had I drunk? had you drunk? had he drunk? had we drunk? had you drunk? had they drunk?	I had not drunk you had not drunk he had not drunk we had not drunk you had not drunk they had not drunk
Future perfect	I shall/will have drunk habré bebido you will have drunk he will have drunk we shall/will have drunk you will have drunk they will have drunk	shall/will I have drunk? will you have drunk? will he have drunk? shall/will we have drunk? will you have drunk? will they have drunk?	I shall/will not have drunk you will not have drunk he will not have drunk we shall/will not have drunk you will not have drunk they will not have drunk

| **Perfect** | I should/would have drunk   habría bebido
you would have drunk
he would have drunk
we should/would have drunk
you would have drunk
they would have drunk | should/would I have drunk?
would you have drunk?
would he have drunk?
should/would we have drunk?
would you have drunk?
would they have drunk? | I should/would not have drunk
you would not have drunk
he would not have drunk
we should/would not have drunk
you would not have drunk
they would not have drunk |

| **Plural** | let us drink   bebamos
drink   bebed
let them drink   beban | * * * * * * * * * * | do not let us (let's not) drink
do not drink
do not let them drink |

| **Present perfect** | I have drunk   haya bebido
you have drunk
he has drunk
we have drunk
you have drunk
they have drunk | * * * * * * * * * * | I have not drunk
you have not drunk
he has not drunk
we have not drunk
you have not drunk
they have not drunk |
| **Past perfect** | I had drunk   hubiera/hubiese bebido
you had drunk
he had drunk
we had drunk
you had drunk
they had drunk | * * * * * * * * * * | I had not drunk
you had not drunk
he had not drunk
we had not drunk
you had not drunk
they had not drunk |

20. Drive - Conducir

affirmative	interrogative	negative

❋ Indicative

Present
I drive conduzco	do I drive?	I do not drive
you drive	do you drive?	you do not drive
he drives	does he drive?	he does not drive
we drive	do we drive?	we do not drive
you drive	do you drive?	you do not drive
they drive	do they drive?	they do not drive

Past
I drove conducía/conduje	did I drive?	I did not drive
you drove	did you drive?	you did not drive
he drove	did he drive?	he did not drive
we drove	did we drive?	we did not drive
you drove	did you drive	you did not drive
they drove	did they drive?	they did not drive

Future
I shall/will drive conduciré	shall/will I drive?	I shall/will not drive
you will drive	will you drive?	you will not drive
he will drive	will he drive?	he will not drive
we shall/will drive	shall/will we drive?	we shall/will not drive
you will drive	will you drive?	you will not drive
they will drive	will they drive?	they will not drive

❋ Conditional

Present
I should/would drive conduciría	should/would I drive?	I should/would not drive
you would drive	would you drive?	you would not drive
he would drive	would he drive?	he would not drive
we should/would drive	should/would we drive?	we should/would not drive
you would drive	would you drive	you would not drive
they would drive	would they drive?	they would not drive

❋ Imperative

Singular
let me drive déjame conducir		do not let me drive
drive conduce	* * * * * * * * *	do not drive
let him/her/it drive conduzca		do not let him/her/it drive

❋ Subjunctive

Present
I drive conduzca		I do not drive
you drive		you do not drive
he drives	* * * * * * * * *	he does not drive
we drive		we do not drive
you drive		you do not drive
they drive		they do not drive

Past
I drove condujera/condujese		I did not drive
you drove		you did not drive
he drove	* * * * * * * * *	he did not drive
we drove		we did not drive
you drove		you did not drive
they drove		they did not drive

❋ Infinitive	❋ Gerund	❋ Participle
to drive	driving	driven

affirmative	interrogative	negative

Present perfect

I have driven he conducido	have I driven?	I have not driven
you have driven	have you driven?	you have not driven
he has driven	has he driven?	he has not driven
we have driven	have we driven?	we have not driven
you have driven	have you driven?	you have not driven
they have driven	have they driven?	they have not driven

Past perfect

I had driven había conducido	had I driven?	I had not driven
you had driven	had you driven?	you had not driven
he had driven	had he driven?	he had not driven
we had driven	had we driven?	we had not driven
you had driven	had you driven?	you had not driven
they had driven	had they driven?	they had not driven

Future perfect

I shall/will have driven habré conducido	shall/will I have driven?	I shall/will not have driven
you will have driven	will you have driven?	you will not have driven
he will have driven	will he have driven?	he will not have driven
we shall/will have driven	shall/will we have driven?	we shall/will not have driven
you will have driven	will you have driven?	you will not have driven
they will have driven	will they have driven?	they will not have driven

Perfect

I should/would have driven habría conducido	should/would I have driven?	I should/would not have driven
you would have driven	would you have driven?	you would not have driven
he would have driven	would he have driven?	he would not have driven
we should/would have driven	should/would we have driven?	we should/would not have driven
you would have driven	would you have driven?	you would not have driven
they would have driven	would they have driven?	they would not have driven

Plural

let us drive conduzcamos	* * * * * * * * *	do not let us (let's not) drive
drive conducid		do not drive
let them drive conduzcan		do not let them drive

Present perfect

I have driven haya conducido	* * * * * * * * *	I have not driven
you have driven		you have not dirven
he has driven		he has not diven
we have driven		we have not driven
you have driven		you have not driven
they have driven		they have not driven

Past perfect

I had driven hubiera/hubiese conducido	* * * * * * * * *	I had not driven
you had driven		you had not driven
he had driven		he had not driven
we had driven		we had not driven
you had driven		you had not driven
they had driven		they had not driven

21. Eat - Comer

affirmative	interrogative	negative

❋ Indicative

Present
I eat como	do I eat?	I do not eat
you eat	do you eat?	you do not eat
he eats	does he eat?	he does not eat
we eat	do we eat?	we do not eat
you eat	do you eat?	you do not eat
they eat	do they eat?	they do not eat

Past
I ate comía/comí	did I eat?	I did not eat
you ate	did you eat?	you did not eat
he ate	did he eat?	he did not eat
we ate	did we eat?	we did not eat
you ate	did you eat?	you did not eat
they ate	did they eat?	they did not eat

Future
I shall/will eat comeré	shall/will I eat?	I shall/will not eat
you will eat	will you eat?	you will not eat
he will eat	will he eat?	he will not eat
we shall/will eat	shall/will we eat?	we shall/will not eat
you will eat	will you eat?	you will not eat
they will eat	will they eat?	they will not eat

❋ Conditional

Present
I should/would eat comería	should/would I eat?	I should/would not eat
you would eat	would you eat?	you would not eat
he would eat	would he eat?	he would not eat
we should/would eat	should/would we eat?	we should/would not eat
you would eat	would you eat?	you would not eat
they would eat	would they eat?	they would not eat

❋ Imperative

Singular
let me eat déjame comer		do not let me eat
eat come	* * * * * * * * *	do not eat
let him/her/it eat coma		do not let him/her/it eat

❋ Subjunctive

Present
I eat coma		I do not eat
you eat		you do not eat
he eats	* * * * * * * * *	he does not eat
we eat		we do not eat
you eat		you do not eat
they eat		they do not eat

Past
I ate comiera/comiese		I did not eat
you ate		you did not eat
he ate	* * * * * * * * *	he did not eat
we ate		we did not eat
you ate		you did not eat
they ate		they did not eat

✿ Infinitive	✿ Gerund	✿ Participle
to eat	eating	eaten

	affirmative	interrogative	negative

Present perfect	I have eaten he comido you have eaten he has eaten we have eaten you have eaten they have eaten	have I eaten? have you eaten? has he eaten? have we eaten? have you eaten? have they eaten?	I have not eaten you have not eaten he has not eaten we have not eaten you have not eaten they have not eaten
Past perfect	I had eaten había comido you had eaten he had eaten we had eaten you had eaten they had eaten	had I eaten? had you eaten? had he eaten? had we eaten? had you eaten? had they eaten?	I had not eaten you had not eaten he had not eaten we had not eaten you had not eaten they had not eaten
Future perfect	I shall/will have eaten habré comido you will have eaten he will have eaten we shall/will have eaten you will have eaten they will have eaten	shall/will I have eaten? will you have eaten? will he have eaten? shall/will we have eaten? will you have eaten? will they have eaten?	I shall/will not have eaten you will not have eaten he will not have eaten we shall/will not have eaten you will not have eaten they will not have eaten
Perfect	I should/would have eaten habría comido you would have eaten he would have eaten we should/would have eaten you would have eaten they would have eaten	should/would I have eaten? would you have eaten? would he have eaten? should/would we have eaten? would you have eaten? would they have eaten?	I should/would not have eaten you would not have eaten he would not have eaten we should/would not have eaten you would not have eaten they would not have eaten
Plural	let us eat comamos eat comed let them eat coman	* * * * * * * * * *	do not let us (let's not) eat do not eat do not let them eat
Present perfect	I have eaten haya comido you have eaten he has eaten we have eaten you have eaten they have eaten	* * * * * * * * * *	I have not eaten you have not eaten he has not eaten we have not eaten you have not eaten they have not eaten
Past perfect	I had eaten hubiera/hubiese comido you had eaten he had eaten we had eaten you had eaten they had eaten	* * * * * * * * * *	I had not eaten you had not eaten he had not eaten we had not eaten you had not eaten they had not eaten

22. Fall - Caer

affirmative	interrogative	negative

✿ Indicative

Present

I fall caigo	do I fall?	I do not fall
you fall	do you fall?	you do not fall
he falls	does he fall?	he does not fall
we fall	do we fall?	we do not fall
you fall	do you fall?	you do not fall
they fall	do they fall?	they do not fall

Past

I fell caía/caí	did I fall?	I did not fall
you fell	did you fall?	you did not fall
he fell	did he fall?	he did not fall
we fell	did we fall?	we did not fall
you fell	did you fall?	you did not fall
they fell	did they fall?	they did not fall

Future

I shall/will fall caeré	shall/will I fall?	I shall/will not fall
you will fall	will you fall?	you will not fall
he will fall	will he fall?	he will not fall
we shall/will fall	shall/will we fall?	we shall/will not fall
you will fall	will you fall?	you will not fall
they will fall	will they fall?	they will not fall

✿ Conditional

Present

I should/would fall caería	should/would I fall?	I should/would not fall
you would fall	would you fall?	you would not fall
he would fall	would he fall?	he would not fall
we should/would fall	should/would we fall?	we should/would not fall
you would fall	would you fall?	you would not fall
they would fall	would they fall?	they would not fall

✿ Imperative

Singular

let me fall déjame caer		do not let me fall
fall cae	* * * * * * * * * *	do not fall
let him/her/it fall caiga		do not let him/her/it fall

✿ Subjunctive

Present

I fall caiga		I do not fall
you fall		you do not fall
he falls	* * * * * * * * * *	he does not fall
we fall		we do not fall
you fall		you do not fall
they fall		they do not fall

Past

I fell cayera/cayese		I did not fall
you fell		you did not fall
he fell	* * * * * * * * * *	he did not fall
we fell		we did not fall
you fell		you did not fall
they fell		they did not fall

❀ **Infinitive**	❀ **Gerund**	❀ **Participle**
to fall	falling	fallen

	affirmative	interrogative	negative

	affirmative	interrogative	negative
Present Perfect	I have fallen he caído you have fallen he has fallen we have fallen you have fallen they have fallen	have I fallen? have you fallen? has he fallen? have we fallen? have you fallen? have they fallen?	I have not fallen you have not fallen he has not fallen we have not fallen you have not fallen they have not fallen
Past Perfect	I had fallen había caído you had fallen he had fallen we had fallen you had fallen they had fallen	had I fallen? had you fallen? had he fallen? had we fallen? had you fallen? had they fallen?	I had not fallen you had not fallen he had not fallen we had not fallen you had not fallen they had not fallen
Future Perfect	I shall/will have fallen habré caído you will have fallen he will have fallen we shall/will have fallen you will have fallen they will have fallen	shall/will I have fallen? will you have fallen? will he have fallen? shall/will we have fallen? will you have fallen? will they have fallen?	I shall/will not have fallen you will not have fallen he will not have fallen we shall/will not have fallen you will not have fallen they will not have fallen
Perfect	I should/would have fallen habría caído you would have fallen he would have fallen we should/would have fallen you would have fallen they would have fallen	should/would I have fallen? would you have fallen? would he have fallen? should/would we have fallen? would you have fallen? would they have fallen?	I should/would not have fallen you would not have fallen he would not have fallen we should/would not have fallen you would not have fallen they would not have fallen
Plural	let us fall caigamos fall caed let them fall caigan	* * * * * * * * * *	do not let us (let's not) fall do not fall do not let them fall
Present Perfect	I have fallen haya caído you have fallen he has fallen we have fallen you have fallen they have fallen	* * * * * * * * * *	I have not fallen you have not fallen he has not fallen we have not fallen you have not fallen they have not fallen
Past Perfect	I had fallen hubiera/hubiese caído you had fallen he had fallen we had fallen you had fallen they had fallen	* * * * * * * * * *	I had not fallen you had not fallen he had not fallen we had not fallen you had not fallen they had not fallen

23. See - Ver

affirmative	interrogative	negative

❀ Indicative

Present	I see veo	do I see?	I do not see
	you see	do you see?	you do not see
	he sees	does he see?	he does not see
	we see	do we see?	we do not see
	you see	do you see?	you do not see
	they see	do they see?	they do not see

Past	I saw veía/vi	did I see?	I did not see
	you saw	did you see?	you did not see
	he saw	did he see?	he did not see
	we saw	did we see?	we did not see
	you saw	did you see?	you did not see
	they saw	did they see?	they did not see

Future	I shall/will see veré	shall/will I see?	I shall/will not see
	you will see	will you see?	you will not see
	he will see	will he see?	he will not see
	we shall/will see	shall/will we see?	we shall/will not see
	you will see	will you see?	you will not see
	they will see	will they see?	they will not see

❀ Conditional

Present	I should/would see vería	should/would I see?	I should/would not see
	you would see	would you see?	you would not see
	he would see	would he see?	he would not see
	we should/would see	should/would we see?	we should/would not see
	you would see	would you see?	you would not see
	they would see	would they see?	they would not see

❀ Imperative

Singular	let me see déjame ver		do not let me see
	see ve	* * * * * * * * * *	do not see
	let him/her/it see vea		do not let him/her/it see

❀ Subjunctive

Present	I see vea		I do not see
	you see		you do not see
	he sees	* * * * * * * * * *	he does not see
	we see		we do not see
	you see		you do not see
	they see		they do not see

Past	I saw viera/viese		I did not see
	you saw		you did not see
	he saw	* * * * * * * * * *	he did not see
	we saw		we did not see
	you saw		you did not see
	they saw		they did not see

87

❀ Infinitive	❀ Gerund	❀ Participle
to see	seeing	seen

	affirmative	interrogative	negative

Present perfect

affirmative	interrogative	negative
I have seen he visto	have I seen?	I have not seen
you have seen	have you seen?	you have not seen
he has seen	has he seen?	he has not seen
we have seen	have we seen?	we have not seen
you have seen	have you seen?	you have not seen
they have seen	have they seen?	they have not seen

Past perfect

affirmative	interrogative	negative
I had seen había visto	had I seen?	I had not seen
you had seen	had you seen?	you had not seen
he had seen	had he seen?	he had not seen
we had seen	had we seen?	we had not seen
you had seen	had you seen?	you had not seen
they had seen	had they seen?	they had not seen

Future perfect

affirmative	interrogative	negative
I shall/will have seen habré visto	shall/will I have seen?	I shall/will not have seen
you will have seen	will you have seen?	you will not have seen
he will have seen	will he have seen?	he will not have seen
we shall/will have seen	shall/will we have seen?	we shall/will not have seen
you will have seen	will you have seen?	you will not have seen
they will have seen	will they have seen?	they will not have seen

Perfect

affirmative	interrogative	negative
I should/would have seen habría visto	should/would I have seen?	I should/would not have seen
you would have seen	would you have seen?	you would not have seen
he would have seen	would he have seen?	he would not have seen
we should/would have seen	should/would we have seen?	we should/would not have seen
you would have seen	would you have seen?	you would not have seen
they would have seen	would they have seen?	they would not have seen

Plural

affirmative	interrogative	negative
let us see veamos	* * * * * * * * * *	do not let us (let's not) see
see ved		do not see
let them see vean		do not let them see

Present perfect

affirmative	interrogative	negative
I have seen haya visto	* * * * * * * * * *	I have not seen
you have seen		you have not seen
he has seen		he has not seen
we have seen		we have not seen
you have seen		you have not seen
they have seen		they have not seen

Past perfect

affirmative	interrogative	negative
I had seen hubiera/hubiese visto	* * * * * * * * * *	I had not seen
you had seen		you had not seen
he had seen		he had not seen
we had seen		we had not seen
you had seen		you had not seen
they had seen		they had not seen

24. Tell - Decir, contar

	affirmative	interrogative	negative
Indicative			

Present

affirmative	interrogative	negative
I tell digo	do I tell?	I do not tell
you tell	do you tell?	you do not tell
he tells	does he tell?	he does not tell
we tell	do we tell?	we do not tell
you tell	do you tell?	you do not tell
they tell	do they tell?	they do not tell

Past

affirmative	interrogative	negative
I told decía/dije	did I tell?	I did not tell
you told	did you tell?	you did not tell
he told	did he tell?	he did not tell
we told	did we tell?	we did not tell
you told	did you tell?	you did not tell
they told	did he tell?	they did not tell

Future

affirmative	interrogative	negative
I shall/will tell diré	shall/will I tell?	I shall/will not tell
you will tell	will you tell?	you will not tell
he will tell	will he tell?	he will not tell
we shall/will tell	shall/will we tell?	we shall/will not tell
you will tell	will you tell?	you will not tell
they will tell	will they tell?	they will not tell

Conditional

Present

affirmative	interrogative	negative
I should/would tell diría	should/would I tell?	I should/would not tell
you would tell	would you tell?	you would not tell
he would tell	would he tell?	he would not tell
we should/would tell	should/would we tell?	we should/would not tell
you would tell	would you tell?	you would not tell
they would tell	would he tell?	they would not tell

Imperative

Singular

affirmative	interrogative	negative
let me tell déjame decir		do not let me tell
tell di	* * * * * * * * *	do not tell
let him/her/it tell diga		do not let him/her/it tell

Subjunctive

Present

affirmative	interrogative	negative
I tell diga		I do not tell
you tell		you do not tell
he tells	* * * * * * * * *	he does not tell
we tell		we do not tell
you tell		you do not tell
they tell		they do not tell

Past

affirmative	interrogative	negative
I told dijera/dijese		I did not tell
you told		you did not tell
he told	* * * * * * * * *	he did not tell
we told		we did not tell
you told		you did not tell
they told		they did not tell

✻ Infinitive	✻ Gerund	✻ Participle
to tell	telling	told

affirmative	interrogative	negative

Present perfect

affirmative	interrogative	negative
I have told he dicho	have I told?	I have not told
you have told	have you told?	you have not told
he has told	has he told?	he has not told
we have told	have we told?	we have not told
you have told	have you told?	you have not told
they have told	have they told?	they have not told

Past perfect

affirmative	interrogative	negative
I had told había dicho	had I told?	I had not told
you had told	had you told?	you had not told
he had told	had he told?	he had not told
we had told	had we told?	we had not told
you had told	had you told?	you had not told
they had told	had they told?	they had not told

Future perfect

affirmative	interrogative	negative
I shall/will have told habré dicho	shall/will I have told?	I will not have told
you will have told	will you have told?	you will not have told
he will have told	will he have told?	he will not have told
we shall/will have told	shall/will we have told?	we shall/will not have told
you will have told	will you have told?	you will not have told
they will have told	will they have told?	they will not have told

Perfect

affirmative	interrogative	negative
I should/would have told habría dicho	should/would I have told?	I should/would not have told
you would have told	would you have told?	you would not have told
he would have told	would he have told?	he would not have told
we should/would have told	should/would we have told?	we should/would not have told
you would have told	would you have told?	you would not have told
they would have told	would they have told?	they would not have told

Plural

affirmative	interrogative	negative
let us tell digamos	* * * * * * * * * *	do not let us (let's not) tell
tell decid		do not tell
let them tell digan		do not let them tell

Present perfect

affirmative	interrogative	negative
I have told haya dicho	* * * * * * * * * *	I have not told
you have told		you have not told
he has told		he has not told
we have told		we have not told
you have told		you have not told
they have told		they have not told

Past perfect

affirmative	interrogative	negative
I had told hubiera/hubiese dicho	* * * * * * * * * *	I had not told
you had told		you had not told
he had told		he had not told
we had told		we had not told
you had told		you had not told
they had told		they had not told

25. Forget · Olvidar

	affirmative	interrogative	negative

❋ Indicative

	affirmative	interrogative	negative
Present	I forget olvido	do I forget?	I do not forget
	you forget	do you forget?	you do not forget
	he forgets	does he forget?	he does not forget
	we forget	do we forget?	we do not forget
	you forget	do you forget?	you do not forget
	they forget	do they forget?	they do not forget
Past	I forgot olvidaba/olvidé	did I forget?	I did not forget
	you forgot	did you forget?	you did not forget
	he forgot	did he forget?	he did not forget
	we forgot	did we forget?	we did not forget
	you forgot	did you forget?	you did not forget
	they forgot	did they forget?	they did not forget
Future	I shall/will forget olvidaré	shall/will I forget?	I shall/will not forget
	you will forget	will you forget?	you will not forget
	he will forget	will he forget?	he will not forget
	we shall/will forget	shall/will we forget?	we shall/will not forget
	you will forget	will you forget?	you will not forget
	they will forget	will they forget?	they will not forget

❋ Conditional

	affirmative	interrogative	negative
Present	I should/would forget olvidaría	should/would I forget?	I should/would not forget
	you would forget	would you forget?	you would not forget
	he would forget	would he forget?	he would not forget
	we should/would forget	should/would we forget?	we should/would not forget
	you would forget	would you forget?	you would not forget
	they would forget	would they forget?	they would not forget

❋ Imperative

	affirmative	interrogative	negative
Singular	let me forget déjame olvidar	* * * * * * * * * *	do not let me forget
	forget olvida		do not forget
	let him/her/it forget olvide		do not let him/her/it forget

❋ Subjunctive

	affirmative	interrogative	negative
Present	I forget olvide		I do not forget
	you forget		you do not forget
	he forgets	* * * * * * * * * *	he does not forget
	we forget		we do not forget
	you forget		you do not forget
	they forget		they do not forget
Past	I forgot olvidara/olvidase		I did not forget
	you forgot		you did not forget
	he forgot	* * * * * * * * * *	he did not forget
	we forgot		we did not forget
	you forgot		you did not forget
	they forgot		they did not forget

❀ Infinitive	❀ Gerund	❀ Participle
to forget	forgeting	forgotten

affirmative	interrogative	negative

Present perfect

affirmative	interrogative	negative
I have forgotten he olvidado	have I forgotten?	I have not forgotten
you have forgotten	have you forgotten?	you have not forgotten
he has forgotten	has he forgotten?	he has not forgotten
we have forgotten	have we forgotten?	we have not forgotten
you have forgotten	have you forgotten?	you have not forgotten
they have forgotten	have they forgotten?	they have not forgotten

Past perfect

affirmative	interrogative	negative
I had forgotten había olvidado	had I forgotten?	I had not forgotten
you had forgotten	had you forgotten?	you had not forgotten
he had forgotten	had he forgotten?	he had not forgotten
we had forgotten	had we forgotten?	we had not forgotten
you had forgotten	had you forgotten?	you had not forgotten
they had forgotten	had they forgotten?	they had not forgotten

Future perfect

affirmative	interrogative	negative
I shall/will have forgotten habré olvidado	shall/will I have forgotten?	I shall/will not have forgotten
you will have forgotten	will you have forgotten?	you will not have forgotten
he will have forgotten	will he have forgotten?	he will not have forgotten
we shall/will have forgotten	shall/will we have forgotten?	we shall/will not have forgotten
you will have forgotten	will you have forgotten?	you will not have forgotten
they will have forgotten	will they have forgotten?	they will not have forgotten

Perfect

affirmative	interrogative	negative
I should/would have fogotten	should/would I have fogotten?	I should/would not have forgotten
habría olvidado	would you have forgotten?	you would not have forgotten
you would have forgotten	would he have forgotten?	he would not have forgotten
he would have forgotten	should/would we have forgotten?	we should/would not have forgotten
we would have forgotten	would you have forgotten?	you would not have forgotten
you would have forgotten	would they have forgotten?	they would not have forgotten
they would have forgotten		

Plural

affirmative	interrogative	negative
let us forget olvidemos	* * * * * * * * * *	do not let us (let's not) forget
forget olvidad		do not forget
let them forget olviden		do not let them forget

Present perfect

affirmative	interrogative	negative
I have forgotten haya olvidado	* * * * * * * * * *	I have not forgotten
you have forgotten		you have not forgotten
he has forgotten		he has not forgotten
we have forgotten		we have not forgotten
you have forgotten		you have not forgotten
they have forgotten		they have not forgotten

Past perfect

affirmative	interrogative	negative
I had forgotten hubiera/hubiese olvidado	* * * * * * * * * *	I had not forgotten
you had forgotten		you had not forgotten
he had forgotten		he had not forgotten
we had forgotten		we had not forgotten
you had forgotten		you had not forgotten
they had forgotten		they had not forgotten

26. Give · Dar

	affirmative	interrogative	negative

❄ Indicative

Present
I give doy	do I give?	I do not give
you give	do you give?	you do not give
he gives	does he give?	he does not give
we give	do we give?	we do not give
you give	do you give?	you do not give
they give	do they give?	they do not give

Past
I gave daba/di	did I give?	I did not give
you gave	did you give?	you did not give
he gave	did he give?	he did not give
we gave	did we give?	we did not give
you gave	did you give?	you did not give
they gave	did they give?	they did not give

Future
I shall/will give daré	shall/will I give?	I shall/will not give
you will give	will you give?	you will not give
he will give	will he give?	he will not give
we shall/will give	shall/will we give?	we shall/will not give
you will give	will you give?	you will not give
they will give	will they give?	they will not give

❄ Conditional

Present
I should/would give daría	should/would I give?	I should/would not give
you would give	would you give?	you would not give
he would give	would he give?	he would not give
we should/would give	should/would we give?	we should/would not give
you would give	would you give?	you would not give
they would give	would they give?	they would not give

❄ Imperative

Singular
let me give déjame dar		do not let me give
give da	* * * * * * * * * *	do not give
let him/her/it give dé		do not let him/her/it give

❄ Subjunctive

Present
I give dé		I do not give
you give		you do not give
he gives	* * * * * * * * * *	he does not give
we give		we do not give
you give		you do not give
they give		they do not give

Past
I gave diera/diese		I did not give
you gave		you did not give
he gave	* * * * * * * * * *	he did not give
we gave		we did not give
you gave		you did not give
they gave		they did not give

❋ **Infinitive** to give	❋ **Gerund** giving	❋ **Participle** given

	affirmative	**interrogative**	**negative**
Present perfect	I have given he dado you have given he has given we have given you have given they have given	have I given? have you given? has he given? have we given? have you given? have they given?	I have not given you have not given he has not given we have not given you have not given they have not given
Past perfect	I had given había dado you had given he had given we had given you had given they had given	had I given? had you given? had he given? had we given? had you given? had they given?	I had not given you had not given he had not given we had not given you had not given they had not given
Future perfect	I shall/will have given habré dado you will have given he will have given we shall/will have given you will have given they will have given	shall/will I have given? will you have given? will he have given? shall/will we have given? will you have given? will they have given?	I shall/will not have given you will not have given he will not have given we shall/will not have given you will not have given they will not have given
Perfect	I should/would have given habría dado you would have given he would have given we should/would have given you would have given they would have given	should/would I have given? would you have given? would he have given? should/would we have given? would you have given? would they have given?	I should/would not have given you would not have given he would not have given we should/would not have given you would not have given they would not have given
Plural	let us give demos give dad let them give den	* * * * * * * * * *	do not let us (let's not) give do not give do not let them give
Present perfect	I have given haya dado you have given he has given we have given you have given they have given	* * * * * * * * * *	I have not given you have not given he has not given we have not given you have not given they have not given
Past perfect	I had given hubiera/hubiese dado you had given he had given we had given you had given they had given	* * * * * * * * * *	I had not given you had not given he had not given we had not given you had not given they had not given

27. Take · Coger, tomar

affirmative	interrogative	negative

❀ Indicative

	affirmative	interrogative	negative
Present	I take cojo	do I take?	I do not take
	you take	do you take?	you do not take
	he takes	does he take?	he does not take
	we take	do we take?	we do not take
	you take	do you take?	you do not take
	they take	do they take?	they do not take
Past	I took cogía/cogí	did I take?	I did not take
	you took	did you take?	you did not take
	he took	did he take?	he did not take
	we took	did we take?	we did not take
	you took	did you take?	you did not take
	they took	did they take?	they did not take
Future	I shall/will take cogeré	shall/will I take?	I shall/will not take
	you will take	will you take?	you will not take
	he will take	will he take?	he will not take
	we shall/will take	shall/will we take?	we shall/will not take
	you will take	will you take?	you will not take
	they will take	will they take?	they will not take

❀ Conditional

	affirmative	interrogative	negative
Present	I should/would take cogería	should/would I take?	I should/would not take
	you would take	would you take?	you would not take
	he would take	would he take?	he would not take
	we should/would take	should/would we take?	we should/would not take
	you would take	would you take?	you would not take
	they would take	would they take?	they would not take

❀ Imperative

	affirmative	interrogative	negative
Singular	let me take déjame coger	* * * * * * * * * *	do not let me take
	take coge		do not take
	let him/her/it take coja		do not let him/her/it take

❀ Subjunctive

	affirmative	interrogative	negative
Present	I take coja	* * * * * * * * * *	I do not take
	you take		you do not take
	he takes		he does not take
	we take		we do not take
	you take		you do not take
	they take		they do not take
Past	I took cogiera/cogiese	* * * * * * * * * *	I did not take
	you took		you did not take
	he took		he did not take
	we took		we did not take
	you took		you did not take
	they took		they did not take

❀ **Infinitive**	❀ **Gerund**	❀ **Participle**
to take	taking	taken

	affirmative	interrogative	negative

Present perfect	I have taken he cogido you have taken he has taken we have taken you have taken they have taken	have I taken? have you taken? has he taken? have we taken? have you taken? have they taken?	I have not taken you have not taken he has not taken we have not taken you have not taken they have not taken
Past perfect	I had taken he cogido you had taken he had taken we had taken you had taken they had taken	had I taken? had you taken? had he taken? had we taken? had you taken? had they taken?	I had not taken you had not taken he had not taken we had not taken you had not taken they had not taken
Future perfect	I shall/will have taken habré cogido you will have taken he will have taken we shall/will have taken you will have taken they will have taken	shall/will I have taken? will you have taken? will he have taken? shall/will we have taken? will you have taken? will they have taken?	I shall/will not have taken you will not have taken he will not have taken we shall/will not have taken you will not have taken they will not have taken
Perfect	I should/would have taken habría cogido you would have taken he would have taken we should/would have taken you would have taken they would have taken	should/would I have taken? would you have taken? would he have taken? should/would we have taken? would you have taken? would they have taken?	I should/would not have taken you would not have taken he would not have taken we should/would not have taken you would not have taken they would not have taken
Plural	let us take cojamos take coged let them take cojan	* * * * * * * * * *	do not let us (let's not) take do not take do not let them take
Present perfect	I have taken haya cogido you have taken he has taken we have taken you have taken they have taken	* * * * * * * * * *	I have not taken you have not taken he has not taken we have not taken you have not taken they have not taken
Past perfect	I had taken hubiera/hubiese cogido you had taken he had taken we had taken you had taken they had taken	* * * * * * * * * *	I had not taken you had not taken he had not taken we had not taken you had not taken they had not taken

28. Wear · Llevar puesto

affirmative	interrogative	negative

❂ Indicative

Present

I wear llevo puesto	do I wear?	I do not weat
you wear	do you wear?	you do not wear
he wears	does he wear?	he does not wear
we wear	do we wear?	we do not wear
you wear	do you wear?	you do not wear
they wear	do they wear?	they do not wear

Past

I wore llevaba/llevé puesto	did I wear?	I did not wear
you wore	did you wear?	you did not wear
he wore	did he wear?	he did not wear
we wore	did we wear?	we did not wear
you wore	did you wear?	you did not wear
they wore	did they wear?	they did not wear

Future

I shall/will wear llevaré puesto	shall/will I wear?	I shall/will not wear
you will wear	will you wear?	you will not wear
he will wear	will he wear?	he will not wear
we shall/will wear	shall/will we wear?	we shall/will not wear
you will wear	will you wear?	you will not wear
they will wear	will they wear?	they will not wear

❂ Conditional

Present

I should/would wear llevaría puesto	should/would I wear?	I should/would not wear
you would wear	would you wear?	you would not wear
he would wear	would he wear?	he would not wear
we should/would wear	should/would we wear?	we should/would not wear
you would wear	would you wear?	you would not wear
they would wear	would they wear?	they would not wear

❂ Imperative

Singular

let me wear déjame llevar puesto		do not let me wear
wear lleva puesto	* * * * * * * * * *	do not wear
let him/her/it wear lleve puesto		do not let him/her/it wear

❂ Subjunctive

Present

I wear lleve puesto		I do not wear
you wear		you do not wear
he wears	* * * * * * * * * *	he does not wear
we wear		we do not wear
you wear		you do not wear
they wear		they do not wear

Past

I wore llevara/llevase puesto		I did not wear
you wore		you did not wear
he wore	* * * * * * * * * *	he did not wear
we wore		we did not wear
you wore		you did not wear
they wore		they did not wear

✿ Infinitive	✿ Gerund	✿ Participle
to wear	wearing	worn

affirmative	interrogative	negative

Present perfect

affirmative	interrogative	negative
I have worn he llevado puesto	have I worn?	I have not worn
you have worn	have you worn?	you have not worn
he has worn	has he worn?	he has not worn
we have worn	have we worn?	we have not worn
you have worn	have you worn?	you have not worn
they have worn	have they worn?	they have not worn

Past perfect

affirmative	interrogative	negative
I had worn había/hube llevado puesto	had I worn?	I had not worn
you had worn	had you worn?	you had not worn
he had worn	had he worn?	he had not worn
we had worn	had we worn?	we had not worn
you had worn	had you worn?	you had not worn
they had worn	had they worn?	they had not worn

Future perfect

affirmative	interrogative	negative
I shall/will have worn habrán llevado puesto	shall/will I have worn?	I shall/will not have worn
you will have worn	will you have worn?	you will not have worn
he will have worn	will he have worn?	he will not have worn
we shall/will have worn	shall/will we have worn?	we shall/will not have worn
you will have worn	will you have worn?	you will not have worn
they will have worn	will they have worn?	they will not have worn

Perfect

affirmative	interrogative	negative
I should/would have worn habría llevado puesto	should/would I have worn?	I should/would not have worn
you would have worn	would you have worn?	you would not have worn
he would have worn	would he have worn?	he would not have worn
we should/would have worn	should/would we have worn?	we should/would not have worn
you would have worn	would you have worn?	you would not have worn
they would have worn	would they have worn?	they would not have worn

Plural

affirmative	interrogative	negative
let us wear llevemos puesto	* * * * * * * * *	do not let us (let's not) wear
wear llevad puesto		do not wear
let them wear lleven puesto		do not let them wear

Present perfect

affirmative	interrogative	negative
I have worn haya llevado puesto	* * * * * * * * *	I have not worn
you have worn		you have not worn
he has worn		he has not worn
we have worn		we have not worn
you have worn		you have not worn
they have worn		they have not worn

Past perfect

affirmative	interrogative	negative
I had worn hubiera/hubiese llevado puesto	* * * * * * * * *	I had not worn
you had worn		you had not worn
he had worn		he has not worn
we had worn		we had not worn
you had worn		you had not worn
they had worn		they had not worn

29. Get · Conseguir, lograr, obtener

	affirmative	interrogative	negative

❀ Indicative

	affirmative	interrogative	negative
Present	I get consigo you get he gets we get you get they get	do I get? do you get? does he get? do we get? do you get? do they get?	I do not get you do not get he does not get we do not get you do not get they do not get
Past	I got conseguía/conseguí you got he got we got you got they got	did I get? did you get? did he get? did we get? did you get? did they get?	I did not get you did not get he did not get we did not get you did not get they did not get
Future	I shall/will get conseguiré you will get he will get we shall/will get you will get they will get	shall/will I get? will you get? will he get? shall/will we get? will you get? will they get?	I shall/will not get you will not get he will not get we shall/will not get you will not get they will not get

❀ Conditional

	affirmative	interrogative	negative
Present	I should/would get conseguiría you would get he would get we should/would get you would get they would get	should/would I get? would you get? would he get? should/would we get? would you get? would they get?	I should/would not get you would not get he would not get we should/would not get you would not get they would not get

❀ Imperative

	affirmative	interrogative	negative
Singular	let me get déjame conseguir get consigue let him/her/it get consiga	* * * * * * * * *	do not let me get do not get do not let him/her/it get

❀ Subjunctive

	affirmative	interrogative	negative
Present	I get consiga you get he gets we get you get they get	* * * * * * * * *	I do not get you do not get he does not get we do not get you do not get they do not get
Past	I got consiguiera/consiguiese you got he got we got you got they got	* * * * * * * * *	I did not get you did not get he did not get we did not get you did not get they did not get

❁ **Infinitive**	❁ **Gerund**	❁ **Participle**
to get	getting	got/gotten

affirmative	interrogative	negative

Present Perfect

affirmative	interrogative	negative
I have got/gotten he conseguido	have I got/gotten?	I have not got/gotten
you have got/gotten	have you got/gotten?	you have not got/gotten
he has got/gotten	has he got/gotten?	he has not got/gotten
we have got/gotten	have we got/gotten?	we have not got/gotten
you have got/gotten	have you got/gotten?	you have not got/gotten
they have got/gotten	have they got/gotten?	they have not got/gotten

Past Perfect

affirmative	interrogative	negative
I had got/gotten había conseguido	had I got/gotten?	I had not got/gotten
you had got/gotten	had you got/gotten?	you had not got/gotten
he had got/gotten	had he got/gotten?	he had not got/gotten
we had got/gotten	had we got/gotten?	we had not got/gotten
you had got/gotten	had you got/gotten?	you had not got/gotten
they had got/gotten	had they got/gotten?	they had not got/gotten

Future Perfect

affirmative	interrogative	negative
I shall/will have got/gotten habré conseguido	shall/will I have got/gotten?	I shall/will not have got/gotten
you will have got/gotten	will you have got/gotten?	you will not have got/gotten
he will have got/gotten	will he have got/gotten?	he will not have got/gotten
we shall/will have got/gotten	shall/will we have got/gotten?	we shall/will have got/gotten
you will have got/gotten	will you have got/gotten?	you will have got/gotten
they will have got/gotten	will they have got/gotten?	they will have got/gotten

Perfect

affirmative	interrogative	negative
I should/would have got/gotten habría conseguido	should/would I have got/gotten?	I should/would not have got/gotten
you would have got/gotten	would you have got/gotten?	you would not have got/gotten
he would have got/gotten	would he have got/gotten?	he would not have got/gotten
we should/would have got/gotten	should/would we have got/gotten?	we should/would not have got/gotten
you would have got/gotten	would you have got/gotten?	you would not have got/gotten
they would have got/gotten	would they have got/gotten?	they would not have got/gotten

Plural

affirmative	interrogative	negative
let us get consigamos	* * * * * * * * * *	do not let us (let's not) get
get conseguid		do not get
let them get consigan		do not let them get

Present Perfect

affirmative	interrogative	negative
I have got/gotten haya conseguido		I have not got/gotten
you have got/gotten	* * * * * * * * * *	you have not got/gotten
he has got/gotten		he has not got/gotten
we have got/gotten		we have not got/gotten
you have got/gotten		you have not got/gotten
they have got/gotten		they have not got/gotten

Past Perfect

affirmative	interrogative	negative
I had got/gotten hubiera/hubiese conseguido		I had not got/gotten
you had got/gotten	* * * * * * * * * *	you had not got/gotten
he had got/gotten		he had not got/gotten
we had got/gotten		we had not got/gotten
you had got/gotten		you had not got/gotten
they had got/gotten		they had not got/gotten

30. Go · Ir

	affirmative	interrogative	negative

☸ Indicative

Present
I go voy	do I go?	I do not go
you go	do you go?	you do not go
he goes	does he go?	he does not go
we go	do we go?	we do not go
you go	do you go?	you do not go
they go	do they go?	they do not go

Past
I went iba/fu	did I go?	I did not go
you went	did you go?	you did not go
he went	did he go?	he did not go
we went	did we go?	we did not go
you went	did you go?	you did not go
they went	did they go?	they did not go

Future
I shall/will go iré	shall/will I go?	I shall/will not go
you will go	will you go?	you will not go
he will go	will he go?	he will not go
we shall/will go	shall/will we go?	we shall/will not go
you will go	will you go?	you will not go
they will go	will they go?	they will not go

☸ Conditional

Present
I should/would go iría	should/would I go?	I should/would not go
you would go	would you go?	you would not go
he would go	would he go?	he would not go
we should/would go	should/would we go?	we should/would not go
you would go	would you go?	you would not go
they would go	would they go?	they would not go

☸ Imperative

Singular
let me go déjame ir		do not let me go
go ve	* * * * * * * * * *	do not go
let him/her/it go vaya		do not let him/her/it go

☸ Subjunctive

Present
I go vaya		I do not go
you go		you do not go
he goes	* * * * * * * * * *	he does not go
we go		we do not go
you go		you do not go
they go		they do not go

Past
I went fuera/fuese		I did not go
you went		you did not go
he went	* * * * * * * * * *	he did not go
we went		we did not go
you went		you did not go
they went		they did not go

❖ **Infinitive**	❖ **Gerund**	❖ **Participle**
to go	going	gone

	affirmative	interrogative	negative

	affirmative	**interrogative**	**negative**
Present Perfect	I have gone he ido	have I gone?	I have not gone
	you have gone	have you gone?	you have not gone
	he has gone	has he gone?	he has not gone
	we have gone	have we gone?	we have not gone
	you have gone	have you gone?	you have not gone
	they have gone	have they gone?	they have not gone
Past Perfect	I had gone había/hube ido	had I gone?	I had not gone
	you had gone	had you gone?	you had not gone
	he had gone	had he gone?	he had not gone
	we had gone	had we gone?	we had not gone
	you had gone	had you gone?	you had not gone
	they had gone	had they gone?	they had not gone
Future Perfect	I shall/will have gone habré ido	shall/will I have gone?	I shall/will not have gone
	you will have gone	will you have gone?	you will not have gone
	he will have gone	will he have gone?	he will not have gone
	we shall/will have gone	shall/will we have gone?	we shall/will not have gone
	you will have gone	will you have gone?	you will not have gone
	they will have gone	will they have gone?	they will not have gone
Perfect	I should/would have gone habría ido	should/would I have gone?	I should/would not have gone
	you would have gone	would you have gone?	you would not have gone
	he would have gone	would he have gone?	he would not have gone
	we should/would have gone	should/would we have gone?	we should/would not have gone
	you would have gone	would you have gone?	you would not have gone
	they would have gone	would they have gone?	they would not have gone
Plural	let us go vayamos	* * * * * * * * * *	do not let us (let's not) go
	go id		go
	let them go vayan		do not let them go
Present Perfect	I have gone haya ido	* * * * * * * * * *	I have not gone
	you have gone		you have not gone
	he has gone		he has not gone
	we have gone		we have not gone
	you have gone		you have not gone
	they have gone		they have not gone
Past Perfect	I had gone hubiera/hubiese ido	* * * * * * * * * *	I had not gone
	you had gone		you had not gone
	he had gone		he had not gone
	we had gone		we had not gone
	you had gone		you had not gone
	they had gone		they had not gone

31. Hear · Oir

affirmative	interrogative	negative

❁ Indicative

	affirmative	interrogative	negative
Present	I hear oigo	do I hear?	I do not hear
	you hear	do you hear?	you do not hear
	he hears	does he hear?	he does not hear
	we hear	do we hear?	we do not hear
	you hear	do you hear?	you do not hear
	they hear	do they hear?	they do not hear
Past	I heard oía/oí	did I hear?	I did not hear
	you heard	did you hear?	you did not hear
	he heard	did he hear?	he did not hear
	we heard	did we hear?	we did not hear
	you heard	did you hear?	you did not hear
	they heard	did they hear?	they did not hear
Future	I shall/will hear oiré	shall/will I hear?	I shall/will not hear
	you will hear	will you hear?	you will not hear
	he will hear	will he hear?	he will not hear
	we shall/will hear	shall/will we hear?	we shall/will not hear
	you will hear	will you hear?	you will not hear
	they will hear	will they hear?	they will not hear

❁ Conditional

	affirmative	interrogative	negative
Present	I should/would hear oiría	should/would I hear?	I should/would not hear
	you would hear	would you hear?	you would not hear
	he would hear	would he hear?	he would not hear
	we should/would hear	should/would we hear?	we should/would not hear
	you would hear	would you hear?	you would not hear
	they would hear	would they hear?	they would not hear

❁ Imperative

	affirmative	interrogative	negative
Singular	let me hear déjame oír	* * * * * * * * * *	do not let me hear
	hear oye		do not hear
	let him/her/it hear oiga		do not let him/her/it hear

❁ Subjunctive

	affirmative	interrogative	negative
Present	I hear oiga		I do not hear
	you hear		you do not hear
	he hears	* * * * * * * * * *	he does not hear
	we hear		we do not hear
	you hear		you do not hear
	they hear		they do not hear
Past	I heard oyera/oyese		I did not hear
	you heard		you did not hear
	he heard	* * * * * * * * * *	he did not hear
	we heard		we did not hear
	you heard		you did not hear
	they heard		they did not hear

❀ Infinitive	❀ Gerund	❀ Participle
to hear	hearing	heard

affirmative	interrogative	negative

Present perfect

affirmative	interrogative	negative
I have heard he oído	have I heard?	I have not heard
you have heard	have you heard?	you have not heard
he has heard	has he heard?	he has not heard
we have heard	have we heard?	we have not heard
you have heard	have you heard?	you have not herd
they have heard	have they heard?	they have not heard

Past perfect

affirmative	interrogative	negative
I had heard había/hube oído	had I heard?	I had not heard
you had heard	had you heard?	you had not heard
he had heard	had he heard?	he had not heard
we had heard	had we heard?	we had not heard
you had heard	had you heard?	you had not heard
they had heard	had they heard?	they had not heard

Future perfect

affirmative	interrogative	negative
I shall/will have heard habré oído	shall/will I have heard?	I shall/will not have heard
you will have heard	will you have heard?	you will not have heard
he will have heard	will he have heard?	he will not have heard
we shall/will have heard	shall/will we have heard?	we shall/will not have heard
you will have heard	will you have heard?	you will not have heard
they will have heard	will they have heard?	they will not have heard

Perfect

affirmative	interrogative	negative
I should/would have heard habría oído	should/would I have heard?	I should/would not have heard
you would have heard	would you have heard?	you would not have heard
he would have heard	would he have heard?	he would not have heard
we should/would have heard	should/would we have heard?	we should/would not have heard
you would have heard	would you have heard?	you would not have heard
they would have heard	would they have heard?	they would not have heard

Plural

affirmative	interrogative	negative
let us hear oigamos	* * * * * * * * * *	do not let us (let's not) hear
hear oíd		do not hear
let them hear oigan		do not let them hear

Present perfect

affirmative	interrogative	negative
I have heard haya oído	* * * * * * * * * *	I have not heard
you have heard		you have not heard
he has heard		he has not heard
we have heard		we have not heard
you have heard		you have not heard
they have heard		they have not heard

Past perfect

affirmative	interrogative	negative
I had heard hubiera/hubiese oído	* * * * * * * * * *	I had not heard
you had heard		you had not heard
he had heard		he had not heard
we had heard		we had not heard
you had heard		you had not heard
they had heard		they had not heard

32. Lay · Poner (huevos, mesa), colocar

affirmative	interrogative	negative

❀ Indicative

	affirmative	interrogative	negative
Present	I lay pongo	do I lay?	I do not lay
	you lay	do you lay?	you do not lay
	he lays	does he lay?	he does not lay
	we lay	do we lay?	we do not lay
	you lay	do you lay?	you do not lay
	they lay	do they lay?	they do not lay
Past	I laid ponía/puse	did I lay?	I did not lay
	you laid	did you lay?	you did not lay
	he laid	did he lay?	he did not lay
	we laid	did we lay?	we did not lay
	you laid	did you lay?	you did not lay
	they laid	did they lay?	they did not lay
Future	I shall/will lay pondré	shall/will I lay?	I shall/will not lay
	you will lay	will you lay?	you will not lay
	he will lay	will he lay?	he will not lay
	we shall/will lay	shall/will we lay?	we shall/will not lay
	you will lay	will you lay?	you will not lay
	they will lay	will they lay?	they will not lay

❀ Conditional

	affirmative	interrogative	negative
Present	I should/would lay pondría	should/would I lay?	I should/would not lay
	you would lay	would you lay?	you would not lay
	he would lay	would he lay?	he would not lay
	we should/would lay	should/would we lay?	we should/would not lay
	you would lay	would you lay?	you would not lay
	they would lay	would they lay?	they would not lay

❀ Imperative

	affirmative	interrogative	negative
Singular	let me lay déjame poner		do not let me lay
	lay pon	* * * * * * * * * *	do not lay
	let him/her/it lay ponga		do not let him/her/it lay

❀ Subjunctive

	affirmative	interrogative	negative
Present	I lay ponga		I do not lay
	you lay		you do not lay
	he lays	* * * * * * * * * *	he does not lay
	we lay		we do not lay
	you lay		you do not lay
	they lay		they do not lay
Past	I laid pusiera/pusiese		I did not lay
	you laid		you did not lay
	he laid	* * * * * * * * * *	he did not lay
	we laid		we did not lay
	you laid		you did not lay
	they laid		they did not lay

❀ **Infinitive**	❀ **Gerund**	❀ **Participle**
to lay	laying	laid

	affirmative	**interrogative**	**negative**

	affirmative	interrogative	negative
Present perfect	I have laid *he puesto* you have laid he has laid we have laid you have laid they have laid	have I laid? have you laid? has he laid? have we laid? have you laid? have they laid?	I have not laid you have not laid he has not laid we have not laid you have not laid they have not laid
Past perfect	I had laid *había puesto* you had laid he had laid we had laid you had laid they had laid	had I laid? had you laid? had he laid? had we laid? had you laid? had they laid?	I had not laid you had not laid he had not laid we had not laid you had not laid they had not laid
Future perfect	I shall/will have laid *habré puesto* you will have laid he will have laid we shall/will have laid you will have laid they will have laid	shall/will I have laid? will you have laid? will he have laid? shall/will we have laid? will you have laid? will they have laid?	I shall/will not have laid you will not have laid he will not have laid we shall/will not have laid you will not have laid they will not have laid
Perfect	I should/would have laid *habría puesto* you would have laid he would have laid we should/would have laid you would have laid they would have laid	should/would I have laid? would you have laid? would he have laid? should/would we have laid? would you have laid? would they have laid?	I should/would not have laid you would not have laid he would not have laid we should/would not have laid you would not have laid they would not have laid
Plural	let us lay *pongamos* lay *poned* let them lay *pongan*	* * * * * * * * * *	do not let us (let's not) lay do not lay do not let them lay
Present perfect	I have laid *haya puesto* you have laid he has laid we have laid you have laid they have laid	* * * * * * * * * *	I have not laid you have not laid he has not laid we have not laid you have not laid they have not laid
Past perfect	I had laid *hubiera/hubiese puesto* you had laid he had laid we had laid you had laid they had laid	* * * * * * * * * *	I had not laid you had not laid he had not laid we had not laid you had not laid they had not laid

33. Lie · Echarse, acostarse, yacer

	affirmative	interrogative	negative

❋ Indicative

Present	I lie yazgo/yazco	do I lie?	I do not lie
	you lie	do you lie?	you do not lie
	he lies	does he lie?	he does not lie
	we lie	do we lie?	we do not lie
	you lie	do you lie?	you do not lie
	they lie	do they lie?	they do not lie

Past	I lay yacía/yací	did I lie?	I did not lie
	you lay	did you lie?	you did not lie
	he lay	did he lie?	he did not lie
	we lay	did we lie?	we did not lie
	you lay	did you lie?	you did not lie
	they lay	did they lie?	they did not lie

Future	I shall/will lie yaceré	shall/will I lie?	I shall/will not lie
	you will lie	will you lie?	you will not lie
	he will lie	will he lie?	he will not lie
	we shall/will lie	shall/will we lie?	we shall/will not lie
	you will lie	will you lie?	you will not lie
	they will lie	will they lie?	they will not lie

❋ Conditional

Present	I should/would lie yacería	should/would I lie?	I should/would not lie
	you would lie	would you lie?	you would not lie
	he would lie	would he lie?	he would not lie
	we should/would lie	should/would we lie?	we should/would not lie
	you would lie	would you lie?	you would not lie
	they would lie	would they lie?	they would not lie

❋ Imperative

Singular	let me lie déjame yacer		do not let me lie
	lie yace	* * * * * * * * * *	do not lie
	let him/her/it lie yazga/yazga		do not let him/her/it lie

❋ Subjunctive

Present	I lie yazga/yazga		I do not lie
	you lie		you do not lie
	he lies	* * * * * * * * * *	he does not lie
	we lie		we do not lie
	you lie		you do not lie
	they lie		they do not lie

Past	I lay yaciera/yaciese		I did not lie
	you lay		you did not lie
	he lay	* * * * * * * * * *	he did not lie
	we lay		we did not lie
	you lay		you did not lie
	they lay		they did not lie

❀ Infinitive	❀ Gerund	❀ Participle
to lie	lying	lain

affirmative	interrogative	negative

Present perfect

I have lain he yacido	have I lain?	I have not lain
you have lain	have you lain?	you have not lain
he has lain	has he lain?	he has not lain
we have lain	have we lain?	we have not lain
you have lain	have you lain?	you have not lain
they have lain	have they lain?	they have not lain

Past perfect

I had lain había yacido	had I lain?	I had not lain
you had lain	had you lain?	you had not lain
he had lain	had he lain?	he had not lain
we had lain	had we lain?	we had not lain
you had lain	had you lain?	you had not lain
they had lain	had they lain?	they had not lain

Future perfect

I shall/will have lain habré yacido	shall/will I have lain?	I shall/will not have lain
you will have lain	will you have lain?	you will not have lain
he will have lain	will he have lain?	he will not have lain
we shall/will have lain	shall/will we have lain?	we shall/will not have lain
you will have lain	will you have lain?	you will not have lain
they will have lain	will they have lain?	they will not have lain

Perfect

I should/would have lain habría yacido	should/would I have lain?	I should/would not have lain
you would have lain	would you have lain?	you would not have lain
he would have lain	would he have lain?	he would not have lain
we should/would have lain	should/would we have lain?	we should/would not have lain
you would have lain	would you have lain?	you would not have lain
they would have lain	would they have lain?	they would not have lain

Plural

let us lie yazcamos	* * * * * * * * * *	do not let us (let's not) lie
lie yaced		do not lie
let them lie yazcan/yazcan		do not let them lie

Present perfect

I have lain haya yacido	* * * * * * * * * *	I have not lain
you have lain		you have not lain
he has lain		he has not lain
we have lain		we have not lain
you have lain		you have not lain
they have lain		they have not lain

Past perfect

I had lain hubiera/hubiese yacido	* * * * * * * * * *	I had not lain
you had lain		you had not lain
he had lain		he has not lain
we had lain		we had not lain
you had lain		you had not lain
they had lain		they had not lain

34. Stand · Estar, poner (de pie), resistir

affirmative	interrogative	negative

✿ Indicative

Present

I stand estoy de pie	do I stand?	I do not stand
you stand	do you stand?	you do not stand
he stands	does he stand?	he does not stand
we stand	do we stand?	we do not stand
you stand	do you stand?	you do not stand
they stand	do they stand?	they do not stand

Past

I stood estaba/estuve de pie	did I stand?	I did not stand
you stood	did you stand?	you did not stand
he stood	did he stand?	he did not stand
we stood	did we stand?	we did not stand
you stood	did you stand?	you did not stand
they stood	did they stand?	they did not stand

Future

I shall/will stand estaré de pie	shall/will I stand?	I shall/will not stand
you will stand	will you stand?	you will not stand
he will stand	will he stand?	he will not stand
we shall/will stand	shall/will we stand?	we shall/will not stand
you will stand	will you stand?	you will not stand
they will stand	will they stand?	they will not stand

✿ Conditional

Present

I should/would stand estaría de pie	should/would I stand?	I should/would not stand
you would stand	would you stand?	you would not stand
he would stand	would he stand?	he would not stand
we should/would stand	should/would we stand?	we should/would not stand
you would stand	would you stand?	you would not stand
they would stand	would they stand?	they would not stand

✿ Imperative

Singular

let me stand déjame estar de pie		do not let me stand
stand esta(te) de pie	* * * * * * * * *	do not stand
let him/her/it stand esté de pie		do not let him/her/it stand

✿ Subjunctive

Present

I stand esté de pie		I do not stand
you stand		you do not stand
he stands	* * * * * * * * *	he does not stand
we stand		we do not stand
you stand		you do not stand
they stand		they do not stand

Past

I stood estuviera/estuviese de pie		I did not stand
you stood		you did not stand
he stood	* * * * * * * * *	he did not stand
we stood		we did not stand
you stood		you did not stand
they stood		they did not stand

❀ **Infinitive**	❀ **Gerund**	❀ **Participle**
to stand	standing	stood

	affirmative	**interrogative**	**negative**

Present perfect	I have stood he estado de pie you have stood he has stood we have stood you have stood they have stood	have I stood? have you stood? has he stood? have we stood? have you stood? have they stood?	I have not stood you have not stood he has not stood we have not stood you have not stood they have not stood
Past perfect	I had stood había/hube estado de pie you had stood he had stood we had stood you had stood they had stood	had I stood? had you stood? had he stood? had we stood? had you stood? had they stood?	I had not stood you had not stood he had not stood we had not stood you had not stood they had not stood
Future perfect	I shall/will have stood habré estado de pie you will have stood he will have stood we shall/will have stood you will have stood they will have stood	shall/will I have stood? will you have stood? will he have stood? shall/will we have stood? will you have stood? will they have stood?	I shall/will not have stood you will not have stood he will not have stood we shall/will not have stood you will not have stood they will not have stood

| **Perfect** | I should/would have stood
                habría estado de pie
you would have stood
he would have stood
we should/would have stood
you would have stood
they would have stood | should/would I have stood?
would you have stood?
would he have stood?
should/would we have stood?
would you have stood?
would they have stood? | I should/would not have stood
you would not have stood
he would not have stood
we should/would not have stood
you would not have stood
they would not have stood |

| **Plural** | let us stand   estemos de pie
stand   estad de pie
let them stand   estén de pie | * * * * * * * * * * | do not let us (let's not) stand
do not stand
do not let them stand |

| **Present perfect** | I have stood   haya estado de pie
you have stood
he has stood
we have stood
you have stood
they have stood | * * * * * * * * * * | I have not stood
you have not stood
he has not stood
we have not stood
you have not stood
they have not stood |
| **Past perfect** | I had stood   hubiera/hubiese estado de pie
you had stood
he had stood
we had stood
you had stood
they had stood | * * * * * * * * * * | I had not stood
you had not stood
he had not stood
we had not stood
you had not stood
they had not stood |

35. Run · Correr

	affirmative	interrogative	negative

❁ Indicative

Present
I run corro	do I run?	I do not run
you run	do you run?	you do not run
he runs	does he run?	he does not run
we run	do we run?	we do not run
you run	do you run?	you do not run
they run	do they run?	they do not run

Past
I ran corría/corrí	did I run?	I did not run
you ran	did you run?	you did not run
he ran	did he run?	he did not run
we ran	did we run?	we did not run
you ran	did you run?	you did not run
they ran	did they run?	they did not run

Future
I shall/will run correré	shall/will I run?	I shall/will not run
you will run	will you run?	you will not run
he will run	will he run?	he will not run
we shall/will run	shall/will we run?	we shall/will not run
you will run	will you run?	you will not run
they will run	will they run?	they will not run

❁ Conditional

Present
I should/would run correría	should/would I run?	I should/would not run
you would run	would you run?	you would not run
he would run	would he run?	he would not run
we should/would run	should/would we run?	we should/would not run
you would run	would you run?	you would not run
they would run	would they run?	they would not run

❁ Imperative

Singular
let me run déjame correr		do not let me run
run corre	* * * * * * * * *	do not run
let him/her/it run corra		do not let him/her/it run

❁ Subjunctive

Present
I run corra		I do not run
you run		you do not run
he runs	* * * * * * * * *	he does not run
we run		we do not run
you run		you do not run
they run		they do not run

Past
I ran corriera/corriese		I did not run
you ran		you did not run
he ran	* * * * * * * * *	he did not run
we ran		we did not run
you ran		you did not run
they ran		they did not run

❋ Infinitive	❋ Gerund	❋ Participle
to run	running	run

	affirmative	interrogative	negative

	affirmative	interrogative	negative
Present perfect	I have run he corrido you have run he has run we have run you have run they have run	have I run? have you run? has he run? have we run? have you run? have they run?	I have not run you have not run he has not run we have not run you have not run they have not run
Past perfect	I had run había corrido you had run he had run we had run you had run they had run	had I run? had you run? had he run? had we run? had you run? had they run?	I had not run you had not run he had not run we had not run you had not run they had not run
Future perfect	I shall/will have run habré corrido you will have run he will have run we shall/will have run you will have run they will have run	shall/will I have run? will you have run? will he have run? shall/will we have run? will you have run? will they have run?	I shall/will not have run you will not have run he will not have run we shall/will not have run you will not have run they will not have run
Perfect	I should/would have run habría corrido you would have run he would have run we should/would have run you would have run they would have run	should/would I have run? would you have run? would he have run? should/would we have run? would you have run? would they have run?	I should/would not have run you would not have run he would not have run we should/would not have run you would not have run they would not have run
Plural	let us run corramos run corred let them run corran	* * * * * * * * * *	do not let us (let's not) run do not run do not let them run
Present perfect	I have run haya corrido you have run he has run we have run you have run they have run	* * * * * * * * * *	I have not run you have not run he has not run we have not run you have not run they have not run
Past perfect	I had run hubiera/hubiese corrido you had run he had run we had run you had run they had run	* * * * * * * * * *	I had not run you had not run he had not run we had not run you had not run they had not run

36. Rise · Elevar, levantar, subir, salir (sol)

	affirmative	interrogative	negative

❋ Indicative

Present I rise   elevo | do I rise? | I do not rise
you rise | do you rise? | you do not rise
he rises | does he rise? | he does not rise
we rise | do we rise? | we do not rise
you rise | do you rise? | you do not rise
they rise | do they rise? | they do not rise

Past I rose   elevaba/elevé | did I rise? | I did not rise
you rose | did you rise? | you did not rise
he rose | did he rise? | he did not rise
we rose | did we rise? | we did not rise
you rose | did you rise? | you did not rise
they rose | did they rise? | they did not rise

Future I shall/will rise   elevaré | shall/will I rise? | I shall/will not rise
you will rise | will you rise? | you will not rise
he will rise | will he rise? | he will not rise
we shall/will rise | shall/will we rise? | we shall/will not rise
you will rise | will you rise? | you will not rise
they will rise | will they rise? | they will not rise

❋ Conditional

Present I should/would rise   elevaría | should/would I rise? | I should/would not rise
you would rise | would you rise? | you would not rise
he would rise | would he rise? | he would not rise
we should/would rise | should/would we rise? | we should/would not rise
you would rise | would you rise? | you would not rise
they would rise | would they rise? | they would not rise

❋ Imperative

Singular let me rise   déjame elevar | * * * * * * * * * | do not let me rise
rise   eleva | | do not rise
let him/her/it rise   eleve | | do not let him/her/it rise

❋ Subjunctive

Present I rise   eleve | * * * * * * * * * | I do not rise
you rise | | you do not rise
he rises | | he does not rise
we rise | | we do not rise
you rise | | you do not rise
they rise | | they do not rise

Past I rose   elevara/elevase | * * * * * * * * * | I did not rise
you rose | | you did not rise
he rose | | he did not rise
we rose | | we did not rise
you rose | | you did not rise
they rose | | they did not rise

❖ Infinitive	❖ Gerund	❖ Participle
to rise	rising	risen

	affirmative	interrogative	negative
Present perfect	I have risen he elevado you have risen he has risen we have risen you have risen they have risen	have I risen? have you risen? has he risen? have we risen? have you risen? have they risen?	I have not risen you have not risen he has not risen we have not risen you have not risen they have not risen
Past perfect	I had risen había/hube elevado you had risen he had risen we had risen you had risen they had risen	had I risen? had you risen? had he risen? had we risen? had you risen? had they risen?	I had not risen you had not risen he had not risen we had not risen you had not risen they had not risen
Future perfect	I shall/will have risen habré elevado you will have risen he will have risen we should/would have risen you would have risen they would have risen	shall/will I have risen? will you have risen? will he have risen? shall/will we have risen? will you have risen? will they have risen?	I shall/will not have risen you will not have risen he will not have risen we shall/will not have risen you will not have risen they will not have risen
Perfect	I should/would have risen habría elevado you would have risen he would have risen we should/would have risen you would have risen they would have risen	should/would I have risen? would you have risen? would he have risen? should/would we have risen? would you have risen? would they have risen?	I should/would not have risen you would not have risen he would not have risen we should/would not have risen you would not have risen they would not have risen
Plural	let us rise elevemos rise elevad let them rise eleven	* * * * * * * * *	do not let us (let's not) rise do not rise do not let them rise
Present perfect	I have risen haya elevado you have risen he has risen we have risen you have risen they have risen	* * * * * * * * *	I have not risen you have not risen he has not risen we have not risen you have not risen they have not risen
Past perfect	I had risen hubiera/hubiese elevado you had risen he had risen we had risen you had risen they had risen	* * * * * * * * *	I had not risen you had not risen he had not risen we had not risen you had not risen they had not risen

37. Choose · Elegir

affirmative	interrogative	negative

h Indicative

Present

I choose elijo	do I choose?	I do not choose
you choose	do you choose?	you do not choose
he chooses	does he choose?	he does not choose
we choose	do we choose?	we do not choose
you choose	do you choose?	you do not choose
they choose	do they choose?	they do not choose

Past

I chose elegía/elegí	did I choose?	I did not choose
you chose	did you choose?	you did not choose
he chose	did he choose?	he did not choose
we chose	did we choose?	we did not choose
you chose	did you choose?	you did not choose
they chose	did they choose?	they did not choose

Future

I shall/will choose eligiré	shall/will I choose?	I shall/will not choose
you will choose	will you choose?	you will not chose
he will choose	will he choose?	he will not choose
we shall/will choose	shall/will we choose?	we shall/will not choose
you will choose	will you choose?	you will not choose
they will choose	will they choose?	they will not choose

h Conditional

Present

I should/would choose elegiría	should/would I choose?	I should/would not choose
you would choose	would you choose?	you would not choose
he would choose	would he choose?	he would not choose
we should/would choose	should/would we choose?	we should/would not chose
you would choose	would you choose?	you would not choose
they would choose	would they choose?	they would not choose

h Imperative

Singular

let me choose déjame elegir		do not let me choose
choose elige	* * * * * * * * *	do not choose
let him/her/it choose elija		do not let him/her/it choose

h Subjunctive

Present

I choose elija		I do not choose
you choose		you do not choose
he chooses	* * * * * * * * *	he does not choose
we choose		we do not choose
you choose		you do not choose
they choose		they do not choose

Past

I chose eligiera/eligiese		I did not choose
you chose		you did not choose
he chose	* * * * * * * * *	he did not choose
we chose		we did not choose
you chose		you did not choose
they chose		they did not choose

h **Infinitive**	h **Gerund**	h **Participle**
to choose	chosing	chosen

	affirmative	interrogative	negative

Present perfect
affirmative	interrogative	negative
I have chosen he elegido	have I chosen?	I have not chosen
you have chosen	have you chosen?	you have not chosen
he has chosen	has he chosen?	he has not chosen
we have chosen	have we chosen?	we have not chosen
you have chosen	have you chosen?	you have not chosen
they have chosen	have they chosen?	they have not chosen

Past perfect
affirmative	interrogative	negative
I had chosen había elegido	had I chosen?	I had not chosen
you had chosen	had you chosen?	you had not chosen
he had chosen	had he chosen?	he had not chosen
we had chosen	had we chosen?	we had not chosen
you had chosen	had you chosen?	you had not chosen
they had chosen	had they chosen?	they had not chosen

Future perfect
affirmative	interrogative	negative
I shall/will have choosen habré elegido	shall/will I have chosen?	I shall/will not have chosen
you will have chosen	will you have chosen?	you will not have chosen
he will have chosen	will he have chosen?	he will not have chosen
we shall/will have chosen	shall/will we have chosen?	we shall/will not have chosen
you will have chosen	will you have chosen?	you will not have chooosen
they will have chosen	will they have chosen?	they will not have chosen

Perfect
affirmative	interrogative	negative
I should/would have chosen habría elegido	should/would I have chosen?	I should/would not have chosen
you would have chosen	would you have chosen?	you would not have chosen
he would have chosen	would he have chosen?	he would not have chosen
we should/would have chosen	should/would we have chosen?	we should/would not have chosen
you would have chosen	would you have chosen?	you would not have chosen
they would have chosen	would they have chosen?	they would not have chosen

Plural
affirmative	interrogative	negative
let us choose elijamos	* * * * * * * * *	do not let us (let's not) choose
choose elegid		do not choose
let them choose elijan		do not let them choose

Present perfect
affirmative	interrogative	negative
I have chosen haya elegido	* * * * * * * * *	I have not chosen
you have chosen		you have not chosen
he has chosen		he has not chosen
we have chosen		we have not chosen
you have chosen		you have not chosen
they have chosen		they have not chosen

Past perfect
affirmative	interrogative	negative
I had chosen hubiera/hubiese elegido	* * * * * * * * *	I had not chosen
you had chosen		you had not chosen
he had chosen		he had not chosen
we had chosen		we had not chosen
you had chosen		you had not chosen
they had chosen		they had not chosen

116

38. Write · Escribir

affirmative	interrogative	negative

❀ Indicative

Present
I write escribo	do I write?	I do not write
you write	do you write?	you do not write
he writes	does he write?	he does not write
we write	do we write?	we do not write
you write	do you write?	you do not write
they write	do they write?	they do not write

Past
I wrote escribía/escribí	did I write?	I did not write
you wrote	did you write?	you did not write
he wrote	did he write?	he did not write
we wrote	did we write?	we did not write
you wrote	did you write?	you did not write
they wrote	did they write?	they did not write

Future
I shall/will write escribiré	shall/will I write?	I shall/will not write
you will write	will you write?	you will not write
he will write	will he write?	he will not write
we shall/will write	shall/will we write?	we shall/will not write
you will write	will you write?	you will not write
they will write	will they write?	they will not write

❀ Conditional

Present
I should/would write escribiría	should/would I write?	I should/would not write
you would write	would you write?	you would not write
he would write	would he write?	he would not write
we should/would write	should/would we write?	we should not write
you would write	would you write?	you would not write
they would write	would they write?	they would not write

❀ Imperative

Singular
let me write déjame escribir		do not let me write
write escribe	* * * * * * * * * *	do not write
let him/her/it write escriba		do not let him/her/it write

❀ Subjunctive

Present
I write escriba		I do not write
you write		you do not write
he writes	* * * * * * * * * *	he does not write
we write		we do not write
you write		you do not write
they write		they do not write

Past
I wrote escribiera/escribiese		I did not write
you wrote		you did not write
he wrote	* * * * * * * * * *	he did not write
we wrote		we did not write
you wrote		you did not write
they wrote		they did not write

❋ **Infinitive**	❋ **Gerund**	❋ **Participle**
to write	writing	written

	affirmative	interrogative	negative

	affirmative	interrogative	negative
Present Perfect	I have written he escrito	have I written?	I have not written
	you have written	have you written?	you have not written
	he has written	has he written?	he has not written
	we have written	have we written?	we have not written
	you have written	have you written?	you have not written
	they have written	have they written?	they have not written
Past Perfect	I had written había/hube escrito	had I written?	I had not written
	you had written	had you written?	you had not written
	he had written	had he written?	he had not written
	we had written	had we written?	we had not written
	you had written	had you written?	you had not written
	they had written	had they written?	they had not written
Future Perfect	I shall/will have written habré escrito	shall/will I have written?	I shall/will not have written
	you will have written	will you have written?	you will not have written
	he will have written	will he have written?	he will not have written
	we shall/will have written	shall/will we have written?	we shall/will not have written
	you will have written	will you have written?	you will not have written
	they will have written	will they have written?	they will not have written
Perfect	I should/would have written habría escrito	should/would I have written?	I should/would not have written
	you would have written	would you have written?	you would not have written
	he would have written	would he have written?	he would not have written
	we should/would have written	should/would we have written?	we should/would not have written
	you would have written	would you have written?	you would not have written
	they would have written	would they have written?	they would not have written
Plural	let us write escribamos		do not let us (let's not) write
	write escribid	* * * * * * * * * *	do not write
	let them write escriban		do not let them write
Present Perfect	I have written haya escrito		I have not written
	you have written		you have not written
	he has written	* * * * * * * * * *	he has not written
	we have written		we have not written
	you have written		you have not written
	they have written		they have not written
Past Perfect	I had written hubiera/hubiese escrito		I had not written
	you had written		you had not written
	he had written	* * * * * * * * * *	he had not written
	we had written		we had not written
	you had written		you had not written
	they had written		they had not written

39. Cast · Arrojar, proyectar, echar

	affirmative	interrogative	negative

✿ Indicative

Present
I cast arrojo	do I cast?	I do not cast
you cast	do you cast?	you do not cast
he casts	does he cast?	he does not cast
we cast	do we cast?	we do not cast
you cast	do you cast?	you do not cast
they cast	do they cast?	they do not cast

Past
I cast arrojaba/arrojé	did I cast?	I did not cast
you cast	did you cast?	you did not cast
he cast	did he cast?	he did not cast
we cast	did we cast?	we did not cast
you cast	did you cast?	you did not cast
they cast	did they cast?	they did not cast

Future
I shall/will cast arrojaré	shall/will I cast?	I shall/will not cast
you will cast	will you cast?	you will not cast
he will cast	will he cast?	he will not cast
we shall/will cast	shall/will we cast?	we shall/will not cast
you will cast	will you cast?	you will not cast
they will cast	will they cast?	they will not cast

✿ Conditional

Present
I should/would cast arrojaría	should/would I cast?	I should/would not cast
you would cast	would you cast?	you would not cast
he would cast	would he cast?	he would not cast
we should/would cast	should/would we cast?	we should/would not cast
you would cast	would you cast?	you would not cast
they would cast	would they cast?	they would not cast

✿ Imperative

Singular
let me cast déjame arrojar	* * * * * * * * * *	do not let me cast
cast arroja		do not cast
let him/her/it cast arroje		do not let him/her/it cast

✿ Subjunctive

Present
I cast arroje	* * * * * * * * * *	I do not cast
you cast		you do not cast
he casts		he does not cast
we cast		we do not cast
you cast		you do not cast
they cast		they do not cast

Past
I cast arrojara/arrojase	* * * * * * * * * *	I did not cast
you cast		you did not cast
he cast		he did not cast
we cast		we did not cast
you cast		you did not cast
they cast		they did not cast

❋ Infinitive	❋ Gerund	❋ Participle
to cast	casting	cast

	affirmative	interrogative	negative

Present Perfect

affirmative	interrogative	negative
I have cast haya arrojado	have I cast?	I have not cast
you have cast	have you cast?	you have not cast
he has cast	has he cast?	he has not cast
we have cast	have we cast?	we have not cast
you have cast	have you cast?	you have not cast
they have cast	have they cast?	they have not cast

Past Perfect

affirmative	interrogative	negative
I had cast había/hube arrojado	had I cast?	I had not cast
you had cast	had you cast?	you had not cast
he had cast	had he cast?	he had not cast
we had cast	had we cast?	we had not cast
you had cast	had you cast?	you had not cast
they had cast	had they cast?	they had not cast

Future Perfect

affirmative	interrogative	negative
I shall/will have cast habré arrojado	shall/will I have cast?	I shall/will not have cast
you will have cast	will you have cast?	you will not have cast
he will have cast	will he have cast?	he will not have cast
we shall/will have cast	shall/will we have cast?	we shall/will not have cast
you will have cast	will you have cast?	you will not have cast
they will have cast	will they have cast?	they will not have cast

Perfect

affirmative	interrogative	negative
I should/would have cast habría arrojado	should/would I have cast?	I should/would not have cast
you would have cast	would you have cast?	you would not have cast
he would have cast	would he have cast?	he would not have cast
we should/would have cast	should/would we have cast?	we should/would not have cast
you would have cast	would you have cast?	you would not have cast
they would have cast	would they have cast?	they would not have cast

Plural

affirmative	interrogative	negative
let us cast arrojemos	* * * * * * * * * *	do not let us (let's not) cast
cast arrojad		do not cast
let them cast arrojen		do not let them cast

Present Perfect

affirmative	interrogative	negative
I have cast haya arrojado	* * * * * * * * * *	I have not cast
you have cast		you have not cast
he has cast		he has not cast
we have cast		we have not cast
you have cast		you have not cast
they have cast		they have not cast

Past Perfect

affirmative	interrogative	negative
I had cast hubiera/hubiese arrojado	* * * * * * * * * *	I had not cast
you had cast		you had not cast
he had cast		he had not cast
we had cast		we had not cast
you had cast		you had not cast
they had cast		they had not cast

40. Modelos verbos regulares. Play · Jugar

	affirmative	interrogative	negative

❀ Indicative

Present
affirmative	interrogative	negative
I play juego	do I play?	I do not play
you play	do you play?	you do not play
he plays	does he play?	he does not play
we play	do we play?	we do not play
you play	do you play?	you do not play
they play	do they play?	they do not play

Past
affirmative	interrogative	negative
I played jugaba/jugué	did I play?	I did not play
you played	did you play?	you did not play
he played	did he play?	he did not play
we played	did we play?	we did not play
you played	did you play?	you did not play
they played	did they play?	they did not play

Future
affirmative	interrogative	negative
I shall/will play jugaré	shall/will I play?	I shall/will not play
you will play	will you play?	you will not play
he will play	will he play?	he will not play
we shall/will play	shall/will we play?	we shall/will not play
you will play	will you play?	you will not play
they will play	will they play?	they will not play

❀ Conditional

Present
affirmative	interrogative	negative
I should/would play jugaría	should/would I play?	I should/would not play
you would play	would you play?	you would not play
he would play	would he play?	he would not play
we should/would play	should/would we play?	we should/would not play
you would play	would you play?	you would not play
they would play	would they play?	they would not play

❀ Imperative

Singular
affirmative	interrogative	negative
let me play déjame jugar		do not let me play
play juega tú	* * * * * * * * *	do not play
let him/her/it play juegue él/ella		do not let them not play

❀ Subjunctive

Present
affirmative	interrogative	negative
I play juegue yo		I do not play
you play		you do not play
he plays	* * * * * * * * *	he does not play
we play		we do not play
you play		you do not play
they play		they do not play

Past
affirmative	interrogative	negative
I played jugara/jugase		I did not play
you played		you did not play
he played	* * * * * * * * *	he did not play
we played		we did not play
you played		you did not play
they played		they did not play

❋ Infinitive	❋ Gerund	❋ Participle
to play	playing	played

	affirmative	interrogative	negative

Present perfect

affirmative	interrogative	negative
I have played he jugado	have I played?	I have not played
you have played	have you played?	you have not played
he has played	has he played?	he has not played
we have played	have we played?	we have not played
you have played	have you played?	you have not played
they have played	have they played?	they have not played

Past perfect

affirmative	interrogative	negative
I had played he jugado	had I played?	I had not played
you had played	had you played?	you had not played
he had played	had he played?	he had not played
we had played	had we played?	we had not played
you had played	had you played?	you had not played
they had played	had they played?	they had not played

Future perfect

affirmative	interrogative	negative
I shall/will have played habré jugado	shall/will I have played?	I shall/will not have played
you will have played	will you have played?	you will not have played
he will have played	will he have played?	he will not have played
we shall/will have played	shall/will we have played?	we shall/will not have played
you will have played	will you have played?	you will not have played
they will have played	will they have played?	they will not have played

Perfect

affirmative	interrogative	negative
I should/would have played habría jugado	should/would have I played?	I should/would not have played
you would have played	would you have played?	you would not have played
he would have played	would he have played?	he would not have played
we should/would have played	should/would we have played?	we should/would not have played
you would have played	would you have played?	you would not have played
they would have played	would they have played?	they would not have played

Plural

affirmative	interrogative	negative
let us play juguemos	* * * * * * * * * *	do not let us (let's not) play
play jugad		do not play
let them play jueguen ellos/ellas		do not let them play

Present perfect

affirmative	interrogative	negative
I have played haya jugado	* * * * * * * * * *	I have not played
you have played		you have not played
he has played		he has not played
we have played		we have not played
you have played		you have not played
they have played		they have not played

Past perfect

affirmative	interrogative	negative
I had played hubiera/hubiese jugado	* * * * * * * * * *	I had not played
you had played		you had not played
he had played		he had not played
we had played		we had not played
you had played		you had not played
they had played		they had not played

41. To love · Amar

	affirmative	interrogative	negative

✿ Indicative

Present	I love amo	do I love?	I do not love
	you love	do you love?	you do not love
	he loves	does he love?	he does not love
	we love	do we love?	we do not love
	you love	do you love?	you do not love
	they love	do they love?	they do not love

Past	I loved amaba/amé	did I love?	I did not love
	you loved	did you love?	you did not love
	he loved	did he love?	he did not love
	we loved	did we love?	we did not love
	you loved	did you love?	you did not love
	they loved	did they love?	they did not love

Future	I shall/will love amaré	shall/will I love?	I shall/will not love
	you will love	will you love?	you will not love
	he will love	will he love?	he will not love
	we shall/will love	shall/will we love?	we shall/will not love
	you will love	will you love?	you will not love
	they will love	will they love?	they will not love

✿ Conditional

Present	I should/would love amaría	should/would I love?	I should/would not love
	you would love	would you love?	you would not love
	he would love	would he love?	he would not love
	we should/would love	should/would we love?	we should/would not love
	you would love	would you love?	you would not love
	they would love	would they love?	they would not love

✿ Imperative

Singular	let me love déjame amar		do not let me love
	love ama tú	* * * * * * * * * *	do not love
	let him/her/it love ame él/ella		do not let him/her/it love

✿ Subjunctive

Present	I love ame		I do not love
	you love		you do not love
	he loves	* * * * * * * * * *	he does not love
	we love		we do not love
	you love		you do not love
	they love		they do not love

Past	I loved amara/amase		I did not love
	you loved		you did not love
	he loved	* * * * * * * * * *	he did not love
	we loved		we did not love
	you loved		you did not love
	they loved		they did not love

❊ Infinitive	❊ Gerund	❊ Participle
to love	loving	loved

	affirmative	interrogative	negative

Present perfect

affirmative	interrogative	negative
I have loved he amado	have I loved?	I have not loved
you have loved	have you loved?	you have not loved
he has loved	has he loved?	he has not loved
we have loved	have we loved?	we have not loved
you have loved	have you loved	you have not loved
they have loved	have they loved?	they have not loved

Past perfect

affirmative	interrogative	negative
I had love había amado	had I loved?	I had not loved
you had loved	had you loved?	you had not loved
he had loved	had he loved?	he had not loved
we had loved	had we loved?	we had not loved
you had loved	had you loved?	you had not loved
they had loved	had they loved?	they had not loved

Future perfect

affirmative	interrogative	negative
I shall/will have loved habré amado	shall/will I have loved?	I shall/will not have loved
you will have loved	will you have loved?	you will not have loved
he will have loved	will he have loved?	he will not have loved
we shall/will have loved	shall/will we have loved?	we shall/will not have loved
you will have loved	will you have loved?	you will not have loved
they will have loved	will they have loved?	they will not have loved

Perfect

affirmative	interrogative	negative
I should/would have loved habría amado	should/would I have loved?	I should/would not have loved
you would have loved	would you have loved?	you would not have loved
he would have loved	would he have loved?	he would not have loved
we should/would have loved	should/would we have loved?	we would not have loved
you would have loved	would you have loved?	you would not have loved
they would have loved	would they have loved?	they would not have loved

Plural

affirmative	interrogative	negative
let us love amemos	* * * * * * * * * *	do not let us (let's not) love
love amad		do not love
let them love amen ellos/ellas		do not let them love

Present perfect

affirmative	interrogative	negative
I have loved haya amado	* * * * * * * * * *	I have not loved
you have loved		you have not loved
he has loved		he has not loved
we have loved		we have not loved
you have loved		you have not loved
they have loved		they have not loved

Past perfect

affirmative	interrogative	negative
I had loved hubiera/hubiese amado	* * * * * * * * * *	I had not loved
you had loved		you had not loved
he had loved		he had not loved
we had loved		we had not loved
you had loved		you had not loved
they had loved		they had not loved

42. To study · Estudiar

affirmative	interrogative	negative

❖ Indicative

	affirmative	interrogative	negative
Present	I study estudio	do I study?	I do not study
	you study	do you study?	you do not study
	he studies	does he study?	he does not study
	we study	do we study?	we do not study
	you study	do you study?	you do not study
	they study	do they study?	they do not study
Past	I studied estudiaba/estudié	did I study?	I did not study
	you studied	did you study?	you did not study
	he studied	did he study?	he did not study
	we studied	did we study?	we did not study
	you studied	did you study?	you did not study
	they studied	did they study?	they did not study
Future	I shall/will study estudiaré	shall/will I study?	I shall/will not study
	you will study	will you study?	you will not study
	he will study	will he study?	he will not study
	we shall/will study	shall/will we study?	we shall/will not study
	you will study	will you study?	you will not study
	they will study	will they study?	they will not study

❖ Conditional

	affirmative	interrogative	negative
Present	I should/would study estudiaría	should/would I study?	I should/would not study
	you would study	would you study?	you would not study
	he would study	would he study?	he would not study
	we should/would study	should/would we study?	we should/would not study
	you would study	would you study?	you would not study
	they would study	would they study?	they would not study

❖ Imperative

	affirmative	interrogative	negative
Singular	let me study déjame estudiar	* * * * * * * * * *	do not let me study
	study estudia tú		do not study
	let him/her/it study estudie él/ella		do not let him/her/it study

❖ Subjunctive

	affirmative	interrogative	negative
Present	I study estudie	* * * * * * * * * *	I do not study
	you study		you do not study
	he studies		he does not study
	we study		we do not study
	you study		you do not study
	they study		they do not study
Past	I studied estudiara/estudiase	* * * * * * * * * *	I did not study
	you studied		you did not study
	he studied		he did not study
	we studied		we did not study
	you studied		you did not study
	they studied		they did not study

❉ Infinitive	❉ Gerund	❉ Participle
to study	studying	studied

affirmative	**interrogative**	**negative**

esent rfect
I have studied he estudiado	have I studied?	I have not studied
you have studied	have you studied?	you have not studied
he has studied	has he studied?	he has not studied
we have studied	have we studied?	we have not studied
you have studied	have you studied?	you have not studied
they have studied	have they studied?	they have not studied

st rfect
I had studied había/hube estudiado	had I studied?	I had not studied
you had studied	had you studied?	you had not studied
he had studied	had he studied?	he had not studied
we had studied	had we studied?	we had not studied
you had studied	had you studied?	you had not studied
they had studied	had they studied?	they had not studied

ture rfect
I shall/will have studied habré estudiado	shall/will I have studied?	I shall/will not have studied
you will have studied	will you have studied?	you will not have studied
he will have studied	will he have studied?	he will not have studied
we shall/will have studied	shall/will we have studied?	we shall/will not have studied
you will have studied	will you have studied?	you will not have studied
they will have studied	will they have studied?	they will not have studied

rfect
I should/would have studied habría estudiado	should/would I have studied?	I should/would not have studied
you would have studied	would you have studied?	you would not have studied
he would have studied	would he have studied?	he would not have studied
we should/would have studied	should/would we have studied?	we should/would not have studied
you would have studied	would you have studied?	you would not have studied
they would have studied	would they have studied?	they would not have studied

ral
let us study estudiemos	* * * * * * * * * *	do not let us (let's not) study
study estudiad		do not study
let them study estudien ellos		do not let them study

sent fect
I have studied haya estudiado	* * * * * * * * * *	I have not studied
you have studied		you have not studied
he has studied		he has not studied
we have studied		we have not studied
you have studied		you have not studied
they have studied		they have not studied

t fect
I had studied hubiera/hubiese estudiado	* * * * * * * * * *	I had not studied
you had studied		you had not studied
he had studied		he had not studied
we had studied		we had not studied
you had studied		you had not studied
they had studied		they had not studied

43. To kiss · Besar

	affirmative	interrogative	negative

❄ Indicative

	affirmative	interrogative	negative
Present	I kiss beso	do I kiss?	I do not kiss
	you kiss	do you kiss?	you do not kiss
	he kisses	does he kiss?	he does not kiss
	we kiss	do we kiss?	we do not kiss
	you kiss	do you kiss?	you do not kiss
	they kiss	do they kiss?	they do not kiss
Past	I kissed besaba/besé	did I kiss?	I did not kiss
	you kissed	did you kiss?	you did not kiss
	he kissed	did he kiss?	he did not kiss
	we kissed	did we kiss?	we did not kiss
	you kissed	did you kiss?	you did not kiss
	they kissed	did they kiss?	they did not kiss
Future	I shall/will kiss besaré	shall/will I kiss?	I shall/will not kiss
	you will kiss	will you kiss?	you will not kiss
	he will kiss	will he kiss?	he will not kiss
	we shall/will kiss	shall/will we kiss?	we shall/will not kiss
	you will kiss	will you kiss?	you will not kiss
	they will kiss	will they kiss?	they will not kiss

❄ Conditional

	affirmative	interrogative	negative
Present	I should/would kiss besaría	should/would I kiss?	I should/would not kiss
	you would kiss	would you kiss?	you would not kiss
	he would kiss	would he kiss?	he would not kiss
	we should/would kiss	should/would we kiss?	we should/would not kiss
	you would kiss	would you kiss?	you would not kiss
	they would kiss	would they kiss?	they would not kiss

❄ Imperative

	affirmative	interrogative	negative
Singular	let me kiss déjame besar	* * * * * * * * *	do not let me kiss
	kiss besa		do not kiss
	let him/her/it kiss bese		do not let him/her/it kiss

❄ Subjunctive

	affirmative	interrogative	negative
Present	I kiss bese	* * * * * * * * *	I do not kiss
	you kiss		you do not kiss
	he kisses		he does not kiss
	we kiss		we do not kiss
	you kiss		you do not kiss
	they kiss		they do not kiss
Past	I kissed besara/besase	* * * * * * * * *	I did not kiss
	you kissed		you did not kiss
	he kissed		he did not kiss
	we kissed		we did not kiss
	you kissed		you did not kiss
	they kissed		they did not kiss

❀ Infinitive	❀ Gerund	❀ Participle
to kiss	kissing	kissed

affirmative	interrogative	negative

esent erfect

affirmative		interrogative	negative
I have kissed	he besado	have I kissed?	I have not kissed
you have kissed		have you kissed?	you have not kissed
he has kissed		has he kissed?	he has not kissed
we have kissed		have we kissed?	we have not kissed
you have kissed		have you kissed?	you have not kissed
they have kissed		have they kissed?	they have not kissed

st erfect

I had kissed	había besado	had I kissed?	I had not kissed
you had kissed		had you kissed?	you had not kissed
he had kissed		had he kissed?	he had not kissed
we had kissed		had we kissed?	we had not kissed
you had kissed		had you kissed?	you had not kissed
they had kissed		had they kissed?	they had not kissed

ture erfect

I shall/will have kissed	habré besado	shall/will I have kissed?	I shall/will not have kissed
you will have kissed		will you have kissed?	you will not have kissed
he will have kissed		will he have kissed?	he will not have kissed
we shall/will have kissed		shall/will we have kissed?	we shall/will not have kissed
you will have kissed		will you have kissed?	you will not have kissed
they will have kissed		will they have kissed?	they will not have kissed

erfect

I should/would have kissed	habría besado	should/would I have kissed?	I should/would not have kissed
you would have kissed		would you have kissed?	you would not have kissed
he would have kissed		would he have kissed?	he would not have kissed
we should/would have kissed		should/would we have kissed?	we should/would not have kissed
you would have kissed		would you have kissed?	you would not have kissed
they would have kissed		would they have kissed?	they would not have kissed

ural

let us kiss	besemos	* * * * * * * * *	do not let us (let's not) kiss
kiss	besad		do not kiss
let them kiss	besen		do not let them kiss

esent rfect

I have kissed	haya besado	* * * * * * * * *	I have not kissed
you have kissed			you have not kissed
he has kissed			he has not kissed
we have kissed			we have not kissed
you have kissed			you have not kissed
they have kissed			they have not kissed

st rfect

I had kissed	hubiera/hubiese besado	* * * * * * * * *	I had not kissed
you had kissed			you had not kissed
he had kissed			he had not kissed
we had kissed			we had not kissed
you had kissed			you had not kissed
they had kissed			they had not kissed

44. To control · Controlar

	affirmative	interrogative	negative

❀ Indicative

Present I control   controlo | do I control? | I do not control
you control | do you control? | you do not control
he controls | does he control? | he does not control
we control | do we control? | we do not control
you control | do you control? | you do not control
they control | do they control? | they do not control

Past I controlled   controlaba/controlé | did I control? | I did not control
you controlled | did you control? | you did not control
he controlled | did he control? | he did not control
we controlled | did we control? | we did not control
you controlled | did you control? | you did not control
they controlled | did they control? | they did not control

Future I shall/will control   controlaré | shall/will I control? | I shall/will not control
you will control | will you control? | you will not control
he will control | will he control? | he will not control
we shall/will control | shall/will we control? | we shall/will not control
you will control | will you control? | you will not control
they will control | will they control? | they will not control

❀ Conditional

Present I should/would control   controlaría | should/would I control? | I should/would not control
you would control | would you control? | you would not control
he would control | would he control? | he would not control
we shall/will control | should/would we control? | we should/would not control
you will control | would you control? | you would not control
they will control | would they control? | they would not control

❀ Imperative

Singular let me control   déjame controlar | | do not let me control
control   controla tú | * * * * * * * * * | do not control
let him/her/it control   controle él/ella/ello | | do not let him/her/it control

❀ Subjunctive

Present I control   controle | | I do not control
you control | | you do not control
he controls | * * * * * * * * * | he does not control
we control | | we do not control
you control | | you do not control
they control | | they do not control

Past I controlled   controlara/controlase | | I did not control
you controlled | | you did not control
he controlled | * * * * * * * * * | he did not control
we controlled | | we did not control
you controlled | | you did not control
they controlled | | they did not control

❄ **Infinitive**	❄ **Gerund**	❄ **Participle**
to control	controlling	controlled

	affirmative	**interrogative**	**negative**

	affirmative	interrogative	negative
Present perfect	I have controlled he controlado you have controlled he has controlled we have controlled you have controlled they have controlled	have I controlled? have you controlled? has he controlled? have we controlled? have you controlled? have they controlled?	I have not controlled you have not controlled he has not controlled we have not controlled you have not controlled they have not controlled
Past perfect	I had controlled había/hube controlado you had controlled he had controlled we had controlled you had controlled they had controlled	had I controlled? had you controlled? had he controlled? had we controlled? had you controlled? had they controlled?	I had not controlled you had not controlled he had not controlled we had not controlled you had not controlled they had not controlled
Future perfect	I shall/will have controlled habré controlado you will have controlled he will have controlled we shall/will have controlled you will have controlled they will have controlled	shall/will I have controlled? will you have controlled? will he have controlled? shall/will we have controlled? will you have controlled? will they have controlled?	I shall/will not have controlled you will not have controlled he will not have controlled we shall/will not have controlled you will not have controlled they will not have controlled
Perfect	I should/would have controlled habría controlado you would have controlled he would have controlled we should/would have controlled you would have controlled they would have controlled	should/would I have controlled? would you have controlled? would he have controlled? should/would we have controlled? would you have controlled? would they have controlled?	I should/would not have controlled you would not have controlled he would not have controlled we should/would not have controlled you would not have controlled they would not have controlled
Plural	let us control controlemos control controlad let them control controlen ellos	* * * * * * * * * *	do not let us (let's not) control do not control do not let them control
Present perfect	I have controlled haya controlado you have controlled he has controlled we have controlled you have controlled they have controlled	* * * * * * * * * *	I have not controlled you have not controlled he has not controlled we have not controlled you have not controlled they have not controlled
Past perfect	I had controlled hubiera/hubiese controlado you had controlled he had controlled we had controlled you had controlled they had controlled	* * * * * * * * * *	I had not controlled you had not controlled he had not controlled we had not controlled you had not controlled they had not controlled

45. To bear · Aguantar, soportar, sostener

	affirmative	interrogative	negative

☀ Indicative

Present
affirmative	interrogative	negative
I bear aguanto	do I bear?	I do not bear
you bear	do you bear?	you do not bear
he bears	does he bear?	he does not bear
we bear	do we bear?	we do not bear
you bear	do you bear?	you do not bear
they bear	do they bear?	they do not bear

Past
affirmative	interrogative	negative
I bore aguantaba / aguanté	did I bear?	I did not bear
you bore	did you bear?	you did not bear
he bore	did he bear?	he did not bear
we bore	did we bear?	we did not bear
you bore	did you bear?	you did not bear
they bore	did they bear?	they did not bear

Future
affirmative	interrogative	negative
I shall/will bear aguantaré	shall/will I bear?	I shall/will not bear
you will bear	will you bear?	you will not bear
he will bear	will he bear?	he will not bear
we shall/will bear	shall/will we bear?	we shall/will not bear
you will bear	will you bear?	you will not bear
they will bear	will they bear?	they will not bear

☀ Conditional

Present
affirmative	interrogative	negative
I should/would bear aguantaría	should/would I bear?	I should/would not bear
you would bear	would you bear?	you would not bear
he would bear	would he bear?	he would not bear
we should/would bear	should/would we bear?	we should/would not bear
you would bear	would you bear?	you would not bear
they would bear	would they bear?	they would not bear

☀ Imperative

Singular
affirmative	interrogative	negative
let me bear déjame aguantar	* * * * * * * * * *	do not let me bear
bear aguanta		do not bear
let him/her/it bear aguante él/ella		do not let him bear

☀ Subjunctive

Present
affirmative	interrogative	negative
I bear aguante	* * * * * * * * * *	I do not bear
you bear		you do not bear
he bears		he does not bear
we bear		we do not bear
you bear		you do not bear
they bear		they do not bear

Past
affirmative	interrogative	negative
I bore aguantara/aguantase	* * * * * * * * * *	I did not bear
you bore		you did not bear
he bore		he did not bear
we bore		we did not bear
you bore		you did not bear
they bore		they did not bear

❋ Infinitive	❋ Gerund	❋ Participle
To bear	bearing	born / borne

	affirmative	interrogative	negative

	affirmative	interrogative	negative
Present perfect	I have born(e) he aguantado you have born(e) he has born(e) we have born(e) you have born(e) they have born(e)	have I born(e)? have you born(e)? has he born(e)? have we born(e)? have you born(e)? have they born(e)?	I have not born(e) you have not born(e) he has not born(e) we have not born(e) you have not born(e) they have not born(e)
Past perfect	I had born(e) había aguantado you had born(e) he had born(e) we had born(e) you had born(e) they had born(e)	had I born(e)? had you born(e)? had he born(e)? had we born(e)? had you born(e)? had they born(e)?	I had not born(e) you had not born(e) he had not born(e) we had not born(e) you had not born(e) they had not born(e)
Future perfect	I shall/will have born(e) habré aguantado you will have born(e) he will have born(e) we shall/will have born(e) you will have born(e) they will have born(e)	shall/will I have born(e)? will you have born(e)? will he have born(e)? shall/will we have born(e)? will you have born(e)? will they have born(e)?	I shall/will not have born(e) you will not have born(e) he will not have born(e) we shall/will not have born(e) you will not have born(e) they will not have born(e)
Perfect	I should/would have born(e) habría aguantado you would have born(e) he would have born(e) we should/would have born(e) you would have born(e) they would have born(e)	should/would I have born(e)? would you have born(e)? would he have born(e)? should/would we have born(e)? would you have born(e)? would they have born(e)?	I should/would not have born(e) you would not have born(e) he would not have born(e) we should/would have not born(e) you would not have born(e) they would not have born(e)
Plural	let us bear aguantemos bear aguantad let them bear aguanten	* * * * * * * * * *	do not let us (let's not) bear do not bear do not let them bear
Present perfect	I have born(e) haya aguantado you have born(e) he has born(e) we have born(e) you have born(e) they have born(e)	* * * * * * * * * *	I have not born(e) you have not born(e) he has not born(e) we have not born(e) you have not born(e) they have not born(e)
Past perfect	I had born(e) hubiera/hubiese aguantado you had born(e) he had born(e) we had born(e) you had born(e) they had born(e)	* * * * * * * * * *	I had not born(e) you had not born(e) he had not born(e) we had not born(e) you had not born(e) they had not born(e)

46. To beat · Golpear, derrotar, pegar

affirmative	interrogative	negative

✿ Indicative

Present

I beat golpeo	do I beat?	I do not beat
you beat	do you beat?	you do not beat
he beats	does he beat?	he does not beat
we beat	do we beat?	we do not beat
you beat	do you beat?	you do not beat
they beat	do they beat?	they do not beat

Past

I beat golpeaba/golpeé	did I beat?	I did not beat
you beat	did you beat?	you did not beat
he beat	did he beat?	he did not beat
we beat	did we beat?	we did not beat
you beat	did you beat?	you did not beat
they beat	did they beat?	they did not beat

Future

I shall/will beat golpearé	shall/will I beat?	I shall/will not beat
you will beat	will you beat?	you will not beat
he will beat	will he beat?	he will not beat
we shall/will beat	shall/will we beat?	we shall/will not beat
you will beat	will you beat?	you will not beat
they will beat	will they beat?	they will not beat

✿ Conditional

Present

I should/would beat golpearía	should/would I beat?	I should/would not beat
you would beat	would you beat?	you would not beat
he would beat	would he beat?	he would not beat
we should/would beat	should/would we beat?	we should/would not beat
you would beat	would you beat?	you would not beat
they would beat	would they beat?	they would not beat

✿ Imperative

Singular

let me beat déjame golpear		do not let me beat
beat golpea	* * * * * * * * * *	do not beat
let him beat golpee él		do not let him beat

✿ Subjunctive

Present

I beat golpee		I do not beat
you beat		you do not beat
he beats	* * * * * * * * * *	he does not beat
we beat		we do not beat
you beat		you do not beat
they beat		they do not beat

Past

I beat golpeara/golpease		I did not beat
you beat		you did not beat
he beat	* * * * * * * * * *	he did not beat
we beat		we did not beat
you beat		you did not beat
they beat		they did not beat

❁ Infinitive	❁ Gerund	❁ Participle
To beat	beating	beaten

affirmative	interrogative	negative

Present perfect

I have beaten he golpeado	have I beaten?	I have not beaten
you have beaten	have you beaten?	you have not beaten
he has beaten	has he beaten?	he has not beaten
we have beaten	have we beaten?	we have not beaten
you have beaten	have you beaten?	you have not beaten
they have beaten	have they beaten?	they have not beaten

Past perfect

I had beaten había golpeado	had I beaten?	I had not beaten
you had beaten	had you beaten?	you had not beaten
he had beaten	had he beaten	he had not beaten
we had beaten	had we beaten?	we had not beaten
you had beaten	had you beaten?	you had not beaten
they had beaten	had they beaten?	they had not beaten

Future perfect

I shall/will have beaten habré golpeado	shall/will I have beaten?	I shall/will not have beaten
you will have beaten	will you have beaten?	you will not have beaten
he will have beaten	will he have beaten?	he will not have beaten
we shall/will have beaten	shall/will we have beaten?	we shall/will not have beaten
you will have beaten	will you have beaten?	you will not have beaten
they will have beaten	will they have beaten?	they will not have beaten

Perfect

I should/would have beaten	should/would I have beaten?	I should/would not have beaten
habría golpeado	would you have beaten?	you would not have beaten
you would have beaten	would he have beaten?	he would not have beaten
he would have beaten	should/would we have beaten?	we should/would not have beaten
we should/would have beaten	would you have beaten?	you would not have beaten
you would have beaten	would they have beaten?	they would not have beaten
they would have beaten		

Plural

let us beat golpeemos	* * * * * * * * * *	do not let us (let's not) beat
beat golpead		do not beat
let them beat golpeen		do not let them beat

Present perfect

I have beaten haya golpeado		I have not beaten
you have beaten	* * * * * * * * * *	you have not beaten
he has beaten		he has not beaten
we have beaten		we have not beaten
you have beaten		you have not beaten
they have beaten		they have not beaten

Past perfect

I had beaten hubiera/hubiese golpeado		I had not beaten
you had beaten	* * * * * * * * * *	you had not beaten
he had beaten		he had not beaten
we had beaten		we had not beaten
you had beaten		you had not beaten
they had beaten		they had not beaten

47. To panic · Asustarse, tener pánico

	affirmative	interrogative	negative

✻ Indicative

Present
I panic tengo pánico	do I panic?	I do not panic
you panic	do you panic?	you do not panic
he panics	does he panic?	he does not panic
we panic	do we panic?	we do not panic
you panic	do you panic?	you do not panic
they panic	do they panic?	they do not panic

Past
I panicked tenía/tuve pánico	did I panic?	I did not panic
you panicked	did you panic?	you did not panic
he panicked	did he panic?	he did not panic
we panicked	did we panic?	we did not panic
you panicked	did you panic?	you did not panic
they panicked	did they panic?	they did not panic

Future
I shall/will panic tendré pánico	shall/will I panic?	I shall/will not panic
you will panic	will you panic?	you will not panic
he will panic	will he panic?	he will not panic
we shall/will panic	shall/will we panic?	we shall/will not panic
you will panic	will you panic?	you will not panic
they will panic	will they panic?	they will not panic

✻ Conditional

Present
I should/would panic tendría pánico	should/would I panic?	I should/would not panic
you would panic	would you panic?	you would not panic
he would panic	would he panic?	he would not panic
we should/would panic	should/would we panic?	we should/would not panic
you would panic	would you panic?	you would not panic
they would panic	would they panic?	they would not panic

✻ Imperative

Singular
let me panic déjame tener pánico		do not let me panic
panic ten pánico	* * * * * * * * * *	do not panic
let him/her/it panic tenga pánico		do not let him/her/it panic

✻ Subjunctive

Present
I panic tenga pánico		I do not panic
you panic		you do not panic
he panics	* * * * * * * * * *	he does not panic
we panic		we do not panic
you panic		you do not panic
they panic		they do not panic

Past
I panicked tuviera/tuviese pánico		I did not panic
you panicked		you did not panic
he panicked	* * * * * * * * * *	he did not panic
we panicked		we did not panic
you panicked		you did not panic
they panicked		they did not panic

❀ **Infinitive**	❀ **Gerund**	❀ **Participle**
To panic	panicking	panicked

	affirmative	**interrogative**	**negative**
Present perfect	I have panicked he tenido pánico you have panicked he has panicked we have panicked you have panicked they have panicked	have I panicked? have you panicked? has he panicked? have we panicked? have you panicked? have they panicked?	I have not panicked you have not panicked he has not panicked we have not panicked you have not panicked they have not panicked
Past perfect	I had panicked había/hube tenido pánico you had panicked he had panicked we had panicked you had panicked they had panicked	had I panicked? had you panicked? had he panicked? had we panicked? had you panicked? had they panicked?	I had not panicked you had not panicked he had not panicked we had not panicked you had not panicked they had not panicked
Future perfect	I shall/will have panicked habré tenido pánico you will have panicked he will have panicked we shall/will have panicked you will have panicked they will have panicked	shall/will I have panicked? will you have panicked? will he have panicked? shall/will we have panicked? will you have panicked? will they have panicked?	I shall/will not have panicked you will not have panicked he will not have panicked we shall/will not have panicked you will not have panicked they will not have panicked
Perfect	I should/would have panicked habría tenido pánico you would have panicked he would have panicked we should/would have panicked you would have panicked they would have panicked	should/would I have panicked? would you have panicked? would he have panicked? should/would we have panicked? would you have panicked? would they have panicked?	I should/would not have panicked you would not have panicked he would not have panicked we should/would not have panicked you would not have panicked they would not have panicked
Plural	let us panic tengamos pánico panic tened pánico let them panic tengan pánico	* * * * * * * * *	do not let us (let's not) panic do not panic do not let them panic
Present perfect	I have panicked haya tenido pánico you have panicked he has panicked we have panicked you have panicked they have panicked	* * * * * * * * *	I have not panicked you have not panicked he has not panicked we have not panicked you have not panicked they have not panicked
Past perfect	I had panicked hubiera/hubiese tenido pánico you had panicked he had panicked we had panicked you had panicked they had panicked	* * * * * * * * *	I had not panicked you had not panicked he had not panicked we had not panicked you had not panicked they had not panicked

48. To be able (can) · Poder

	affirmative	interrogative	negative

❋ Indicative

Present

I can / I am able puedo	can I? / am I able?	I cannot / I am not able
you can / you are able	can you? / are you able?	you cannot / you arenot able
he can / he is able	can he? / is he able?	he cannot / he is not able
we can / we are able	can we? / are we able?	we cannot / we are not able
you can / you are able	can you? / are you able?	you cannot / you are not able
they can / they are able	can they? / are they able?	they cannot / they are not able

Past

I could / I was able podía/pude	could I? /was I able?	I could not / I was not able
you could / you were able	could you? / were you able?	you could not / you were not able
he could / he was able	could he? / was he able?	he could not / he were not able
we could / we were able	could we? / were we able?	we could not / we were not able
you could / you were able	could you? / were you able?	you could not / you were not able
they could / they were able	could they? / were they able?	they could not / they were not able

Future

I shall/will be able podré	shall/will I be able?	I shall/will not be able
you will be able	will you be able?	you will not be able
he will be able	will he be able?	he will not be able
we shall/will be able	shall/will we be able?	we shall/will not be able
you will be able	will you be able?	you will not be able
they will be able	will they be able?	they will not be able

❋ Conditional

Present

I could / would be able podría	could I? / would I be able?	I could not / I would not be able
you could / would be able	could you? / would you be able?	you could not / would not be able
he could / would be able	could he? / would he be able?	he could not / would not be able
we could / would be able	could we? / would we be able?	we could not / would not be able
you could / would be able	could you? / would you be able?	you could not / would not be able
they could / would be able	could they? / would they be able?	they could not / would not be able

❋ Imperative

Singular

* * * * * * * * * *	* * * * * * * * * *	* * * * * * * * * *

❋ Subjunctive

Present

I can / I am able pueda		I cannot / I am not able
you can / you are able		you cannot / you are not able
he can / he is able	* * * * * * * * * *	he cannot / he is not able
we can / we are able		we cannot / we are not able
you can / you are able		you cannot / you are not able
they can / they are able		they cannot / they are not able

Past

I could / I was able pudiera/pudiese		I could not / I was not able
you could / you were able		you could not / you were not able
he could / he was able	* * * * * * * * * *	he could not / he was not able
we could / we were able		we could not / we were not able
you could / you were able		you could not / you were not able
they could / they were able		they could not / they were not able

✤ **Infinitive** To be able	✤ **Gerund** being able	✤ **Participle** been able

	affirmative	**interrogative**	**negative**
Present Perfect	I have been able he podido you have been able he has been able we have been able you have been able they have been able	have I been able? have you been able? has he been able? have we been able? have you been able? have they been able?	I have not been able you have not been able he has not been able we have not been able you have not been able they have not been able
Past Perfect	I had been able había podido you had been able he had been able we had been able you had been able they had been able	had I been able? had you been able? had he been able? had we been able? had you been able? had they been able?	I had not been able you had not been able he had not been able we had not been able you had not been able they had not been able
Future Perfect	I shall/will have been able habré podido you will have been able he will have been able we shall/will have been able you will have been able they will have been able	shall/will I have been able? will you have been able? will he have been able? shall/will we have been able? will you have been able? will they have been able?	I shall/will not have been able you will not have been able he will not have been able we shall/will not have been able you will not have been able they will not have been able
Perfect	I should/would have been able habría podido you would have been able he would have been able we should/would have been able you would have been able they would have been able	should/would I have been able? would you have been able? would he have been able? should/would we have been able? would you have been able? would they have been able?	I should/would not have been able you would not have been able he would not have been able we should/would not have been able you would not have been able they would not have been able
Plural	* * * * * * * * *	* * * * * * * * *	* * * * * * * * *
Present Perfect	I have been able haya podido you have been able he has been able we have been able you have been able they have been able	* * * * * * * * *	I have not been able you have not been able he has not been able we have not been able you have not been able they have not been able
Past Perfect	I had been able hubiera/hubiese podido you had been able he had been able we had been able you had been able they had been able	* * * * * * * * *	I had not been able you had not been able he had not been able we had not been able you had not been able they had not been able

49. Must · Debo, etc.

	affirmative	interrogative	negative

❀ Indicative

Present	I must / I have to debo you must / you have to he must / he has to we must / we have to you must / you have to they must /they have to	must I? / have I to? must you? / have you to? must he? / has he to? must we? / have we to? must you? / have you to? must they? / have they to?	I must not / I don't have to you must not / you don't have to he must not / he doesn't have to we must not / we don't have to you must not / you don't have to they must not / they don't have to
Past	I had to debía/debí you had to he had to we had to you had to they had to	had I to? / did I have to? had you to? / did you have to? had he to? / did he have to? had we to? / did we have to? had you to? / did you have to? had they to? / did they have to?	I had not / didn't have to you had not / didn't have to he had not / didn't have to we had not / didn't have to you had not / didn't have to they had not / didn't have to
Future	I shall/will have to deberé you will have to he will have to we shall/will have to you will have to they will have to	shall/will I have to? will you have to? will he have to? shall/will we have to? will you have to? will they have to?	I shall/will not have to you will not have to he will not have to we shall/will not have to you will not have to they will not have to

❀ Conditional

Present	I should/would have to debería you would have to he would have to we should/would have to you would have to they would have to	should/would I have to? would you have to? would he have to? should/would we have to? would you have to? would they have to?	I should/would not have to you would not have to he would not have to we should/would not have to you would not have to they would not have to

❀ Imperative

Singular	* * * * * * * * *	* * * * * * * * *	* * * * * * * * *

❀ Subjunctive

Present	I must / I have to deba you must / you have to he must / he has to we must / we have to you must / you have to they must /they have to	* * * * * * * * *	I must not / I don't have to you must not / you don't have to he must not / he doesn't have to we must not / we don't have to you must not / you don't have to they must not / they don't have to
Past	I had to debiera/debieses you had to he had to we had to you had to they had to	* * * * * * * * *	I had not / didn't have to you had not / didn't have to he had not / didn't have to we had not / didn't have to you had not / didn't have to they had not / didn't have to

❊ Infinitive	❊ Gerund	❊ Participle
To have to	having to	had to

	affirmative	interrogative	negative

Present perfect	I have had to he debido you have had to he has had to we have had to you have had to they have had to	have I had to? have you had to? has he had to? have we had to? have you had to? have they had to?	I have not had to you have not had to he has not had to we have not had to you have not had to they have not had to
Past perfect	I had had to había debido you had had to he had had to we had had to you had had to they had had to	had I had to? had you had to? had he have to? had we had to? had you had to? had they had to?	I had not had to you had not had to he had not had to we had not had to you had not had to they had not had to
Future perfect	I shall/will have had to habré debido you will have had to he will have had to we shall/will have had to you will have had to they will have had to	shall/will I have to? will you have to? will he have to? shall/will we have to? will you have to? will they have to?	I shall/will not have had to you will not have had to he will not have had to we shall/will not have had to you will not have had to they will not have had to
Perfect	I should/would have had to habría debido you would have had to he would have had to we should/would have had to you would have had to they would have had to	should/would I have had to? would you have had to? would he have had to? should/would we have had to? would you have had to? would they have had to?	I should/would not have had to you would not have had to he would not have had to we should/would not have had to you would not have had to they would not have had to
Plural	* * * * * * * * * *	* * * * * * * * * *	* * * * * * * * * *
Present perfect	I have had to haya debido you have had to he has had to we have had to you have had to they have had to	* * * * * * * * * *	I have not had to you have not had to he has not had to we have not had to you have not had to they have not had to
Past perfect	I had had to hubiera/hubiese debido you had had to he had had to we had had to you had had to they had had to	* * * * * * * * * *	I had not had to you had not had to he had not had to we had not had to you had not had to they had not had to

50. There to be · Haber (impersonal)

	affirmative	interrogative	negative

✿ Indicative

Present singular: there is   hay
plural: there are   hay   * * * * * * * * * *   * * * * * * * * * *

Past singular: there was   había
plural: there were   había   * * * * * * * * * *   * * * * * * * * * *

Future singular: there will be   habrá
plural: there will be   * * * * * * * * * *   * * * * * * * * * *

✿ Conditional

Present singular: there would be   habría
plural: there would be   * * * * * * * * * *   * * * * * * * * * *

✿ Imperative

Singular let there be   haya   * * * * * * * * * *   * * * * * * * * * *

✿ Subjunctive

Present singular: there is/be   haya
plural: there are/be   * * * * * * * * * *   * * * * * * * * * *

Past singular: there was   hubiera/hubiese
plural: there were   * * * * * * * * * *   * * * * * * * * * *

	Infinitive	Gerund	Participle
	there to be	there being	there having been

		affirmative	interrogative	negative

Present perfect singular: there has been ha habido
plural: there have been
* * * * * * * * * *   * * * * * * * * * *

Past perfect singular: there had been había habido
plural: there had been
* * * * * * * * * *   * * * * * * * * * *

Future perfect singular: there will have been habrá habido
plural: there will have been
* * * * * * * * * *   * * * * * * * * * *

Perfect singular: there would have been habría habido
plural: there would have been
* * * * * * * * * *   * * * * * * * * * *

Plural let there be haya
* * * * * * * * * *   * * * * * * * * * *

Present perfect singular: there have/has been haya habido
plural: there have been
* * * * * * * * * *   * * * * * * * * * *

Past perfect singular: there had been hubiera/hubiese habido
plural: there had been
* * * * * * * * * *   * * * * * * * * * *

Forma continua

51. To be playing · Estar jugando

affirmative	interrogative	negative

❋ Indicative

Present

I am playing estoy jugando	am I playing?	I am not playing
you are playing	are you playing?	you are not playing
he is playing	is he playing?	he is not playing
we are playing	are we playing?	we are not playing
you are playing	are you playing?	you are not playing
they are playing	are they playing?	they are not playing

Past

I was playing estaba jugando	was I playing?	I was not playing
you were playing	were you playing?	you were not playing
he was playing	was he playing?	he was not playing
we were playing	were we playing?	we were not playing
you were playing	were you playing?	you were not playing
they were playing	were they playing?	they were not playing

Future

I shall/will be playing estaré jugando	shall/will I be playing?	I shall/will not be playing
you will be playing	will you be playing?	you will not be playing
he will be playing	will he be playing?	he will not be playing
we shall/will be playing	shall/will we be playing?	we shall/will not be playing
you will be playing	will you be playing?	you will not be playing
they will be playing	will they be playing?	they will not be playing

❋ Conditional

Present

I should/would be playing estaría jugando	should/would I be playing?	I should/would not be playing
you would be playing	would you be playing?	you would not be playing
he would be playing	would he be playing?	he would not be playing
we should/would be playing	should/would we be playing?	we should/would not be playing
you would be playing	would you be playing?	you would not be playing
they would be playing	would they be playing?	they would not be playing

❋ Imperative

Singular

Let me be playing esté yo jugando	* * * * * * * * *	do not let me be playing
Be playing está [te] tú jugando		do not be playing
Let him/her/it be playing esté él/ella jugando		do not let him/her/ it be playing

❋ Subjunctive

Present

I am playing esté jugando		I am not playing
you are playing		you are not playing
he is playing	* * * * * * * * *	he is not playing
we are playing		we are not playing
you are playing		you are not playing
they are playing		they are not playing

Past

I was/were playing estuviera/estuviese jugando		I was/were not playing
you were playing		you were not playing
he was/were playing	* * * * * * * * *	he was/were not playing
we were playing		we were not playing
you were playing		you were not playing
they were playing		they were not playing

* Infinitive	* Gerund	* Participle
To be playing	being playing	been playing

	affirmative	interrogative	negative

Present perfect

I have been playing   he estado jugando
you have been playing
he has been playing
we have been playing
you have been playing
they have been playing

have I been playing?
have you been playing?
has he been playing?
have we been playing?
have you been playing?
have they been playing?

I have not been playing
you have not been playing
he has not been playing
we have not been playing
you have not been playing
they have not been playing

Past perfect

I had been playing   había estado jugando
you had been playing
he had been playing
we had been playing
you had been playing
they had been playing

had I been playing?
had you been playing?
had he been playing?
had we been playing?
had you been playing?
had they been playing?

I had not been playing
you had not been playing
he had not been playing
we had not been playing
you had not been playing
they had not been playing

Future perfect

I shall/will have been playing   estaré jugando
you will have been playing
he will have been playing
we shall/will have been playing
you will have been playing
they will have been playing

shall/will I have been playing?
will you have been playing?
will he have been playing?
shall/will we have been playing?
will you have been playing?
will they have been playing?

I shall/will not have been playing
you will not have been playing
he will not have been playing
we shall/will not have been playing
you will not have been playing
they will not have been playing

Perfect

I should/would have been playing
   habría estado jugando
you would have been playing
he would have been playing
we should/would have been playing
you would have been playing
they would have been playing

should/would I have been playing?
would you have been playing?
would he have been playing?
should/would we have been playing?
would you have been playing?
would they have been playing?

should/would I not have been playing?
would you not have been playing?
would he not have been playing?
should/would we not have been playing?
would you not have been playing?
would they not have been playing?

Plural

Let us be playing   estemos jugando
Be playing   estad jugando
Let them be playing   estén ellos/ellas jugando

* * * * * * * * * *

do not let us be (let's not) playing
do not be playing
do not let them be playing

Present perfect

I have been playing   haya estado jugando
you have been playing
he has been playing
we have been playing
you have been playing
they have been playing

* * * * * * * * * *

I have not been playing
you have not been playing
he has not been playing
we have not been playing
you have not been playing
they have not been playing

Past perfect

I had been playing   hubiera/hubiese estado jugando
you had been playing
he had been playing
we had been playing
you had been playing
they had been playing

* * * * * * * * * *

I had been playing
you had been playing
he had been playing
we had been playing
you had been playing
they had been playing

52. Passive voice · To be seen

	affirmative	interrogative	negative

✿ Indicative

	affirmative	interrogative	negative
Present	I am seen soy visto	am I seen?	I am not seen
	you are seen	are you seen?	you are not seen
	he is seen	is he seen?	he is not seen
	we are seen	are we seen?	we are not seen
	you are seen	are you seen?	you are not seen
	they are seen	are they seen?	they are not seen
Past	I was seen era/fui visto	was I seen?	I was not seen
	you were seen	were you seen?	you were not seen
	he was seen	was he seen?	he was not seen
	we were seen	were we seen?	we were not seen
	you were seen	were you seen?	you were not seen
	they were seen	were they seen?	they were not seen
Future	I shall/will be seen seré visto	shall/will I be seen?	I shall/will not be seen
	you will be seen	will you be seen?	you will not be seen
	he will be seen	will he be seen?	he will not be seen
	we shall/will be seen	shall/will we be seen?	we shall/will not be seen
	you will be seen	will you be seen?	you will not be seen
	they will be seen	will they be seen?	they will not be seen

✿ Conditional

	affirmative	interrogative	negative
Present	I should/would be seen sería visto	should/would I be seen?	I should/would not be seen
	you would be seen	would you be seen?	you would not be seen
	he would be seen	would he be seen?	he would not be seen
	we should/would be seen	should/would we be seen?	we should/would not be seen
	you would be seen	would you be seen?	you would not be seen
	they would be seen	would they be seen?	they would not be seen

✿ Imperative

	affirmative	interrogative	negative
Singular	let me be seen déjame ser visto	* * * * * * * * * *	do not let me be seen
	be seen sé visto		do not be seen
	let him/her/it be seen sea visto él		do not let him/her/it be seen

✿ Subjunctive

	affirmative	interrogative	negative
Present	I am/be seen déjame ser visto	* * * * * * * * * *	I am not seen
	you are/be seen		you are not seen
	he is/be seen		he is not seen
	we are/be seen		we are not seen
	you are/be seen		you are not seen
	they are/be seen		they are not seen
Past	I was/were seen fuera/fuese visto	* * * * * * * * * *	I was not seen
	you were seen		you were not seen
	he was/were seen		he was not seen
	we were seen		we were not seen
	you were seen		you were not seen
	they were seen		they were not seen

❊ Infinitive	❊ Gerund	❊ Participle
To be seen	being seen	been seen

	affirmative	interrogative	negative

	affirmative	interrogative	negative
Present Perfect	I have been seen he sido visto you have been seen he has been seen we have been seen you have been seen they have been seen	have I been seen? have you been seen? has he been seen? have we been seen? have you been seen? have they been seen?	I have not been seen you have not been seen he has not been seen we have not been seen you have not been seen they have not been seen
Past Perfect	I had been seen había sido visto you had been seen he had been seen we had been seen you had been seen they had been seen	had I been seen? had you been seen? had he been seen? had we been seen? had you been seen? had they been seen?	I had not been seen you had not been seen he had not been seen we had not been seen you had not been seen they had not been seen
Future Perfect	I shall/will have been seen habré sido visto you will have been seen he will have been seen we shall/will have been seen you will have been seen they will have been seen	shall/will I have been seen? will you have been seen? will he/she/it have been seen? shall/will we have been seen? will you have been seen? will they have been seen?	I shall/will not have been seen you will not have been seen he will not have been seen we will not have been seen you will not have been seen they will not have been seen
Perfect	I should/would have been seen habría sido visto you would have been seen he would have been seen we should/would have been seen you would have been seen they would have been seen	should/would I have been seen? would you have been seen? would he have been seen? should/would we have been seen? would you have been seen? would they have been seen?	I should/would not have been seen you would not have been seen he would not have been seen we should/would not have been seen you would not have been seen they would not have been seen
Plural	let us be seen seamos vistos be seen sed vistos let them be seen sean vistos	* * * * * * * * * *	do not let us be (let's not) seen do not be seen do not let them be seen
Present Perfect	I have been seen haya sido visto you have been seen he has been seen we have been seen you have been seen they have been seen	* * * * * * * * * *	I have not been seen you have not been seen he has not been seen we have not been seen you have not been seen they have not been seen
Past Perfect	I had been seen hubiera/hubiese sido visto you had been seen he had been seen we had been seen you had been seen they had been seen	* * * * * * * * * *	I had not been seen you had not been seen he had not been seen we had not been seen you had not been seen they had not been seen

53. May · Might · Poder

	affirmative	interrogative	negative

✿ Indicative

Present	I may *puedo* you may he may we may you may they may	may I? may you? may he? may we? may you? may they?	I may not you may not he may not we may not you may not they may not
Past	I might *podía/pude* you might he might we might you might they might	might I? might you? might he? might we? might you? might they?	I might not you might not he might not we might not you might not they might not
Future	* * * * * * * * * *	* * * * * * * * * *	* * * * * * * * * *

✿ Conditional

Present	I might *podría* you might he might we might you might they might	might I? might you? might he? might we? might you? might they?	I might not you might not he might not we might not you might not they might not

✿ Imperative

Singular	* * * * * * * * * *	* * * * * * * * * *	* * * * * * * * * *

✿ Subjunctive

Present	* * * * * * * * * *	* * * * * * * * * *	* * * * * * * * * *
Past	* * * * * * * * * *	* * * * * * * * * *	* * * * * * * * * *

✸ Infinitive	✸ Gerund	✸ Participle
* * * * * * * * * *	* * * * * * * * * *	* * * * * * * * * *

	affirmative	interrogative	negative
Present perfect	* * * * * * * * * *	* * * * * * * * * *	* * * * * * * * * *
Past perfect	* * * * * * * * * *	* * * * * * * * * *	* * * * * * * * * *
Future perfect	* * * * * * * * * *	* * * * * * * * * *	* * * * * * * * * *
Perfect	* * * * * * * * * *	* * * * * * * * * *	* * * * * * * * * *
Plural	* * * * * * * * * *	* * * * * * * * * *	* * * * * * * * * *
Present perfect	* * * * * * * * * *	* * * * * * * * * *	* * * * * * * * * *
Past perfect	* * * * * * * * * *	* * * * * * * * * *	* * * * * * * * * *

Part Three
Tercera Parte

Irregular Verbs · Verbos Irregulares

infinitive	past	participle	infinitive	past	participle
abide	abode or abided	abode or abided	dwell	dwelt	dwelt
arise	arose	arisen	eat	ate	eaten
awake	awoke	awaked	fall	fell	fallen
be	was, were	been	feed	fed	fed
bear	bore	(llevado) borne, (nacido) born	feel	felt	felt
			fight	fought	fought
beat	beat	beaten	find	found	found
become	became	become	flee	fled	fled
beget	begot, (**) begat	begotten	fling	flung	flung
			fly	flew	flown
begin	began	begun	forbid	forbad (e)	forbidden
bend	bent	bent	forget	forgot	forgotten
beseech	besought	besought	forsake	forsook	forsaken
bet	bet or betted	bet or betted	freeze	froze	frozen
bid (ordenar) (licitar etc)	bade bid	bidden bid	get	got	got, (US) gotten
bind	bound	bound	gild	gilded	gilded or gilt
bite	bit	bitten	gird	girded or girt	girded or girt
bleed	bled	bled	give	gave	given
blow	blew	blown	go	went	gone
break	broke	broken	grind	ground	ground
breed	bred	bred	grow	grew	grown
bring	brought	brought	hang (colgar) (ahorcar)	hung, hanged	hung, hanged
build	built	built	have	had	had
burn	burned or burnt	burned or burnt	hear	heard	heard
burst	burst	burst	heave	heaved, (Naut) hove	heaved, (Naut) hove
buy	bought	bought			
can	could	-	hew	hewed	hewed or hewn
cast	cast	cast	hide	hid	hidden
catch	caught	caught	hit	hit	hit
choose	chose	chosen	hold	held	held
cleave1(vt)	clove or cleft	cloven or cleft	hurt	hurt	hurt
cleave2(vi)	cleaved	cleaved	keep	kept	kept
cling	clung	clung	kneel	knelt	knelt
come	came	come	know	knew	known
cost	cost	cost	lade	laded	laden
creep	crept	crept	lay	laid	laid
cut	cut	cut	lead	led	led
deal	dealt	dealt	lean	leaned or leant	leaned or leant
dig	dug	dug	leap	leaped or leapt	leaped or leapt
do	did	done	learn	learned or learnt	learned or learnt
draw	drew	drawn	leave	left	left
dream	dreamed or dreamt	dreamed or dreamt	lend	lent	lent
			let	let	let
drink	drank	drunk	lie	lay	lain
drive	drove	driven	light	lit or lighted	lit or lighted

infinitive	past	participle	infinitive	past	participle
lose	lost	lost	speak	spoke	spoken
make	made	made	speed (vt)	speeded	speeded
may	might	-----	(vi)	sped	sped
mean	meant	meant	spell	spelled or spelt	spelled or spelt
meet	met	met	spend	spent	spent
mow	mowed	mown or mowed	spill	spilled or spilt	spilled or spilt
pay	paid	paid	spin	spun or span	spun
put	put	put	spit	spat	spat
quit	quit or quitted	quit or quitted	split	split	split
read	read	read	spoil	spoiled or spoilt	spoiled or spoilt
rend	rent	rent	spread	spread	spread
rid	rid	rid	spring	sprang	sprung
ride	rode	ridden	stand	stood	stood
ring	rang	rung	stave	stove or staved	stove or staved
rise	rose	risen	steal	stole	stolen
run	ran	run	stick	stuck	stuck
saw	sawed	sawed or sawn	sting	stung	stung
say	said	said	stink	stank	stunk
see	saw	seen	strew	strewed	strewed or strewn
seek	sought	sought	stride	strode	stridden
sell	sold	sold	strike	struck	struck
send	sent	sent	string	strung	strung
set	set	set	strive	strove	striven
sew	sewed	sewn	swear	swore	sworn
shake	shook	shaken	sweep	swept	swept
shave	shaved	shaved or shaven	swell	swelled	swollen
shear	sheared	shorn	swim	swam	swum
shed	shed	shed	swing	swung	swung
shine	shone	shone	take	took	taken
shoe	shod	shod	teach	taught	taught
shoot	shot	shot	tear	tore	torn
show	showed	shown	tell	told	told
shrink	shrank	shrunk	think	thought	thought
shut	shut	shut	thrive	throve	thriven
sing	sang	sung	throw	threw	thrown
sink	sank	sunk	thrust	thrust	thrust
sit	sat	sat	tread	trod	trodden
slay	slew	slain	wake	woke	woken or waked
sleep	slept	slept	wear	wore	worn
slide	slid	slid	weave	wove	woven
sling	slung	slung	weep	wept	wept
slink	slunk	slunk	win	won	won
slit	slit	slit	wind	wound	wound
smell	smelled or smelt	smilled or smelt	wring	wrung	wrung
smite	smote	smitten	write	wrote	written
sow	sowed	sown			

List of Verbs · Lista de Verbos

40 abandon	41 adhere	41 allude	40 appertain	43 attach	42 bandy
41 abase	40 adjoin	41 allure	40 applaud	40 attain	40 bang
43 abash	40 adjourn	42 ally	42 apply	40 attaint	43 banish
41 abate	41 adjudge	40 alter	40 appoint	40 attempt	40 bank
41 abbreviate	41 adjudicate	41 altercate	40 apportion	40 attend	40 bankrupt
41 abdicate	40 adjure	41 alternate	41 appose	41 attenuate	40 banquet
40 abduct	40 admire	41 aluminate	41 appraise	40 attest	40 banter
44 abet	44 admit	41 amalgamate	41 appreciate	41 attire	41 baptize
44 abhor	40 admix	43 amass	40 apprehend	41 attitudinize	44 bar
41 abide	43 admonish	41 amaze	41 apprentice	40 attract	40 barb
41 abjure	40 adopt	40 ambition	41 apprise/	41 attribute	41 barbarize
41 abnegate	41 adore	41 amble	apprize	41 attune	41 barbecue
41 abode	40 adorn	43 ambush	40 approach	40 auction	40 bard
43 abolish	40 adsorb	41 ameliorate	41 approbate	40 audit	41 bare
41 abominate	41 adulate	40 amend	40 appropriate	40 audition	40 bargain
40 abort	41 adulterate	41 amerce	41 approve	40 augment	41 barge
40 abound	41 advance	41 americanize	41 approximate	40 augur	40 barhop
41 abrade	41 advantage	41 amortize	41 arabize	41 aureole	40 bark
41 abridge	41 adventure	40 amount	41 arbitrate	41 auscultate	40 barnstorm
41 abrogate	40 advert	42 amplifly	41 archaize	41 authenticate	40 barrack
40 abscond	41 advertise/	41 amputate	41 argue	41 authorize	41 barrage
40 absent	advertize	41 amuse	41 arise	40 autograph	40 barrel
41 absolve	41 advise	41 anaesthetize	40 armor/armour	41 automate	41 barricade
40 absorb	41 aerate	41 analogize	41 arouse	40 automatize	40 barter
40 abstain	42 aerify	41 analyse	40 arpeggio	41 autopsy	41 base
40 abstract	41 aestivate	41 analyze	40 arraign	40 avail	43 bash
41 abuse	40 affect	41 anastomose	41 arrange	41 avenge	40 bask
44 abut	41 affiance	41 anathematize	40 array	44 aver	40 basset
41 accede	41 affiliate	41 anatomize	40 arrest	41 average	41 bastardize
41 accelerate	40 affirm	40 anchor	41 arrive	40 avert	41 baste
40 accent	40 affix	41 anchylose	41 arrogate	40 avoid	40 bat
41 accentuate	40 afflict	41 anesthetize	41 article	40 avouch	41 bate
40 accept	40 afford	40 anger	40 ascend	40 await	40 bath
40 acclaim	40 afforest	41 angle	40 ascertain	41 awake	41 bathe
41 acclimate	41 affranchise	41 anglicize	41 ascribe	40 award	40 batten
41 acclimatize	40 affront	43 anguish	40 asepticize	41 awe	40 batter
41 accommodate	41 age	40 animadvert	40 ask	40/41 ax/axe	41 battle
42 accompany	41 agglomerate	41 animalize	41 asperse	40 babbit	40 bawl
43 accomplish	41 agglutinate	41 animate	40 asphalt	41 babble	40 bay
40 accord	41 aggrandize	41 ankylose	41 asphyxiate	44 baby-sit	40 bayonet
40 account	41 aggravate	40 anneal	41 aspirate	43 bach	1 be
40 accoutre/	41 aggregate	40 annex	41 aspire	40 back	43 beach
accouter	41 agitate	41 annihilate	40 assail	41 backbite	40 beacon
40 accredit	41 agonize	41 annotate	41 assassinate	41 backdate	40 bead
41 accrue	41 agree	41 announce	40 assault	41 backfire	40 beam
41 accumulate	40 aid	40 annoy	40 assay	40 backpedal	45 bear
41 accuse	40 ail	44 annul	41 assemble	41 backslide	40 beard
42 acetify	40 aim	41 annunciate	40 assent	43 backstitch	46 beat
41 ache	40 air	40 anoint	40 assert	40 backtrack	42 beatify
41 achieve	40 alarm	40 answer	40 assess	40 badger	42 beautify
42 acidify	41 alcoholize	41 antagonize	41 asseverate	41 baffle	40 becalm
41 acidulate	40 alert	41 ante	40 assign	44 bag	40 beckon
41 acknowledge	41 alienate	41 antedate	41 assimilate	40 bail	14 become
41 acquaint	40 alight	41 anticipate	40 assist	40 bait	44 bed
41 acquiesce	40 align	41 apocopate	41 associate	41 bake	40 bedaub
41 acquire	41 aline	41 apologize	41 assonate	41 balance	40 bedeck
44 acquit	41 alkalinize	41 apostatize	40 assort	41 bale	44 bedevil
40 act	41 alkalize	41 apostemate	41 assuage	40 balk	41 bee
41 activate	40 allay	41 apostrophize	41 assume	40 ball	40 beef
41 actualize	41 allege	41 apotheosize	41 assure	40 ballast	41 beetle
41 actuate	41 allegorize	44 appal/appall	40 asterisk	40 balloon	22 befall
40 add	41 alleviate	40 apparel	43 astonish	40 ballot	44 befit
41 addle	41 alliterate	44 appeal	40 astound	40 ballyhoo	44 befog
43 address	41 allocate	40 appear	40 astrict	41 bamboozle	40 befool
41 adduce	44 allot	41 appease	41 astringe	44 ban	40 befoul
40 adduct	40 allow	40 append	41 atomize	40 band	40 befriend
40 adept	40 alloy	41 apperceive	42 atrophy	41 bandage	44 beg
41 adequate					

29 beget
40 beggar
3 begin
41 begrime
41 begrudge
41 beguile
41 behave
40 behead
23 behold
40/44 bejewel
40 belabo(u)r
40 belaud
40 belay
40 belch
41 beleaguer
41 belie
41 believe
41 belittle
40 bell
40 bellow
42 belly
41 bellyache
40 bellyflop
40 belong
40 belt
42 baly
41 bemire
40 bemoan
41 bench
40 bend
40 benefit
40 benumb
40 bequeath
41 berate
41 bereave
42 berry
40 berth
11 beseech
40 bessem
40 beset
41 besiege
40 besmear
43 besmirch
44 besot
41 bespangle
40 bespatter
10 bespeak
41 besprinkle
40 best
41 bestialize
44 bestir
40 bestow
41 bestraddle
40 bestrew
20 bestride
5 bet
27 betake
11 bethink
41 betide
40 betoken
40 betray
40 betroth
40 better
40/44 bevel
40 bewail
41 beware
40 bewilder
43 bewitch
40/44 bias
40 bicker
5 bid

41 bide
40 biff
41 bifurcate
41 bike
41 bilge
40 bilk
40 billet
40 billow
7 bind
43 birch
41 bisect
43 bitch
2 bite
40 bivouac
44 blab
40 black
40 blackball
40 blacken
40 blackguard
40 blackjack
40 blackleg
40 blacklist
40 blackmail
41 blame
43 blanch
43 blandish
40 blank
40 blanket
41 blare
40 blarney
41 blaspheme
40 blast
40 blather
41 blaze
43 bleach
40 blear
40 bleat
8 bleed
43 blemish
43 blench
40 blend
43 bless
40 blight
40 blind
40 blindfold
40 blink
40 blister
40 blitz
40 bloat
40 blob
40 block
41 blockade
40 blood
42 bloody
40 bloom
40 blossom
44 blot
43 blotch
9 blow
44 blub
40 blubber
40 bludgeon
41 blue
40 bluff
40 blunder
40 blunt
44 blur
40 blurt
43 blush
40 bluster
40 board
40 boast

40 boat
44 bob
40 bobtail
41 bode
42 body
44 bog
40 boggle
40 boil
40 bolster
40 bolt
40 bomb
40 bombard
40 bond
41 bone
40 boo
40 book
40 boom
40 boomerang
40 boost
40 boot
40 bootleg
40 bootlick
41 booze
44 bop
40 border
41 bore
40 borrow
40 bosom
43 boss
41 botanize
43 botch
40 bother
41 bottle
40 bottom
42 bottomry
41 bounce
40 bound
40 bow
41 bowdlerize
40 bowl
43 box
40 boxhaul
40 boycott
41 brace
40 bracket
44 brag
40 braid
40 brail
40 brain
43 brainwash
41 braise
41 brake
43 branch
40 brand
43 brandish
41 brattle
41 brave
40 brawl
40 bray
41 braze
40 brazen
43 breach
10 break
40 breakfast
40 breast
41 breathe
8 breed
41 breeze
40 brevet
40 brew
41 bribe
40 brick

41 bridge
41 bridle
40 brief
41 brigade
40 brighten
40 brim
11 bring
40 brisk
41 bristle
43 broach
25 broadcast
40 broaden
41 brocade
40 broil
41 bronze
40 brood
40 brook
40 broom
40 brother
40 browbeat
40 brown
41 browse
41 bruise
40 bruit
43 brush
41 brutalize
41 bubble
40 buccaneer
40 buck
41 bucket
41 buckle
40 buckler
44 bud
41 buddle
41 budge
40 budget
40 buff
40 buffalo
40 buffet
44 bug
41 bugle
12 build
41 bulge
40 bulk
40 bull
44 bulldog
41 bulldoze
42 bully
40 bum
41 bumble
40 bump
42 bunch
41 bundle
40 bung
41 bungle
40 bunk
40 bunker
40 bunt
42 buoy
41 burble
40 burden
40 burgeon
41 burgle
40 burl
41 burlesque
41 burp
40 burr
40 burrow
5 burst
43 bury

40/43 bus
43 bush
40 bust
41 bustle
42 busy
40 butcher
40 butt
40 butter
40 button
41 buttonhole
43 buttress
11 buy
40 buzz
43 bypass
40 cabal
41 cable
41 cache
41 cachinnate
41 cackle
41 cadge
41 cage
41 cajole
41 cake
42 calcify
41 calcimine
41 calcine
41 calculate
40 calendar
40 calender
41 calibrate
40 calk
40 call
40 calligraph
40 calm
41 calumniate
41 calve
41 camouflage
40 camp
40 campaign
41 camphorate can
41 canalize
40 cancel
41 candle
42 candy
41 cane
40 canker
41 cannibalize
40 cannon
41 cannonade
41 canoe
41 canonize
41 cannoodle
42 canopy
40 cant
40 canter
40 canton
43 canvass
44 cap
41 capacitate
40 caparison
40 caper
41 capitalize
41 capitulate
41 capsize
40 captain
40 caption
41 capture
41 caracole
41 caramelize
41 carbonate
41 carbonize

41 carburate
40 carburet
41 carburize
40 card
41 care
40 careen
40 career
43 caress
41 caricature
40 carillon
40 carol
41 carouse
40 carp
40 carpet
42 carry
40 cart
41 carve
41 case
43 cash
40 cashier
40 cask
39 cast
41 castigate
41 castle
41 castrate
44 cat
41 catalogue
41 catalyse
41 catalyze
40 catapult
40 catcall
43 catch
41 catechize
41 categorize
41 catenate
40 cater
40 caterwaul
41 catholicize
41 caucus
41 caulk
41 cause
41 cauterize
40 caution
41 cave
40 cavil
40 cavort
40 caw
41 cesse
41 cede
40 ceil
41 celebrate
40 cement
41 cense
40 censor
41 censure
41 centralize
41 centre
41 centrifuge
41 centuple
41 cerebrate
41 certificate
42 certify
40 chafe
40 chaff
40 chain
40 chair
40 chairman
40 chalk
41 challenge
40 chamfer
40 champ
40 champion

41 chance	41 circumfuse	41 coddle	40 compost	40 consent	40 copyright
41 change	41 circumnavigate	41 code	40 compound	41 conserve	40 corbel
40 channel	41 circumscribe	42 codify	40 comprehend	40 consider	40 cord
40 chant	41 circumstantiate	41 coerce	43 compress	40 consign	40 cordon
44 chap	41 circumvallate	40 coexist	41 comprise/	40 consist	41 core
40 chapter	40 circumvent	40 coffer	comprize	41 console	40 cork
44 char	41 cite	40 coffin	41 compromise	41 consolidate	40 corkscrew
41 characterize	42 citify	44 cog	41 compute	40 consort	40 corn
41 charge	41 civilize	41 cogitate	41 computerize	41 conspire	40 corner
40 charm	40 clack	41 cognize	44 con	41 constellate	40 corral
40 chart	40 clad	40 cohabit	41 concatenate	41 consternate	40 correct
40 charter	40 claim	41 cogere	44 conceal	41 constipate	41 correlate
41 chase	44 clam	40 cohibit	41 concede	41 constitute	40 correspond
40 chasten	40 clamber	40 coil	41 conceive	41 constitutionalize	41 corroborate
41 chastise	40 clamor/	40 coin	40 concenter	40 constrain	41 corrode
44 chat	clamour	41 coincide	41 concentrate	40 constrict	40 corrugate
40 chatter	40 clamp	41 coke	41 concentre	41 construct	40 corrupt
40 chauffeur	40 clang	40 colander	40 concern	41 construe	41 coruscate
40 chaw	40 clank	41 collaborate	40 concert	41 consubstantiate	43 cosh
40 cheapen	44 clap	41 collapse	41 conciliate	40 consult	40 cosher
40 cheat	40 clapboard	40 collar	41 conclude	41 consume	5 cost
40 check	42 clarify	40 collect	40 concoct	41 consummate	41 costume
40 checker	43 clash	40 collectivize	41 concrete	40 contact	40 cotton
41 checkmate	40 clasp	40 collet	41 concretize	40 contain	43 couch
40 cheek	43 class	41 colligate	44 concur	41 containerize	40 cough
40 cheep	42 classify	41 collocate	43 concuss	41 contaminate	40 counsel
40 cheer	40 clatter	41 collogue	40 condemn	40 contemn	40 count
40 chequer	40 claw	41 collude	40 condense	41 contemplate	41 countenance
43 cherish	40 clean	41 colonize	40 condescend	41 contemporize	40 counter
40 chew	41 cleanse	40 color/colour	40 condition	40 contend	40 counteract
41 chicane	40 clear	40 colorcast	41 condole	41 content	40 counterattack
40 chicken	16/20 cleave	40 comb	41 condone	40 contest	41 counterbalance
2/8 chide	43 clench	40 combat	41 conduce	40 continue	41 counterbrace
40 chill	40 clew	41 combine	40 conduct	40 contort	41 countercharge
41 chime	40 click	14 come	41 cone	40 contour	40 countercheck
41 chine	40 climax	40 comfort	40 confab	40 contract	40 counterclaim
40 chink	40 climb	40 command	41 confabulate	40 contradict	40 counterfeit
44 chip	43 clinch	40 commandeer	40 confect	41 contraindicate	40 countermand
40 chirp	13 cling	41 commemorate	41 confederate	40 contrast	43 countermarch
40 chirr	40 clink	41 commence	40 confer	41 contravene	41 countermine
40 chisel	44 clip	41 commend	43 confess	41 contribute	40 counterplot
42 chivy/chivvy	40 cloak	40 comment	41 confide	40 contrive	41 counterpoise
41 chlorinate	40 clobber	41 commentate	41 configurate	40 contriver	40 counterseal
40 chloroform	44 clog	41 commercialize	41 configure	44 control	40 countersign
40 chock	40 cloister	41 comminate	41 confine	40 controvert	40 countersink
40 choir	41 close	41 commingle	40 confirm	41 contuse	40 countervail
41 choke	40 closet	41 comminute	41 confiscate	41 convalesce	40 counterweight
37 choose	44 clot	41 commiserate	40 conflict	41 convene	41 couple
44 chop	8/40 clothe	40 commission	40 conform	41 conventionalize	41 course
41 chortle	40 cloud	44 commit	40 confound	41 converge	40 court
40 chorus	40 clout	40 commix	40 confront	40 converse	40 court-martial
41 chouse	40 clown	41 communicate	41 confuse	40 convert	41 cove
40 christen	42 cloy	41 communize	41 confute	40 convey	40 covenant
41 christianize	40 club	41 commutate	40 congeal	40 convict	40 cover
41 chrome	40 clubhaul	41 commute	40 congest	41 convince	40 covet
41 chronicle	41 cluck	40 compact	41 conglobate	41 convoke	40 cow
40 chuck	40 clump	41 compare	41 conglomerate	41 convolute	40 cower
41 chuckle	40 cluster	43 compass	41 conglutinate	41 convolve	40 cox
44 chug	43 clutch	41 compassionate	41 congratulate	41 convoy	40 crab
44 chum	40 clutter	44 compel	41 congregate	41 convulse	40 crack
40 church	43 coach	41 compensate	41 conjecture	40 coo	41 crackle
40 churn	41 coagulate	41 compere	40 conjoin	40 cook	41 cradle
41 cicatrize	40 coal	41 compete	41 conjugate	40 cool	44 cram
40 cinch	41 coalesce	40 complain	41 conjure	40 coop	40 cramp
40 cipher	40 coarsen	40 complement	40 conk	40 cooper	41 crane
41 circle	40 coast	41 complete	40 conn	41 cooperate	40 crank
40 circuit	40 coat	41 complicate	40 connect	41 coordinate	43 crash
41 circularize	41 coax	40 compliment	41 connive	44 cop	41 crate
41 circulate	41 cobble	40 complot	41 connote	41 cope	41 crave
41 circumambulate	41 cocainize	42 comply	40 conquer	40 copper	40 crawl
41 circumcise	40 cock	40 comport	40 conscript	41 copulate	40 crayon
40 circumflex	41 cockle	41 compose	41 consecrate	42 copy	41 craze

40 creak	41 curve	41 decline	41 delete	41 depredate	40 diagram
40 cream	40 curvet	40 declutch	41 deliberate	43 depress	40 dial
41 crease	40 cushion	40 decoct	40 delight	41 depressurize	41 dialogue
41 create	43 cuss	41 decode	41 delineate	41 deprive	41 dialyze
40 credit	5 cut	41 decoke	41 deliquesce	41 depurate	40 diamond
40/15 creep	41 cycle	41 decolonize	40 deliver	41 depute	40 diaper
41 cremate	44 dab	41 decolo(u)rize	41 delouse	41 deputize	40 diaphragm
41 crenel(l)ate	41 dabble	41 decompose	41 delude	41 deracinate	41 dibble
41 creosote	42 dally	40 decompound	41 deluge	40 derail	41 dice
41 crepitate	44 dam	43 decompress	41 delve	41 derange	41 dichotomize
40 crest	41 damage	41 deconsecrate	41 demagnetize	40 derat	40 dicker
44 crib	41 damascene	41 decontaminate	40 demand	41 derate	41 dictate
40 crick	40 damask	40 decontrol	41 demarcate	41 deride	41 diddle
41 criminate	40 damn	41 decorate	41 dematerialize	41 derive	41 die
40 crimp	42 damnify	41 decorticate	40 demean	41 derogate	40 diet
40 crimson	40 damp/dampen	40 decoy	40 dement	41 desalinate	40 differ
41 cringe	41 dance	41 decrease	40 demilitarize	40 desalt	41 differentiate
41 crinkle	42 dandify	41 decree	41 demineralize	41 descale	40 diffract
41 cripple	41 dandle	41 decrepitate	41 demise	40 descant	41 diffuse
40 crisp	41 dangle	42 decry	40 demist	40 descend	13 dig
40 crisscross	44 dap	41 decuple	40 demit	41 describe	40 digest
41 criticize	41 dapple	41 dedicate	44 demob	42 descry	42 dignify
40 croak	5/41 dare	41 deduce	41 demobilize	41 desecrate	43 digress
40 crochet	40 darken	40 deduct	41 democratize	41 desegregate	41 dilacerate
40 crock	40 darkle	40 deem	43 demolish	41 desensitize	41 dilapidate
40 crook	40 darn	40 deepen	41 demonetize	40 desert	41 dilate
40 croon	40 dart	41 deface	41 demonstrate	41 deserve	41 dilute
44 crop	43 dash	41 defaecate	41 demoralize	41 desiccate	44 dim
43 cross	41 date	41 defalcate	41 demote	40 design	43 diminish
40 crossbreed	40 daub	41 defame	40 demount	41 designate	41 dimple
40 crosscut	40 daunt	40 default	44 demur	41 desilverize	44 din
43 crosshatch	41 dawdle	40 defeat	41 denationalize	41 desire	41 dine
43 croutch	40 dawn	41 defeature	41 denaturalize	40 desist	40 ding
9/40 crow	40 daydream	41 defecate	41 denature	41 desolate	40 dint
40 crowd	41 daze	40 defect	41 denicotinize	40 despair	44 dip
40 crown	41 dazzle	40 defend	41 denigrate	43 despatch	41 diphthongize
42 crucify	40 deacon	40 defer	41 denitrate	41 despise	40 direct
41 cruise	41 deadlock	41 defilade	42 denitrify	40 despoil	40 dirk
40 crumb	40 deafen	41 defile	41 denominate	40 despond	42 dirty
41 crumble	40/16 deal	41 define	41 denote	41 despumate	41 disable
41 crumple	44 debar	41 deflagrate	41 denounce	41 desquamate	41 disabuse
43 crunch	40 debark	41 deflate	42 densify	41 destine	40 disaccord
41 crusade	41 debase	40 deflect	40 dent	40 destroy	40 disaccustom
43 crush	41 debate	40 deflower	41 denudate	43 detach	41 disadvantage
40 crust	40 debauch	41 defoliate	41 denude	40 detail	40 disaffect
42 cry	41 debilitate	40 deforest	42 deny	40 detain	40 disaffirm
41 crystallize	40 debit	40 deform	41 deodorize	40 detect	41 disagree
44 cub	40 debouch	40 defraud	41 deoxidize	44 deter	40 disallow
41 cube	41 debride	40 defray	41 deoxygenate	41 deterge	40 disannul
40 cuckold	40 debunk	40 defrock	40 depart	41 deteriorate	40 disappear
41 cuddle	41 decaffeinate/	40 defrost	41 depauperate	41 determine	40 disappoint
40 cudgel	decaffeinize	42 defy	40 depend	40 detest	41 disapprove
40 cuff	42 decalcify	43 degauss	41 depeople	41 dethrone	40 disarm
43 cuirass	40 decamp	41 degenerate	41 depersonalize	41 detonate	41 disarrange
40 cull	40 decant	41 degrade	41 dephase	41 detoxicate	40 disarray
40 cullender	41 decapitate	41 degrease	41 dephosphorize	40 detract	41 disarticulate
41 culminate	41 decarbonate	40 degust	40 depict	40 detrain	41 disassemble
41 cultivate	41 decarbonize	41 dehisce	41 depilate	41 detruncate	41 disassociate
41 culture	41 decarburize	40 dehorn	43 deplenish	41 devaluate	40 disavow
40 cumber	40 decay	41 dehumanize	41 deplete	41 devalue	40 disband
41 cumulate	41 decease	42 dehumidify	41 deplore	41 devastate	44 disbar
44 cup	41 deceive	41 dehydrate	40 deploy	40 develop	41 disbelieve
40 cupel	41 decelerate	41 dehydrogenate	41 deplume	41 deviate	43 disbranch
40 curb	41 decentralize	41 dehydrogenize	41 depolarize	40 devil	40 disbud
41 cure	41 decentre	41 deice	41 depone	41 devirginate	40 disburden
41 curette	41 dechristianize	42 deify	41 depopulate	41 devise	41 dusburse
40 curl	41 decide	40 deign	40 deport	41 devitalize	40 discard
42 curry	41 decimalize	40 deject	41 depose	42 devitrify	40 discern
41 curse	40 decipher	41 delate	40 deposit	41 devolve	41 discharge
40 curtail	40 deck	40 delay	41 deprave	41 devote	41 discipline
40 curtain	40 declaim	41 dele	41 deprecate	40 devour	40 disclaim
42 curtsy/curtsey	41 declare	41 delegate	41 depreciate	41 diagnose	41 disclose

40 discolo(u)r	41 disorganize	42 dizzy	44 drum	41 eliminate	41 endamage
40 discomfit	41 disorientate	17 do	42 dry	41 elongate	40 endanger
40 discomfort	40 disown	40 dock	44 dub	41 elope	40 endear
41 discommode	41 disparage	40 docket	40 duck	41 elucidate	40 endeavo(u)r
41 discompose	43 dispatch	40 doctor	40 duel	41 elude	41 endorse
40 disconcert	44 dispel	40 document	40 duff	41 emanciate	40 endow
40 disconnect	41 dispense	40 dodder	42 dulcify	41 emanate	41 endue
40 discontent	41 dispeople	41 dodge	40 dull	41 emancipate	41 endure
41 discontinue	41 disperse	40 doff	40 dumbfound	41 emasculate	41 energize
40 discord	40 dispirit	44 dog	40 dumfound	40 embalm	41 enervate
40 discount	41 displace	41 dogmatize	42 dummy	10 embank	41 enfeeble
41 discountenance	40 display	41 dole	40 dump	40 embargo	40 enfeoff
41 discourage	41 displease	40 doll	44 dun	40 embark	41 enfetter
41 discourse	40 disport	41 dome	41 dung	43 embarrass	41 enfilade
40 discover	41 dispose	41 domesticate	40 dunk	41 embattle	40 enfold
40 discredit	43 dispossess	41 domicile	41 dupe	44 embed	41 enforce
41 discriminate	41 dispraise	41 domiciliate	40 duplex	43 embellish	41 enframe
40 discrown	40 disproportion	41 dominate	41 duplicate	41 embezzle	41 enfranchise
43 discuss	41 disprove	40 domineer	40 dusk	40 embitter	41 engage
40 disdain	41 dispute	44 don	40 dust	41 emblaze	40 engarland
40 disembark	42 disqualify	41 donate	40 dwarf	40 emblazon	40 engender
43 disembarrass	40 disquiet	41 doodle	16/40 dwell	41 emblematize	40 engineer
42 disembody	41 disrate	44 doom	41 dwindle	42 embody	40 engird
41 disembogue	40 disregard	41 dope	41 dye	44 embog	40 englut
40 disembowel	43 disrelish	41 dose	41 dynamite	40 embolden	41 engorge
40 disembroil	40 disrespect	43 doss	41 ear	40 embosom	40 engraft
40 disenchant	41 disrobe	44 dot	40 earmark	43 emboss	40 engrain
40 disencumber	40 disroot	41 dote	40 earn	40 embowel	41 engrave
40 disendow	40 disrupt	41 double	40 earth	40 embower	43 engross
41 disengage	42 dissastify	40 doubt	41 ease	41 embrace	40 engulf
40 disentail	40 dissect	41 douche	21 eat	41 embrocate	41 enhance
41 disentangle	41 disseize	41 douse	44 eavesdrop	40 embroider	40 enjoin
40 disentomb	41 dissemble	40 dovetail	40 ebb	40 embroil	40 enjoy
43 disestablish	41 disseminate	40 dowel	40 echelon	40 embrown	41 enkindle
40 disesteem	40 dissent	40 dower	40 echo	40 emend	41 enlace
40 disfavo(u)r	41 dissertate	40 down	41 eclipse	41 emerge	41 enlarge
41 disfeature	41 disserve	41 downgrade	41 economize	41 emigrate	40 enligten
41 disfigure	41 dissever	41 dowse	41 ecstasize	44 emit	40 enlist
41 disfranchise	41 dissimilate	41 doze	42 eddy	41 emote	40 enliven
41 disgorge	41 dissimulate	41 drabble	41 edge	41 empale	42 enmesh
41 disgrace	41 dissipate	40 draft	42 edify	40 empanel	41 ennoble
41 disgruntle	41 dissociate	44 drag	40 edit	41 emphasize	41 enounce
41 disguise	41 dissolve	41 draggle	41 educate	40 employ	41 enplane
40 disgust	41 dissuade	40 dragoon	41 educe	40 empoison	41 enquire
43 dish	41 distance	40 drain	41 edulcorate	40 empower	41 enrage
41 disharmonize	40 distemper	41 dramatize	41 efface	42 empty	41 enrapture
40 dishearten	40 distend	41 drape	40 effect	41 empurple	42 enrich
40 dishevel	40 distil/distill	40 draught	41 effectuate	41 emulate	41 enrobe
40 dishono(u)r	43 distinguish	18 draw	41 effeminate	42 emulsify	40 enrol/enroll
41 dishouse	40 distort	40 drawl	41 effervesce	41 enable	40 enroot
40 disillusion	40 distract	40 dread	41 effloresce	40 enact	41 ensanguine
41 disincline	40 distrain	16 dream	41 effuse	40 enamel	41 ensconce
40 disinfect	40 distress	41 dredge	40 egg	40 enamour/	41 enshrine
40 disinfest	41 distribute	43 drench	41 ejaculate	enamor	40 enshroud
40 disinherit	40 distrust	43 dress	40 eject	40 encamp	41 ensilage/ensile
41 disintegrate	40 disturb	41 dribble	41 eke	41 encase	41 enslave
40 disinter	41 disunite	40 drift	41 elaborate	42 encash	41 ensnare
40 disinterest	41 disuse	40 drill	41 elapse	40 enchain	41 ensphere
40 disjoin	43 ditch	19 drink	41 elate	40 enchant	41 ensure
40 disjoint	40 dither	40 drip	40 elbow	41 enchase	41 enswathe
41 dislike	41 divagate	20 drive	40 elect	41 encircle	40 entail
41 dislocate	41 divaricate	40 drivel	40 electioneer	40 enclasp	41 entangle
41 dislodge	41 dive	41 drizzle	42 electrify	41 enclave	40 enter
41 dismantle	41 diverge	41 drone	41 electrize	41 enclose	40 entertain
40 dismast	42 diversify	41 droop	41 electrocute	42 encompass	40 enthral/
40 dismay	40 divert	40 drop	41 electrolyze	41 encore	enthrall
40 dismember	40 divest	41 drove	41 electroplate	40 encounter	41 enthrone
41 dismiss	41 divide	40 drown	41 electrotype	41 encourage	41 enthuse
40 dismount	41 divine	41 drowse	41 elegize	43 encroach	41 entice
40 disobey	41 divinize	40 drub	41 elevate	40 encrust	41 entitle
41 disoblige	41 divorce	41 drudge	40 elicit	40 encumber	40 entomb
40 disorder	41 divulge	44 drug	41 elide	40 end	41 entrain

41 entrance	41 evidence	40 exsert	8 feed	41 flame	40 follow
40 entrap	41 evince	41 exsiccate	16 feel	41 flange	40 foment
40 entreat	41 evoke	41 extemporize	40 feign	40 flank	41 fondle
43 entrench	41 evolve	40 extend	40 feint	40 flannel	40 fool
40 entrust	41 exacerbate	41 extenuate	41 felicitate	44 flap	40 foot
41 entwine	40 exact	41 exteriorize	40 fell	41 flare	41 footle
40 entwist	41 exaggerate	41 exterminate	40 fellow	43 flash	40 footslog
41 enucleate	40 exalt	41 externalize	40 felt	44 flat	41 foozle
41 enumerate	41 examine	43 extinguish	41 feminize	40 flatten	40 foray
41 enunciate	41 exasperate	41 extirpate	41 fence	40 flatter	45 forbear
40 envelop	41 excavate	40 extol/extoll	40 fend	40 flaunt	6 forbid
40 envenom	40 exceed	40 extort	40 feoff	40 flavo(u)r	41 force
40 environ	44 excel	40 extract	40 ferment	40 flaw	40 ford
41 envisage	40 except	41 extradite	40 ferret	40 flay	40 forearm
40 envision	40 excerpt	41 extrapolate	42 ferry	40 fleck	41 forebode
42 envy	41 exchange	41 extravasate	41 fertilize	41 fledge	45 forecast
40 enwrap	41 excise	41 extricate	41 ferule	8 flee	41 foreclose
41 enwreathe	41 excite	41 extrude	40 fester	41 fleece	40 foredoom
41 epitomize	40 exclaim	41 exude	40 festoon	43 flench	40 foregather
40 equal	41 exclude	40 exult	43 fetch	43 flesh	30 forego
41 equalize	41 excogitate	41 exuviate	40 fetter	43 fletch	41 forejudge
41 equate	41 excommunicate	41 eye	41 fettle	43 flex	18 foreknow
41 equilibrate	41 excoriate	41 fable	40 feud	40 flick	40 foreordain
44 equip	41 excrete	41 fabricate	41 feudalize	40 flicker	43 forereach
41 equiponderate	41 excruciate	41 face	40 fever	40 flight	35 forerun
41 equivocate	41 exculpate	40 facet	40 fiat	43 flinch	23 foresee
41 eradiate	41 excuse	41 facilitate	44 fib	13 fling	40 foreshadow
41 eradicate	41 execrate	41 factorize	41 fictionalize	44 flip	40 foreshorten
41 erase	41 execute	41 fade	41 fictionize	40 flirt	40 foreshow
40 erect	42 exemplify	44 fag	41 fiddle	44 flit	40 forest
41 ergotize	40 exempt	40 faggot/fagot	40 fidget	40 flitter	40 forestall
41 erode	41 exercise	40 fail	40 field	40 float	41 foretaste
40 eruct	40 exert	40 faint	41 fife	41 flocculate	24 foretell
40 erupt	41 exfoliate	40 fair	40/11 fight	40 flock	40 foretoken
41 escalade	41 exhale	41 fake	41 figure	44 flog	40 forewarn
41 escalate	40 exhaust	22 fall	41 filagree	40 flood	40 forfeit
41 escape	40 exhibit	40 fallow	43 filch	40 floodlight	40 forgather
41 escarp	41 exhilerate	42 falsify	41 file	40 floor	41 forge
40 escheat	40 exhort	40 falter	40 filibuster	44 flop	25 forget
40 eschew	41 exhume	41 familiarize	41 filigree	41 flounce	26 forgive
40 escort	41 exile	43 famish	40 fill	40 flounder	30 forgo
40 escrow	40 exist	44 fan	40 fillet	40 flour	40 fork
41 espouse	40 exit	41 fanaticize	40 fillip	43 flourish	40 form
42 espy	41 exonerate	42 fancy	40 film	40 flout	41 formalize
42 essay	41 exorcise	41 farce	40 filter	40 flow	41 formularize
43 establish	41 exorcize	41 fare	41 filtrate	40 flower	41 formulate
40 esteem	40 expand	40 farm	44 fin	41 fluctuate	41 formulize
42 esterify	41 expatiate	40 farrow	41 finalize	40 fluff	41 fornicate
41 estimate	41 expatriate	40 fart	41 finance	42 fluidify	27 forsake
41 estivate	40 expect	41 fascinate	40/7 find	41 fluke	28 forswear
40 estop	41 expectorate	40 fashion	41 fine	43 flummox	42 fortify
41 estrange	41 expedite	40 fast	41 finesse	40 flump	40 forward
43 etch	44 expel	40 fasten	40 finger	40 flung	41 fossilize
41 eternize	40 expend	44 fat	40 fingerprint	41 fluoresce	40 foster
42 etherify	41 experience	41 fate	43 finish	42 flurry	40 foul
41 etherize	40 experiment	40 father	41 fire	43 flush	40 found
41 etiolate	41 expiate	40 fathom	40 fireproof	40 fluster	40 founder
41 etymologize	41 expire	41 fatigue	40 firm	41 flute	40 fowl
41 euchre	40 explain	40 fatten	43 fish	40 flutter	43 fox
41 eulogize	41 explicate	40 fault	40 fishtail	43 flux	40 fraction
41 euphemize	41 explode	40 favo(u)r	41 fissure	9 fly	41 fractionalize
41 europeanize	40 exploit	40 fawn	40 fist	40 foal	41 fractionate
41 evacuate	41 explore	41 faze	44 fit	40 foam	41 fracture
41 evade	40 export	40 fear	43 fix	44 fob	40 fragment
41 evaginate	41 expose	40 feast	41 fixate	41 focalize	41 frame
41 evaluate	41 expostulate	40 feather	40 fizz	43 focus	41 franchise
41 evanesce	40 expound	40 featherbed	41 fizzle	40 fodder	40 frank
41 evangelize	43 express	41 feature	40 flabbergast	44 fog	44 frap
41 evaporate	41 expropriate	41 fecundate	44 flag	40 foil	41 fraternize
40 even	41 expunge	41 federalize	41 flagellate	40 foist	40 fray
41 eventuate	41 expurgate	41 federate	40 flail	40 fold	41 frazzle
40 evert	40 exscind	41 fee	41 flake	41 foliate	40 freak

41 freckle	40 gallop	41 glance	41 gripe	41 handwrite	41 hike
41 free	40 glare	41 glare	44 grit	40/13 hang	40 hilt
40 freewheel	41 galvanize	41 glaze	41 grizzle	40 hanker	40 hinder
20 freeze	44 gam	40 gleam	40 groan	44 hap	41 hinge
40 freight	41 gamble	40 glean	40 groin	40 happen	40 hint
42 frenchify	40 gambol	41 glide	40 groom	41 harangue	41 hire
42 frenzy	41 game	40 glimmer	41 groove	43 harass	41 hispanicize/
40 frequent	40 gammon	41 glimpse	41 grope	40 harbinger	hispanize
40 freshen	40 gang	40 glint	43 gross	40 harbo(u)r	43 hiss
44 fret	41 gangrene	40 glisten	43 grouch	40 harden	5 hit
41 fribble	40 gaol	40 glitter	40 ground	41 hare	43 hitch
40 frighten	41 gape	40 gloat	40 group	40 hark	41 hitchhike
40 frill	41 garage	40 gloom	41 grouse	40 harken	41 hive
41 fringe	40 garb	42 glorify	40 grout	40 harm	40 hoard
40 frisk	41 garble	42 glory	40 grovel	41 harmonize	43 hoax
44 frit	40 garden	43 gloss	9 grow	43 harness	41 hobble
40 fritter	41 gargle	41 glove	40 growl	40 harp	40 hobnob
40 frivol	40 garland	40 glow	41 groyne	40 harpoon	40 hock
43 frizz	40 garner	40 glower	44 grub	40 harrow	43 hocus
41 frizzle	43 garnish	41 gloze	41 grudge	42 harry	41 hoe
40 frolic	41 garnishee	41 glue	41 grumble	40 harvest	44 hog
40 frost	41 garotte	44 glut	41 guarantee	43 hash	40 hoist
41 frostbite	40 garrison	43 gnash	40 guard	41 haste	23 hold
40 froth	41 garrotte	40 gnaw	43 guess	40 hasten	41 hole
40 frown	40 garter	30 go	40 guffaw	43 hatch	40 holiday
42 fructify	43 gas	40 goad	41 guggle	41 hate	40 holler
40 fruit	43 gash	41 gobble	41 guide	40 haul	40 hollow
41 frustrate	42 gasify	40 goffer	41 guillotine	40 haunt	40 holystone
42 fry	40 gasp	41 goggle	40 gull	2 have	41 home
40 fuck	41 gate	40 goldbrick	42 gully	40 hawk	41 homogenize
41 fuddle	43 gatecrash	40 goof	40 gulp	40 hay	41 homologize
41 fudge	40 gather	41 gore	44 gum	40 hazard	41 hone
40 fuel	40 gauffer	41 gorge	44 gun	41 haze	40 honey
41 fulfil	41 gauge	41 gorgonize	41 gurgle	40 head	40 honeycomb
41 fulgurate	40 gawk	41 gormandize	43 gush	40 heal	40 honeymoon
40 full	41 gaze	40 gossip	44 gut	40 heap	40 hono(u)r
41 fulminate	41 gazette	41 gouge	40 gutter	31 hear	40 hood
41 fumble	40 gear	40 govern	41 gutturalize	40 hearken	40 hoodoo
41 fume	44 gel	40 gown	44 guy	40 hearten	40 hoodwink
41 fumigate	40 geld	44 grab	41 guzzle	40 heat	40 hoof
44 fun	44 gem	41 grabble	41 gybe	41 heathenize	40 hook
40 function	41 gemmate	41 grace	44 gyp	5/40 heave	40 hoop
40 fund	40 gender	41 gradate	40 gypsum	41 hebetate	40 hoot
40 funk	41 generalize	41 grade	41 gyrate	41 heckle	40 hoover
40 funnel	41 generate	41 graduate	41 gyre	40 hector	44 hop
44 fur	40 genuflect	40 graft	40 habit	41 hedge	41 hope
43 furbish	41 geologize	40 grain	41 habituate	40 heed	41 hopple
41 furcate	41 geometrize	40 grant	41 hachure	40 hee-haw	40 horn
40 furl	41 germinate	41 granulate	40 hack	40 heel	40 hornswoggle
40 furlough	40 gerrymander	41 grapple	41 hackle	40 heft	42 horrify
41 furnace	41 gestate	40 grasp	41 hade	40 heighten	41 horse
42 furnish	41 gesticulate	43 grass	40 haft	40 heliograph	40 horsewhip
40 furrow	41 gesture	41 grate	41 haggle	41 hellenize	41 hose
40 further	29 get	42 gratify	41 hail	40 helm	41 hospitalize
41 fuse	40 ghost	40 grave	40 hallo	40 help	44 hot
41 fusillade	40 gibb	40 gravel	40 halloo	44 hem	40 hotfoot
42 fuss	40 gibber	41 gravitate	40 hallow	43 hemstitch	40 hound
41 fustigate	40 gibbet	41 graze	41 hallucinate	40 henpeck	41 house
41 fuze	41 gibe	41 grease	40 halo	40 herald	40 hover
43 fuzz	40 gift	41 grecize	40 halt	41 herborize	40 howl
44 gab	41 giggle	40 green	40 halter	40 herd	40 huckster
41 gabble	5/40 gild	40 greet	41 halve	41 hesitate	41 huddle
44 gad	40 gill	40 grey	44 ham	9/40 hew	40 huff
40 gaff	40 gimlet	41 griddle	40 hammer	43 hex	44 hug
44 gag	44 gin	41 gride	40 hamper	41 hibernate	40 hull
41 gage	40 ginger	41 grieve	40 hamstring	40 hiccup	44 hum
40 gain	5/40 gird	40 grill	40 hand	6 hide	41 humanize
42 gainsay	41 girdle	41 grimace	40 handcuff	41 hierarchize	41 humble
40 gail	40 girth	41 grime	41 handicap	40 higgle	40 humbug
40 gallant	26 give	44 grin	41 handle	40 highjack	42 humidify
41 gallicize	40 gladden	7 grind	40 handpick	40 highlight	41 humiliate
40 gallivant	41 glamorize	44 grip	40 handsel	40 hijack	40 humour

40 hump	40 implant	41 industrialize	8 interbreed	41 invigilate	43 josh
43 hunch	41 impledge	40 indwell	41 intercalate	41 invirogate	41 jostle
40 hunger	40 implement	41 intercede	41 intercede	41 invite	44 jot
40 hunt	41 implicate	41 infatuate	40 intercept	41 invoice	41 journalize
41 hurdle	41 implore	40 infect	41 interchange	41 invoke	40 journey
40 hurl	42 imply	44 infer	40 interconnect	41 involve	40 joust
42 hurry	40 import	40 infest	40 intercrop	40 inwall	41 jubilate
5 hurt	41 importune	41 infiltrate	40 interdepend	41 inweave	41 judaize
41 hurtle	41 impose	40 infirm	40 interdict	40 inwrap	41 judge
40 husband	40 impound	43 infix	40 interest	41 iodate	44 jug
43 hush	42 impoverish	41 inflame	41 interfere	41 iodize	41 juggle
40 husk	41 imprecate	41 inflate	41 interfuse	41 ionize	41 jugulate
41 hustle	41 impregnate	40 inflect	40 interject	40 irk	41 jumble
41 hybridize	43 impress	40 inflict	41 interlace	40 iron	40 jump
41 hydrate	40 imprint	41 influence	40 interlard	41 irradiate	40 junk
41 hydrogenate	40 imprison	40 inform	41 interline	41 irrigate	40 junket
41 hidrogenize	41 impropriate	41 infringe	40 interlock	41 irritate	42 justify
40 hymn	41 improve	41 infuriate	41 interlope	40 irrupt	44 jut
42 hypertrophy	41 improvise	41 infuse	42 intermarry	40 island	41 juxtapose
40 hyphen	40 impugn	41 ingeminate	41 intermeddle	41 isolate	41 kedge
41 hypnotize	41 impute	40 ingest	41 intermediate	41 issue	40 keel
41 hypothecate	41 inactivate	40 ingrain	41 intermingle	41 italicize	40 keen
41 ice	42 inarch	41 ingratiate	40 intermit	43 itch	16 keep
41 idealize	40 inarm	41 ingurgigate	43 intermix	41 itemize	44 ken
41 ideate	41 inaugurate	40 inhabit	40 intern	41 iterate	40 kennel
42 identify	41 inbreathe	41 inhale	41 internationalize	41 itinerate	40 key
41 idiotize	40 inbreed	41 here	41 interpage	44 jab	40 kick
41 iddle	41 incandesce	40 inherit	41 interpellate	41 jabber	44 kid
41 idolatrize	41 incapacitate	40 inhibit	41 interpenetrate	40 jack	40 kidnap
41 idolize	41 incarcerate	41 inhume	40 interplay	40 jacket	40 kill
41 ignite	41 incarnadine	40 initial	41 interpolate	41 jackknife	40 kilt
41 ignore	41 incarnate	41 initiate	41 interpose	44 jag	41 kindle
41 illegitimate	41 incase	40 inject	40 interpret	40 jail	40 kink
41 illuminate	41 incense	41 injure	41 interrogate	44 jam	44 kip
41 illumine	40 incept	40 ink	40 interrupt	41 jangle	40 kipper
41 illustrate	43 inch	32 inlay	40 intersect	41 jape	43 kiss
41 image	41 incinerate	41 innervate	41 interspace	44 jar	44 kit
41 imagine	41 incise	41 innerve	41 intersperse	41 jaundice	40 kitten
44 imbed	41 incite	41 innovate	41 intertwine	40 jaunt	44 knap
41 imbide	41 incline	41 inoculate	41 intervene	40 jaw	40 knead
41 imbricate	41 inclose	41 inosculate	40 interview	40 jaywalk	41 knee
41 imbrue	41 include	41 inquire	41 interweave	43 jazz	40 knife
41 imbrute	41 incommode	41 insalivate	41 intimate	40 jeer	40 knight
41 imbue	41 inconvenience	41 inscribe	41 intimidiate	40 jell	5/44 knit
41 imitate	41 incorporate	41 inseminate	41 intitule	42 jellify	40 knock
41 immerge/	41 increase	40 insert	41 intonate	41 jeopardize	44 knot
immerse	41 incriminate	40 inset	41 intone	40 jerk	41 knout
43 immesh	40 incrust	41 insinuate	41 intoxicate	40 jarrymander	18 know
41 immigrate	41 incubate	40 insist	40 intreat	40 jest	41 knuckle
43 immix	41 inculcate	41 insolate	43 intrench	44 jet	40 label
41 immobilize	41 inculpate	40 inspect	41 intrigue	40 jettison	41 labialize
41 immolate	44 incur	41 inspire	41 introduce	40 jewel	40 labour/labor
41 immortalize	41 incurvate	40 inspirit	40 intromit	40 jib/jibb	41 lace
41 immunize	41 incurve	41 inspissate	40 introspect	41 jibe	41 lacerate
41 immure	42 indemnify	40 install	40 introvert	44 jig	40 lack
40 impact	40 indent	41 instance	41 intrude	41 jiggle	40 lacquer
40 impair	41 indenture	41 instigate	41 intubate	40 jilt	41 lactate
41 impale	43 index	40 instil/instill	40 intuit	42 jimmy	40 ladder
41 imparadise	41 indicate	41 institute	41 intumesce	41 jingle	46 lade
40 impark	40 indict	41 institutionalize	41 inundate	43 jinx	41 ladle
40 impart	41 indispose	40 instruct	41 inure	40 jitter	44 lag
40 impassion	41 indite	40 instrument	40 inurn	41 jive	41 laicize
41 impaste	41 individualize	41 insufflate	41 invade	44 job	40 lair
40 impawn	41 individuate	40 insulate	41 invaginate	40 jockey	44 lam
42 impeach	41 indoctrinate	40 insult	41 invalidate	44 jog	40 lamb
41 impede	41 indorse	41 insure	40 inveigh	41 joggle	41 lame
44 impel	41 induce	41 integrate	41 inveigle	40 join	40 lament
40 impend	40 induct	41 intellectualize	40 invent	40 joint	41 laminate
40 imperil	41 indue	40 intend	42 inventory	41 joke	40 lamp
41 impersonate	41 indulge	42 intensify	40 invert	42 jollify	40 lampoon
41 impetrate	41 indulgence	40 inter	40 invest	42 jolly	41 lance
41 impinge	41 indurate	40 interact	41 investigate	40 jolt	

41 lancinate
40 land
41 landscape
43 languish
44 lap
41 lapidate
42 lapidify
41 lapse
40 lard
40 lark
40 larrup
43 lash
40 lasso
40 last
43 latch
40 laten
40 lath
41 lathe
40 lather
41 latinize
41 lattice
40 laud
40 laugh
43 launch
40 launder
40 laurel
41 lave
43 lavish
32 lay
40 layer
41 laze
43 leach
8 lead
40 leaf
41 league
40 leak
16 lean
17 leap
40 leapfrog
16 learn
41 lease
43 leash
40 leather
16 leave
40 leaven
41 lecture
40 leer
44 leg
41 legalize
41 legate
41 legislate
41 legitimate
41 legitimize
16 lend
40 lengthen
40 lessen
40 lesson
5 let
41 lethargize
41 letter
40 level
40 lever
41 levitate
42 levy
41 liaise
40 libel
41 liberalize
41 liberate
41 librate
41 licence/license
40 lick
33 lie

40 lift
41 ligate
41 ligature
12/40 light
40 lighten
40 lighter
42 lignify
41 like
40 liken
40 lilt
40 limb
40 limber
41 lime
40 limit
40 limn
40 limp
41 line
40 linger
40 link
41 lionize
44 lip
41 liquate
42 liquefy
41 liquidate
41 liquidize
40 liquor
40 lisp
40 list
40 listen
41 literalize
40 lithograph
40 lithoprint
41 litigate
40 litter
41 live
40 liven
41 lixiviate
40 load
40 loaf
40 loan
41 loathe
44 lob
42 lobby
41 localize
41 locate
40 lock
41 lodge
40 loft
44 log
40 loiter
40 loll
40 lollop
40 long
41 longe
40 look
40 loom
40 loop
41 loose
40 loosen
40 loot
44 lop
41 lope
40 lord
16 lose
40 louden
41 lounge
40 lour
41 louse
40 love
40 low
40 lower
41 lubricate

41 lucubrate
40 luff
44 lug
40 lull
42 lullaby
40 lumber
40 lump
43 lunch
41 lunge
43 lurch
41 lure
40 lurk
40 lust
40 luster
41 lustrate
41 lustre
41 lute
41 luxate
41 luxuriate
43 lynch
41 lyophilize
41 macerate
41 machinate
41 machine
40 machine-gun
41 mackle
41 maculate
40 madden
41 magnetize
42 magnify
40 mail
40 maim
40 maintain
16 make
41 malaxate
40 malign
40 malinger
40 malt
40 maltreat
44 man
41 manacle
41 manage
41 mandate
41 manducate
40 maneuver
41 mangle
41 manhandle
41 manicure
40 manifest
40 manifold
41 manipulate
41 manoeuvre
41 mantle
41 manufacture
40 manumit
41 manre
44 map
44 mar
40 maraud
41 marble
41 marbleize
43 march
40 margin
41 marginate
41 marinade/marinate
40 mark
40 market
40 maroon
42 marry
40 marshal
40 martyr

41 martyrize
40 marvel
43 mash
40 mask
40 mason
41 masquerade
43 mass
41 massacre
41 massage
40 mast
40 master
40 mastermind
40 masthead
41 masticate
41 masturbate
40 mat/matt
43 match
41 mate
41 materialize
41 matriculate
40 matter
41 maturate
41 mature
40 maul
40 maunder
41 maximize may
41 maze
16 mean
40 meander
41 measure
41 mechanize
40 medal
41 meddle
41 mediate
41 mediatize
41 medicate
41 medicine
41 meditate
16 meet
40 meld
41 meliorate
40 mellow
41 melodize
41 melodramatize
40 melt
41 memorialize
41 memorize
41 menace
40 mend
41 menstruate
40 mention
40 meow
41 mercerize
41 merchandise
41 merge
40 merit
43 mesh
41 mesmerize
43 mess
41 message
40 metal
41 metallize/metalize
41 metamorphose
41 metaphorize
41 metaphrase
41 mete
40 meter
41 methodize
41 methylate
42 metrify
40 mew

40 mewl
40 miaow
40 miaul
41 micturate
41 middle
40 miff
41 migrate
40 milden
40 mildew
41 militarize
41 militate
40 milk
40 mill
40 milt
40 mimeograph
41 mince
40 mind
41 mine
41 mineralize
41 mingle
41 miniaturize
41 minimize
40 minister
40 minor
40 mint
41 minute
41 mire
40 mirror
41 misadvise
42 misapply
40 misapprehend
41 misbehave
41 miscalculate
40 miscall
42 miscarry
39 miscast
40 miscolo(u)r
41 misconceive
40 misconduct
41 misconstrue
40 miscount
41 miscue
40 misdeal
40 misdemean
40 misdirect
40 misdoubt
41 misestimate
41 misfire
26 misgive
40 misgovern
41 misguide
41 mishandle
31 mishear
40 misinterpret
41 misjudge
32 mislay
8 mislead
41 mismanage
42 mismatch
41 misname
41 misplace
40 misprint
41 mispronounce
41 misquote
5 misread
40 misremember
40 misrepresent
41 misrule
40 miss
40 misspell
40 mist
27 mistake

41 mistime
34 misunderstand
41 misuse
40 miter
41 mistigate
41 mitre
43 mix
41 mizzle
40 moan
44 mob
41 mobilize
40 mock
40 model
41 moderate
41 modernize
42 modify
41 modulate
40 moil
40 moisten
41 moisturize
40 mold
40 molder
40 molest
42 mollify
41 monetize
40 monitor
40 monkey
41 monologize
41 monopolize
41 monumentalize
40 moo
40 moon
40 moor
40 moot
44 mop
40 mope
41 moralize
40 mortar
41 mortgage
41 mortice
42 mortify
41 mortise
40 mosey
40 moss
40 mother
40 motion
41 motivate
41 motive
40 motor
41 motorcycle
41 motorize
41 mottle
40 mould
40 moulder
40 moult
40 mound
40 mount
40 mountaineer
40 mourn
41 mouse
40 mouth
41 move
9/40 mow
40 muck
41 muckrake
40 muddle
42 muddy
40 muff
41 muffle
44 mug
42 mulch
40 mull

40 mullion	41 nitrogenize	41 orchestrate	40 overcloud	40 paraph	43 percuss
43 multiplex	40 nock	40 ordain	14 overcome	41 paraphrase	41 peregrinate
42 multiply	44 nod	40 order	40 overcook	40 parboil	40 perfect
44 mum	41 noise	41 organize	44 overcrop	41 parbuckle	41 perforate
41 mumble	41 nominate	40 orient	40 overcrowd	40 parcel	40 perform
42 mummify	41 noose	41 orientalize	40 overdevelop	43 parch	41 perfume
42 mummy	41 normalize	41 orientate	17 overdo	40 pardon	41 perfuse
43 munch	41 nose	41 originate	18 overdraw	41 pare	41 periphrase
41 municipalize	41 notarize	40 ornament	40 overdress	41 parenthesize	43 perish
40 munition	43 notch	40 orphan	19 overdrink	40 parget	41 perjure
40 murder	41 note	41 orphanize	20 overdrive	40 park	40 perk
40 murmur	41 notice	41 oscillate	17 overfeed	40 parley	40 perm
41 muscle	42 notify	41 osculate	20 override	42 parody	41 permeate
41 muse	43 nourish	42 ossify	40 overrule	41 parole	40 permit
43 mush	41 novelize	41 ostracize	35 overrun	40 parquet	41 permute
40 mushroom	41 nucleate	40 ought	27 overtake	40 parrot	41 perorate
43 muss must	41 nudge	40 oust	9 overthrow	42 parry	40 perpend
40 muster	42 nullify	40 out	40 overweight	41 parse	41 perpetrate
41 mutate	40 numb	41 outbalance	40 overwhelm	40 part	41 perpetuate
41 mute	40 number	5 outbid	40 overwind	41 partake	43 perplex
41 mutilate	41 nurse	41 outbrave	40 overwork	41 participate	41 persecute
42 mutiny	41 nurture	8 outbreed	40 oviposit	41 particularize	41 persevere
40 mutter	41 nuzzle	40 outclass	41 ovulate	40 partition	40 persist
41 muzzle	40 oar	44 outcrop	41 owe	40 partner	41 personalize
42 mystify	40 obey	41 outdistance	40 own	43 pass	41 personate
41 mythicize	41 obfuscate	17 outdo	41 oxidize	41 paste	42 personify
44 nab	40 object	41 outface	41 oxygenate	41 pasteurize	41 perspire
44 nag	42 objectify	44 outfit	41 oxigenize	41 pasture	41 pervade
40 nail	41 onjurgate	40 outflank	41 ozonize	44 pat	40 pervert
41 name	41 obligate	30 outgo	41 pace	43 patch	41 pester
44 nap	41 oblige	9 outgrow	42 pacify	40 patent	41 pestle
41 narcotize	41 oblique	40 outlaw	40 pack	41 patinate	44 pet
40 nark	41 obliterate	41 outline	41 package	40 patrol	40 peter
41 narrate	41 obscure	40 outlook	40 packet	41 patronize	40 petition
40 narrow	41 observe	40 outmarch	44 pad	40 patter	42 petrify
41 nasalize	43 obsess	40 outmatch	41 paddle	40 pattern	41 phase
41 nationalize	40 obstruct	40 outnumber	40 padlock	43 paunch	40 philander
40 natter	40 obtain	41 outpace	41 paganize	41 pauperize	41 philosophize
41 naturalize	41 obtrude	40 outplay	41 page	41 pause	41 phlebotomize
41 nauseate	41 obturate	40 outpoint	41 paginate	41 pave	41 phonate
41 navigate	40 obvert	41 outrage	40 pain	40 paw	41 phone
40 near	41 obviate	41 outrange	40 paint	40 pawn	41 phosphatize
41 nebulize	40 occasion	40 outrank	40 pair	8 pay	41 phosphorate
41 necessitate	41 occidentalize	43 outreach	41 palatalize	43 peach	41 phosphoresce
40 neck	41 occlude	40 outrival	40 palaver	40 peak	40 photo
40 need	40 occult	35 outrun	41 pale	40 peal	42 photocopy
41 needle	42 occupy	40 outsail	41 palisade	40 pearl	41 photoengrave
41 mavegate	44 occur	41 outscore	40 pall	41 pebble	40 photograph
41 negative	41 octuple	24 outsell	41 palliate	40 peck	40 photolithograph
40 neglect	40 off	24 outshine	40 palm	41 peculate	40 photostat
41 negotiate	40 offend	24 outshoot	41 palpate	40 pedal	41 phrase
40 neigh	44 offer	40 outsmart	41 palpitate	41 peddle	40 pick
40 neigbo(u)r	40 officer	41 outstare	40 palter	41 pee	40 picket
41 nerve	41 officiate	44 outstrip	40 pamper	40 peek	41 pickle
40 nest	40 offset	41 outvalue	40 pamphleteer	40 peel	47 picnic
41 nestle	41 ogle	40 outwalk	44 pan	40 peep	40 picot
44 net	40 oil	28 outwear	41 pancake	40 peer	41 picture
40 nett	40 okay	40 outweigh	40 pander	41 peeve	41 piece
41 nettle	40 omen	44/44 outwit	41 panegyrize	44 peg	41 pierce
41 neuter	44 omit	40 outwork	40 panel	40 pelt	41 piffle
41 neutralize	41 ooze	41 ovalize	41 panhandle	44 pen	44 pig
41 nibble	40 oopen	40 overact	40 paper	41 penalize	40 pigment
41 niche	41 operate	41 overawe	41 parabolize	40 pencil	40 pile
40 nick	41 opiate	41 overbalance	41 parachute	41 penetrate	40 pilfer
40 nickel	41 opine	45 overbear	41 parade	40 pension	41 pillage
41 nickname	41 oppose	5 overbid	40 paraffin	41 people	40 pillar
42 nidify	43 oppress	12 overbuild	40 paragraph	44 pep	42 pillory
40 niff	40 oppugn	40 overburden	40 parallel	40 pepper	40 pillow
41 niggle	40 opt	40 overcall	41 paralyse	41 perambulate	
44 nip	41 optimize	41 overcapitalize	41 paralyze	41 perceive	
41 nitrate	41 orate	39 overcast		43 perch	
42 nitrify	40 orbit	41 overcharge		41 percolate	

40 pilot	41 polarize	41 predetermine	44 prod	41 puddle	44 quiz
40 pimp	41 pole	41 predicate	41 produce	40 puff	41 quote
44 pin	41 polemicize	40 predict	41 profane	44 pug	40 quoth
43 pinch	41 police	41 predispose	43 profess	41 puke	40 rabbet
41 pine	43 polish	41 predominate	41 professionalize	40 pull	40 rabbit
40 ping	41 politicize	40 preempt	40 proffer	41 pullulate	41 rabble
40 pinion	40 poll	40 preen	41 profile	40 pulp	41 race
40 pink	41 pollinate	43 preestablish	40 profit	41 pulsate	40 rack
41 pinnacle	41 pollute	40 preexist	40 profiteer	41 pulse	40 racket
40 pinpoint	41 polymerize	41 preface	41 prognosticate	41 pulverize	41 raddle
40 pioneer	40 pommel	44 prefer	41 programme	41 pumice	41 radiate
44 pip	40 ponder	41 prefigure	40 program	40 pummel	41 radicate
41 pipe	40 pong	43 prefix	43 progress	40 pump	40 radio
41 pique	40 poniard	40 preform	40 prohibit	44 pun	40 radiograph
41 pirate	41 pontificate	40 preheat	40 project	43 punch	41 raffle
41 pirouette	40 pool	41 prejudge	41 proletarianize	41 punctuate	40 raft
43 piss	40 poop	41 prejudice	41 proliferate	41 puncture	44 rag
44 pit	44 pop	40 prelect	41 prologize	43 punish	41 rage
43 pitch	41 popple	41 prelude	41 prologue	40 punt	40 raid
40 pitchfork	41 popularize	41 premeditate	41 prologuize	44 pup	40 rail
40 pith	41 populate	41 premise	40 prolong	41 purchase	40 railroad
42 pity	41 pore	43 premonish	41 prolongate	41 purge	40 rain
40 pivot	40 port	42 preoccupy	41 promenade	42 purify	40 rainproof
40 placard	40 portend	40 preordain	41 promise	40 purl	41 raise
41 place	40 portion	41 prepare	41 promote	40 purloin	41 rake
41 plagiarize	40 portray	32 prepay	40 prompt	41 purple	42 rally
40 plait	41 pose	41 preponderate	41 promulgate	40 purport	44 ram
44 plan	43 posh	41 presage	41 pronate	41 purpose	41 ramble
41 plane	40 posit	40 prescind	40 prong	40 purr	42 ramify
43 planish	40 position	41 prescribe	41 pronounce	41 purse	40 ramp
40 plank	43 possess	40 present	40 proof	41 pursue	41 rampage
40 plant	40 post	41 preserve	40 proofread	40 purvey	40 rampart
43 plash	41 postdate	41 preside	44 prop	43 push	43 ranch
40 plaster	43 postfix	43 press	41 propagandize	41 put	41 range
41 plasticize	40 postmark	41 pressure	41 propagate	5 put	40 rank
44 plat	41 postpone	41 pressureize	44 propel	42 putrefy	41 rankle
41 plate	41 postulate	43 prestress	42 prophesy	40 putt	40 ransack
41 platinize	41 posture	41 presume	41 propitiate	40 putter	40 ransom
41 platitude	44 pot	41 presuppose	40 proportion	42 putty	40 rant
40 play	41 pothole	40 pretend	41 proportionate	41 puzzle	44 rap
43 pleach	40 potter	40 pretermit	41 propose	40 quack	41 rape
40 plead	43 pouch	40 pretext	40 proposition	41 quadrate	41 rapture
41 please	41 poultice	42 prettify	40 propound	41 quadruple	42 rarefy
40 pleat	41 pounce	40 prevail	41 prorate	41 quadruplicate	41 rase
41 pledge	40 pound	41 prevaricate	41 prorogue	40 quaff	40 rasp
40 plight	40 pour	40 prevent	41 proscribe	40 quail	44 rat
44 plod	40 pout	41 preview	41 prose	41 quake	41 rate
40 plonk	40 powder	41 previse	41 prosecute	42 qualify	42 ratify
44 plop	40 power	41 prevue	41 proselyte	42 quantify	41 ratiocinate
44 plot	41 practice	40 prey	41 proselytize	41 quarantine	40 ration
40 plugh	41 practise	41 price	40 prospect	40/44 quarrel	41 rationalize
40 plow	41 praise	40 prick	40 prosper	42 quarry	41 rattle
40 pluck	41 prance	41 prickle	41 prostitute	40 quarter	41 ravage
44 plug	40 prang	41 pride	41 prostrate	43 quash	41 rave
40 plumb	40 prank	44 prim	40 protect	40 queen	40/44 ravel
41 plume	41 prate	41 prime	40 protest	40 queer	40 raven
40 plummet	41 prattle	40 primp	40 protocol	40 quell	43 ravish
40 plump	40 pray	40 prink	41 protocolize	43 quench	41 raze
40 plunder	43 preach	40 print	40 protract	42 query	43 razz
41 plunge	42 preachify	41 prise	41 protrude	40 quest	43 reach
40 plunk	41 prearrange	40 prison	41 prove	40 question	40 react
41 pluralize	40 prebook	41 privilege	41 provide	41 queue	41 reactivate
42 ply	41 precede	41 prize	40 provision	41 quibble	5 read
43 poach	41 precipitate	41 probate	41 provoke	40 quicken	40 readapt
40 pocket	41 preclude	41 probe	40 prowl	40 quiet	43 readdress
44 pod	41 preconceive	40 proceed	41 prune	40 quieten	40 readjust
41 poeticize	40 preconcert	43 process	42 pry	40 quill	40 readmit
41 poetize	41 preconize	40 procession	41 psychoanalise	40 quilt	42 ready
40 point	41 predate	40 proclaim	41 psychoanalize	41 quintuple	40 reaffirm
41 poise	41 predecease	41 procrastinate	41 publicize	44 quip	41 realise
40 poison	41 predestinate	41 procreate	43 publish	40 quirt	41 realize
41 poke	41 predestine	41 procure	40 pucker	5/44 quit	40 ream
				40 quiver	

41 reanimate	41 recuperate	41 regurgitate	41 renounce	41 resonate	41 revolutionize
40 reap	44 recur	41 rehabilitate	41 renovate	40 resorb	41 revolve
40 reappear	41 recuse	43 rehash	40 rent	40 resort	40 reward
40 reappoint	40 redact	41 rehearse	40 renumber	40 resound	8 rewind
40 reapportion	40 redden	41 rehydrate	42 reoccupy	40 respect	41 rhyme
40 rear	40 redeem	42 reify	40 reopen	40 respell	44 rib
40 rearm	40 redemand	40 reign	40 reorder	41 respire	41 rice
41 rearrange	40 redeploy	41 reimburse	41 reorganize	41 respite	40 rick
40 reason	41 redintegrate	40 reimport	40 reorient	40 respond	40 ricochet
41 reassemble	40 redirect	40 rein	40 repack	40 rest	5/44 rid
40 reassert	40 rediscover	41 reincarnate	41 repackage	40 restart	41 riddle
43 reassess	41 redistribute	40 reinforce	40 repaint	41 restate	20 ride
41 reassume	41 redouble	40 reinsert	40 repair	40 restitute	41 ridge
41 reassure	40 redound	40 reinstall	43 repass	40 restock	41 ridicule
40 reattack	40 redraft	41 reinstate	41 repatriate	40 restore	41 riffle
40 reawaken	43 redress	41 reinsure	8 repay	40 restrain	41 rifle
41 rebaptize	41 reduce	41 reintegrate	40 repeal	40 restrict	44 rig
41 rebate	41 reduplicate	40 reinter	40 repeat	40 result	40 right
44 rebel	40 reed	41 reintroduce	44 repel	41 resume	41 rile
41 rebore	41 reeducate	40 reinvest	40 repent	41 resurface	44 rim
40 rebound	40 reef	41 reinvigorate	41 repeople	40 resurrect	41 rime
40 rebuff	40 reek	41 reissue	41 rephrase	40 retail	19 ring
41 rebuke	40 reel	41 reiterate	41 repine	40 retain	41 rinse
44 rebut	40 reelect	40 reject	41 replace	41 retake	40 riot
41 recalcitrate	40 reembark	40 rejoice	40 replant	41 retaliate	44 rip
41 recalculate	41 reemerge	40 rejoin	40 replay	40 retard	40 ripen
40 recall	40 reemploy	41 rejuvenate	43 replenish	42 retch	41 ripple
40 recant	40 reenact	41 rekindle	40 replevin	41 reticulate	36 rise
44 recap	41 reenforce	41 relapse	42 replevy	41 retile	40 risk
41 recapitulate	41 reengage	41 relate	41 replicate	40 retin	41 rivalize
41 recapture	41 reeve	43 relax	42 reply	41 retire	41 rive
41 recede	41 reexamine	40 relay	43 repolish	40 retort	40 rivet
40 receipt	40 reexport	41 release	41 repopulate	43 retouch	40 roam
41 receive	41 reface	40 relegate	40 report	41 retrace	40 roar
43 recess	40 refashion	40 relent	41 repose	40 retract	40 roast
41 recharge	44 refer	40 relet	40 reprehend	40 retrain	44 rob
40 rechristen	41 referee	41 relieve	40 represent	40 retreat	41 robe
41 reciprocate	41 reference	41 reline	43 repress	43 retrench	40 rock
41 recite	40 refill	43 relinquish	41 reprieve	41 retrieve	40 rocket
40 reck	41 refinance	43 relish	40 reprimand	40 retroact	40 roil
40 reckon	41 refine	41 relive	40 reprint	41 retrocede	40 roister
41 recline	44 refit	40 reload	43 reproach	41 retrograde	40 roll
41 recognize	40 reflect	41 relocate	41 reprobate	43 retrogress	40 rollick
40 recoil	40 refloat	40 reluct	41 reproduce	40 retrospect	41 romance
40 recoin	43 reflourish	42 rely	41 reprove	42 retry	41 romanize
40 recollect	40 reforest	40 remain	41 republicanize	40 return	41 romanticize
41 recommence	40 reform	40 remainder	43 republish	42 reunify	40 romp
40 recommend	40 refract	41 remake	41 repudiate	41 reunite	40 roof
41 recompense	40 refrain	40 reman	40 repulse	41 reuse	40 rook
41 recompose	43 refresh	40 remand	41 repurchase	44 rev	40 room
41 reconcile	41 refrigerate	40 remark	41 repute	41 revaccinate	40 roost
40 reconfirm	42 refry	42 remarry	40 request	41 revalorize	40 root
41 reconnoitre	40 refuel	42 remedy	41 require	41 revalue	41 rope
40 reconnoiter	40 refund	40 remember	40 requisition	40 revamp	40 rosin
40 reconquer	43 refurbish	41 remilitarize	41 requite	40 reveal	44 rot
40 reconsider	43 refurnish	40 remind	40 reroute	44 revel	41 rotate
41 reconsitute	41 refuse	41 reminisce	40 rescind	41 revenge	41 rouge
40 reconstruct	41 refute	41 remise	41 rescue	41 reverberate	40 rough
41 reconvene	40 regain	44 remit	43 research	41 revere	40 roughen
40 reconvert	40 regale	40 remodel	40 reseat	41 reverence	41 roulette
40 reconvey	40 regard	41 remonetize	40 resect	41 reverse	40 round
40 recook	41 regenerate	41 remonstrate	40 reseed	40 revert	41 rouse
40 record	40 regiment	40 remount	41 resemble	40 review	40 rout
40 recount	40 regionalize	41 remove	40 resent	41 revigorate	41 route
40 recoup	40 register	41 remunerate	41 reserve	41 revile	40 rove
40 recover	41 registrate	41 rename	5 reset	41 revindicate	41 row
41 recreate	41 regorge	8 rend	41 reside	41 revise	40 rowel
41 recriminate	43 regreess	40 render	40 resign	41 revitalize	44 rub
43 recross	40 regret	40 rendezvous	41 resinate	41 revive	41 rubberize
41 recrudesce	41 regroup	41 renegade	40 resist	42 revivify	40 rubberneck
40 recruit	41 regularize	41 renege	41 resole	41 revoke	42 rubefy
42 rectify	41 regulate	40 renew	41 resolve	40 revolt	41 ruckle

41 rue	44 scar	40 sear	40 shelter	40 silt	40 sleigh
40 ruff	41 scare	43 search	41 shelve	40 silver	41 slenderize
41 ruffle	40 scarf	40 season	40 shepherd	40 simmer	40 sleuth
40 ruin	42 scarify	40 seat	40 shield	40 simper	40 slew
41 rule	40 scarp	41 secede	40 shift	42 simplify	41 slice
41 rumble	44 scat	41 seclude	44 shim	42 simulate	40 slick
41 ruminate	41 scathe	40 second	40 shimmer	44 sin	12 slide
41 rummage	40 scatter	41 secrete	42 shimmy	19 sing	40 slight
41 rumour/rumor	41 scavenge	40 section	44 shin	41 singe	44 slim
41 rumple	40 scent	41 sectionalize	24 shine	41 single	41 slime
35 run	41 schedule	41 secularize	41 shingle	41 singularize	13 sling
41 rupture	41 schematize	41 secure	42 shinny	19 sink	13 slink
43 rush	41 scheme	41 seduce	44 ship	40 sinter	44 slip
40 rust	40 school	23 see	40 shipwreck	44 sip	5 slit
41 rusticate	43 schuss	40 seed	40 shirk	40 siphon	40 slither
41 rustle	41 scintillate	11 seek	40 shirr	44 sir	40 sliver
44 rut	40 scissor	40 seem	44 shit	41 sire	40 slobber
40 saber	40 scoff	40 seesaw	40 shiver	8 sit	44 slog
41 sabotage	40 scold	41 seethe	40 shoal	41 site	44 slop
41 sabre	40 scollop	40 segment	40 shock	41 situate	41 slope
42 saccharify	40 scoop	41 segregate	24/41 shoe	41 size	40 slosh
40 sack	40 scoot	41 seine	40 shoo	41 sizzle	44 slot
41 sacrifice	43 scorch	41 seize	24 shoot	41 skate	40 slouch
40 sadden	41 score	40 select	44 shop	41 skedaddle	40 slough
41 saddle	42 scorify	24 sell	40 shore	41 skeletonize	40 slow
40 safeguard	40 scorn	41 semaphore	40 short	40 sketch	44 slub
44 sag	43 scotch	8 send	41 shortchange	40 skew	41 slue
40 sail	40 scour	41 sense	40 shorten	40 skewer	44 slug
40 saint	41 scourge	41 sensitize	should	40 ski	41 sluice
42 salify	40 scout	41 sensualize	40 shoulder	44 skid	44 slum
41 salivate	40 scowl	41 sentence	40 shout	40 skiddoo	40 slumber
40 sallow	41 scrabble	41 sentimentalize	41 shove	44 skim	40 slump
42 sally	44 scrag	41 separate	40 shovel	40 skimp	44 slur
40 salt	40 scram	41 septuple	9/40 show	44 skin	40 slush
41 salute	41 scramble	40 sepulcher	40 shower	44 skip	40 smack
41 salvage	40 scrap	41 sepulchre	44 shred	40 skipper	40 smarm
41 salve	41 scrape	40 sequester	40 shriek	40 skirl	40 smart
41 sample	43 scratch	41 sequestrate	40 shrill	40 skirmish	40 smarten
42 sanctify	40 scrawl	41 serenade	40 shrimp	40 skirr	40 smash
40 sanction	40 screak	41 serialize	19 shrink	40 skirt	40 smear
40 sand	40 scream	41 seriate	41 shrive	40 skitter	16/40 smell
41 sanitate	43 screech	41 sermonize	40 shrivel	41 stive	41 smile
44 sap	40 screen	41 serve	40 shroud	40 skulk	40 smirch
42 saponify	40 screw	41 service	44 shrug	40 skunk	40 smirk
43 sass	41 scribble	5 set	40 shuck	42 sky	38 smite
41 sate	41 scribe	41 settle	40 shudder	40 skyjack	40 smock
41 satiate	41 scrimmage	40 sever	41 shuffle	40 skylark	41 smoke
40 satin	40 scrimp	9/40 sew	44 shun	40 skyrocket	40 smolder
41 satirize	40 scrimshaw	40 shack	40 shunt	44 slab	43 smooch
42 satisfy	40 scroll	41 shackle	40 shush	40 slabber	40 smooth
41 saturate	41 scrounge	41 shade	5 shut	40 slack	40 smother
41 sauce	44 scrub	40 shadow	40 shutter	40 slacken	40 smoulder
40 saunter	41 scrummage	27 shake shall	41 shuttle	44 slag	41 smudge
41 saute	43 scrunch	40 shallow	42 shy	41 slake	41 smuggle
41 savage	41 scruple	44 sham	41 sibilate	41 slame	44 smut
41 save	41 scruinize	41 shamble	40 sick	40 slander	40 snack
40 savour/savor	44 scud	41 shame	41 side	40 slang	41 snaffle
42 savvy	40 scuff	40 shampoo	41 sidle	40 slant	44 snag
9/40 saw	41 scuffle	40 shank	41 sieve	44 slap	41 snake
8 say	40 scull	9/40 shape	40 sift	43 slash	44 snap
44 scab	40 sculpt	41 share	40 sigh	40 slat	41 snare
41 scabble	41 sculpture	40 sharp	40 sight	41 slate	40 snarl
40 scaffold	40 scum	40 sharpen	40 sign	40 slaughter	43 snatch
40 scald	41 scumble	40 shatter	40 signal	41 slave	40 sneak
41 scale	40 scupper	9/40 shave	41 signalize	40 slaver	40 sneer
40 scallop	42 scurry	40 sheaf	42 signify	33 slay	41 sneeze
40 scalp	43 scutch	40/45 shear	40 signpost	40 sled	40 snick
40 scamp	40 scutter	41 sheave	41 silage	41 sledge	40 snicker
40 scamper	41 scuttle	5 shed	41 silence	40 sledgehammer	40 sniff
44 scan	41 scythe	40 sheer	41 silhouette	40 sleek	41 sniffle
41 scandalize	40 seal	40 sheet	40 silk	16 sleep	40 snigger
40 scant	40 seam	40 shell	40 silo	40 sleet	44 snip

41 snipe	41 speculate	43 squelch	41 stone	41 subscribe	40 suspect
43 snitch	42 spechify	40 squint	40 stook	41 subside	40 suspend
40 snivel	8/40 speed	41 squire	40 stook	41 subsidize	40 suspicion
40 snooker	16/40 spell	40 squirm	40 stoop	41 subsist	41 suspire
41 snooze	16 spend	40 squirt	44 stop	41 substantiate	40 sustain
41 snore	40 spew	44 stab	40 stopper	41 substantivate	41 suture
40 snort	41 spice	41 stabilize	41 store	41 substitute	44 swab
40 snow	40 spiel	41 stable	40 storm	40 subtract	41 swaddle
40 snowball	41 spike	40 stack	40 stow	40 subvert	44 swag
44 snub	41 spile	40 staff	41 straddle	40 succeed	40 swagger
40 snuff	16/40 spill	41 stage	41 strafe	40 succor	40 swallow
41 snuffle	19 spin	40 stagger	41 straggle	40 succour	40 swamp
44 snug	41 spindle	40 stain	40 straighten	40 succumb	40 swank
41 snuggle	40 spiral	41 stake	40 strain	40 suck	44 swap
40 soak	41 spire	41 stale	40 straiten	41 suckle	40 swarm
40 soap	40 spirit	40 stalk	40 strand	41 sue	43 swash
40 soar	41 spiritualize	40 stall	41 strangle	40 suffer	44 swat
44 sob	40 spirt	40 stammer	41 strangulate	41 suffice	41 swathe
40 sober	19 spit	40 stamp	44 strap	40 suffix	40 sway
41 socialize	41 spite	41 stampede	40 straphang	41 suffocate	28 swear
40 sock	43 splash	43 stanch	42 stratify	41 suffuse	5/40 sweat
44 sod	40 splatter	34 stand	40 stray	40 sugar	16 sweep
40 soften	40 splay	41 staple	40 streak	40 sugarcoat	40 sweeten
40 soil	41 splice	44 star	40 stream	40 suggest	9/40 swell
40 sojourn	41 spline	43 starch	41 streamline	40 suit	40 swelter
41 solace	40 spint	41 stare	40 strengthen	41 sulfate	41 swerve
40 solder	40 splinter	41 stargaze	43 stress	40 sulfur	44 swig
40 soldier	5 split	40 start	43 stretch	41 sulfurate	40 swill
41 sole	41 splodge	41 starve	9/40 strew	41 sulfurize	19 swim
41 solemnize	43 slotch	41 state	41 striate	40 sulk	41 swindle
40 sol-fa	41 splurge	40 station	41 strickle	42 sully	13 swing
40 solicit	40 splutter	40 staunch	20 stride	41 sulphate	41 swipe
42 solidify	16 spoil	24 stave	13 strike	41 sulphurate	40 swirl
41 soliloquize	41 spoke	40 stay	13 string	41 sulphurize	43 swish
41 solve	41 spoliate	42 steady	44 strip	44 sum	43 switch
41 somnambulate	41 sponge	20 steal	41 stripe	41 summarize	40 swivel
40 soot	40 sponsor	40 steam	20 strive	40 summer	40 swoon
41 soothe	40 spoof	40 steamroller	41 stroke	40 summersault	40 swoop
44 sop	40 spool	40 steel	40 stroll	40 summon	43 swoosh
41 sophisticate	40 spoon	40 steep	44 strop	44 sun	44 swop
40 sorrow	40 spoor	40 steepen	41 structure	41 sunbathe	44 swot
40 sort	40 sport	40 steer	41 struggle	40 sunder	41 syllabicate
40 sough	44 spot	41 steeve	44 strum	44 sup	41 syllable
40 sound	40 spotlight	44 stem	44 strut	41 superpose	41 syllogize
40 soundproof	40 spout	40 stencil	44 stub	41 supersede	41 symbolize
40 soup	44 sprag	40 stenograph	40 stucco	41 supervene	41 symmetrize
40 sour	40 sprain	44 step	44 stud	41 supervise	41 sympathize
41 souse	40 sprawl	41 stereotype	42 study	41 supinate	41 synchronize
40 south	40 spray	41 sterilize	40 stuff	41 supple	41 syncopate
41 sovietize	5 spread	41 stevedore	42 stultify	40 supplant	41 syndicate
9/40 sow	44 sprig	40 stew	41 stumble	40 supplement	41 synthesize
41 space	19 spring	20 stick	40 stump	41 supplicate	41 syntonize
41 spade	41 springe	41 stickle	44 stun	42 supply	41 syringe
40 spall	41 sprinkle	40 stiffen	40 stunt	40 support	41 systematize
40 span	40 sprint	41 stifle	42 stupefy	41 suppose	41 systemize
41 spangle	40 sprout	40 stigmatize	40 stutter	43 suppress	42 tabby
40 spank	41 spruce	40 still	42 sty	41 suppurate	41 table
44 spar	44 spud	41 stimulate	41 style	41 surbase	40 taboo
41 spare	41 spume	42 stimy	41 stylize	41 surcharge	41 tabulate
40 spark	44 spur	13 sting	44 sub	41 surface	40 tack
41 sparkle	40 spurn	19 stink	41 subdue	40 surfeit	41 tackle
44 spat	40 spurt	40 stint	40 subject	41 surge	44 tag
40 spatter	40 sputter	41 stipple	40 subjoin	41 surmise	40 tail
40 spawn	42 spy	41 stipulate	41 subjugate	40 surmount	40 tailor
40 spay	41 squabble	44 stir	41 sublimate	41 surname	40 taint
10 speak	40 squall	43 stitch	41 sublime	43 surpass	27 take
40 spear	40 squander	40 stock	41 submerge	41 surprise	40 talk
40 spearhead	41 square	41 stockade	41 submerse	40 surrender	42 tally
41 specialize	43 squash	41 stockpile	40 submit	40 surround	40 tambour
42 specify	44 squat	41 stodge	41 subordinate	43 surtax	41 tame
40 speck	40 squawk	41 stoke	40 suborn	40 survey	40 tamp
41 speckle	41 squeeze	43 stomach	41 subrogate	41 survive	40 tamper

40 tampon	40 threaten	41 topple	41 tremble	41 ulcerate	41 upstage
44 tan	43 thresh	40 torment	43 trench	41 ululate	40 upturn
40 tang	40 thrill	40 torpedo	40 trend	41 umpire	41 urbanize
41 tangle	20 thrive	42 torrefy	40 trepan	40 unarm	41 urge
40 tango	44 throb	42 torrify	41 trephine	41 unbalance	41 urinate
40 tank	41 throne	41 torture	43 trespass	40 unballast	41 use
44 tap	40 throng	43 toss	41 triangulate	41 unbandage	40 usher
41 tape	41 throttle	44 tot	41 trice	44 unbar	40 usufruct
40 taper	9 throw	40 total	40 trick	4 unbend	40 usurp
44 tar	44 thrum	41 totalize	41 trickle	7 unbind	41 utilize
41 tare	5 thrust	41 tote	41 trifle	40 underact	40 utter
40 tariff	44 thud	40 totter	44 trig	5 underbid	41 vacate
43 tarnish	40 thumb	43 touch	40 trigger	41 undercharge	40 vacation
40 task	40 thump	40 toughen	40 trill	5 undercut	41 vaccinate
40 tassel	40 thunder	40 tour	44 trim	17 underdo	41 vacillate
41 taste	40 thwack	41 tousle	44 trip	43 underdress	40 vacuum
44 tat	40 thwart	40 tout	41 triplicate	41 underestimate	40 vagabond
41 tattle	40 tick	40 tow	40 trisect	41 underexpose	41 vagabondize
40 tattoo	40 ticket	40 towel	41 triturate	8 underfeed	40 valet
40 taunt	41 tickle	40 tower	40 triumph	30 undergo	41 validate
40 tauten	41 tide	40 toy	40 troat	32 underlay	41 valorize
40 taw	42 tidy	41 trace	40 troll	41 underline	41 value
43 tax	41 tie	40 track	40 troop	41 undermine	40 vamp
40 taxi	40 tier	41 trade	44 trot	34 understand	41 vandalize
11 teach	40 tiff	40 trademark	41 trouble	41 understate	43 vanish
40 team	40 tighten	47 traffic	41 trounce	33 undertake	43 vanquish
45 tear	41 tile	40 trail	40 truck	41 undervalue	40 vapor
41 tease	40 till	40 train	41 truckle	17 undo	41 vaporize
40 teasel	40 tiller	41 traipse	41 trudge	43 undress	40 vapour
44 ted	40 tilt	40 trammel	41 true	41 undulate	41 variegate
41 tee	40 timber	40 tramp	40 trump	40 unearth	43 varnish
40 teem	41 time	41 trample	40 trumpet	40 unfasten	42 vary
40 teeter	44 tin	41 tranquillize/	41 truncate	40 unfold	44 vat
41 teethe	40 tincture	tranquilize	41 trundle	40 unhook	41 vaticinate
41 tehee	40 ting	40 transact	43 truss	40 uniform	40 vault
40 telegram	41 tinge	40 transcend	40 trust	41 uniformize	40 vaunt
40 telegraph	41 tingle	41 transcribe	42 try	42 unify	40 veer
41 telephone	40 tinker	40 transect	44 tub	41 unionize	41 vegetate
41 telescope	40 tinkle	44 transfer	41 tube	41 unite	40 veil
41 televise	40 tinsel	41 transfigure	40 tuck	41 universalize	40 vend
43 telex	40 tint	43 transfix	40 tucker	41 unlace	40 veneer
24 tell	44 tip	40 transform	40 tuft	43 unlash	41 venerate
40 temper	41 tipple	41 transfuse	44 tug	43 unlatch	40 vent
41 temporize	41 tiptoe	43 transgress	41 tumble	40 unload	41 ventilate
40 tempt	41 tire	40 transit	41 tune	40 unlock	41 ventriloquize
40 tenant	41 tithe	41 translate	40 tunnel	40 unmask	41 venture
40 tend	41 titillate	41 translocate	40 turf	40 unmast	41 verbalize
40 tender	41 titivate	41 transmigrate	40 turn	40 unpack	41 verge
41 tenderize	41 title	44 transmit	41 turtle	41 unpave	42 verify
40 tenon	41 titrate	41 transmute	41 tussle	44 4unplug	41 verse
41 tense	40 titter	41 transpire	40 tutor	40 unreel	42 versify
40 tent	41 tittivate	40 transplant	41 twaddle	41 unriddle	41 vesicate
40 term	40 tittup	40 transport	40 twang	44 unrig	40 vest
41 terminate	40 toast	41 transpose	40 tweak	41 unrobe	44 vet
41 terrace	40 toboggan	44 transship	40 tweet	40 unroll	40 veto
42 teffify	41 toddle	41 transude	41 twiddle	40 unroof	43 vex
41 terrorize	41 toe	41 transvase	44 twig	41 unsaddle	41 vibrate
40 test	44 tog	44 trap	40 twill	40 unscrew	41 victimize
42 testify	41 toggle	43 trapes	40 twin	40 unseal	40 victual
41 tetanize	40 toil	43 trash	41 twine	40 unseat	41 vide
40 tether	41 tolerate	40 travail	41 twinge	41 unsettle	41 vie
40 thank	40 toll	40/44 travel	41 twinkle	40 unveil	40 view
40 thaw	40 tomb	41 traverse	40 twirl	11 unwind	42 vilify
41 theologize	41 tone	42 travesty	40 twist	40 unwrap	40 vilipend
41 theorize	41 tongue	40 trawl	44 twit	44 unzip	41 vindicate
40 thicken	41 tonsure	9/24 tread	43 twitch	44 up	41 violate
41 thieve	40 tool	41 treadle	40 twitter	23 uphold	40 visa
44 thin	40 toot	41 treasure	40 type	40 uplift	40 vision
11 think	40 tooth	40 treat	42 typify	41 upraise	40 visit
40 thrall	41 tootle	41 treble	41 tyrannize	41 uprise	41 visualize
40 thrash	44 top	41 tree	41 tyre	40 uproot	41 vitalize
40 thread	41 tope	44 trek	42 uglify	5 upset	41 vitiate

42 vitrify	40 weatherproof	40 wiredraw
40 vitriol	10 weave	43 wireless
41 vituperate	5/44 wed	41 wise
42 vivify	41 wedge	43 wish
40 vivisect	40 weed	40 wisp
41 vocalize	40 ween	44 wit
41 vociferate	16 weep	43 witch
41 voice	41 wee-wee	18 withdraw
40 void	40 weigh	40 wither
41 volatilize	40 weight	23 withhold
41 volcanize	43 welch	34 withstand
40 volley	41 welcome	43 witness
41 volplane	40 weld	41 wobble
40 volunteer	40 well	40 wolf
40 vomit	43 welsh	41 womanize
40 voodoo	40 welt	40 wonder
41 vote	40 welter	40 woo
43 vouch	43 wench	40 word
43 vouchsafe	40 wend	40 work
40 vow	40 wester	40 worm
41 voyage	41 westernize	42 worry
41 vulcanize	5/44 wet	40 worsem
41 vulgarize	40 whack	40 worship
44 wad	41 whale	40 worst
41 wade	44 wham	40 worth
40 wafer	40 whang	would
41 wafle	40 wharf	40 wound
40 waft	41 wheedle	40 wrack
44 wag	40 wheel	44 wrap
41 wage	41 wheeze	40 wreak
40 wager	40 whelm	41 wreathe
41 waggle	40 whelp	40 wreck
40 wail	44 whet	43 wrench
40 wainscot	40 whiff	40 wrest
40 wait	41 while	41 wrestle
10 wake	40 whimper	41 wriggle
40 waken	41 whine	13 wring
41 wale	42 whinny	41 wrinkle
40 walk	44 whip	38 write
40 wall	44 whir	41 writhe
40 wallop	40 whirl	40 wrong
40 wallow	40 whirr	40 x-ray
40 wallpaper	43 whish	40 yacht
40 waltz	40 whisk	40 yammer
40 wander	40 whisper	40 yank
41 wane	41 whistle	44 yap
41 wangle	40 whiten	40 yard
40 want	43 whitewash	40 yarn
44 war	41 whittle	40 yaup
41 warble	40 whiz/whizz	40 yaw
40 ward	40 whoop	40 yawn
41 ware	44 whop	40 yawp
41 warehouse	41 whore	40 yearn
40 warm	40 widen	40 yell
40 warn	40 widow	40 yellow
40 warp	40 wield	40 yelp
40 warrant	44 wig	41 yen
43 wash	41 wiggle	40 yield
40 wassail	41 wile	44 yip
41 waste	40 will	40 yodel
43 watch	40 willow	41 yoke
40 water	40 wilt	40 yowl
41 wattle	44/24 win	40 zero
41 wave	41 wince	44 zigzag
40 waver	11 wind	47 zinc
43 wax	40 windrow	44 zip
40 waylay	40 wink	41 zone
40 weaken	41 winkle	40 zoom
40 wean	40 winnow	
28 wear	41 winterize	
42 weary	41 wipe	
40 weather	41 wire	

FONDO EDITORIAL STANLEY

INGLÉS

3000 TESTS ELEMENTARY LEVEL

KEYS 3000 TESTS

2000 TESTS ADVANCED LEVEL

KEYS 2000 TESTS

1500 STRUCTURED TESTS
· NIVELES 1, 2 Y 3

KEYS 1500 STRUCTURED TESTS

2000 BILINGUAL PHRASES · FRASES
BILINGÜES · NIVELES 1, 2, 3, 4 Y 5

TRANSLATIONS · TRADUCCIONES
· NIVELES 1, 2, 3 Y 4

FILL IN THE GAPS · NIVELES 1, 2 Y 3

KEYS FILL IN THE GAPS

DIDACTIC CROSSWORDS   NIVEL 1
(EDICIÓN FOTOCOPIABLE)

NEW GUIDE TO PHRASAL VERBS

EXERCISES - GUIDE TO PHRASAL
VERBS

ENGLISH GRAMMAR
· NIVELES 1, 2, 3 Y 4

KEYS ENGLISH GRAMMAR

GUIDE TO PREPOSITIONS
ENGLISH TO SPANISH

USING PREPOSITIONS

ENGLISH VERBS ONE BY ONE

IRREGULAR VERBS AND MODALS

MY ENGLISH TELLTALE

DICTATIONS IN ENGLISH
· NIVELES 1 Y 2

CONVERSATION IN ACTION

NEW GUIDE TO BUSINESS LETTERS

A TO ZED, A TO ZEE A GUIDE TO THE
DIFFERENCES BETWEEN BRITISH AND
AMERICAN ENGLISH

EVERYDAY IDIOMS IN BUSINESS

EL INGLÉS PROHIBIDO

FALSOS AMIGOS-FALSE FRIENDS

E-MAIL ENGLISH

ODDS & ENDS OF ENGLISH USAGE

HELLO... AND NOW WHAT?
STRATEGIES FOR SUCESSFUL SOCIALIZING

**FRONT LINE ENGLISH
GRAMMAR SERIES:**
MODAL VERBS

PREPOSITIONS

PHRASAL VERBS

REPORTED SPEECH

ESPAÑOL

TESTS ESPAÑOL
· NIVELES 1, 2, 3, 4 Y 5

CLAVES TESTS ESPAÑOL

CRUCIGRAMAS DIDÁCTICOS
· NIVELES 1, 2 Y 3

DICTADOS EN ESPAÑOL
· NIVELES A, B Y C

GRAMÁTICA ESPAÑOLA EN MARCHA

CLAVES GRAMÁTICA ESPAÑOLA

LOS VERBOS ESPAÑOLES

DIFERENCIAS ENTRE SER O ESTAR

CLAVES DIFERENCIAS SER O ESTAR

LECTURAS GRADUADAS EN ESPAÑOL

NIVEL 0 LA FAMILIA PEREZ

"   ¿QUIÉN SABE?

"   LA CLASE DE YOGA

NIVEL 1 LA ISLA MISTERIOSA

"   20.000 LEGUAS VIAJE SUBMARINO

"   EL CONDE DE MONTECRISTO

"   DON QUIJOTE DE LA MANCHA

NIVEL 2 LOS TRES MOSQUETEROS

"   UN CAPITÁN DE 15 AÑOS

"   MIGUEL STROGOFF

"   URDANETA. EL TORNAVIAJE

FRANCÉS

1000 TESTS EN FRANÇAIS
· NIVELES 1, 2, 3, 4 Y 5

CLÉS POUR LES TESTS EN FRANÇAIS

TRADUIRE AUJOURD'HUI
· NIVELES 1, 2 Y 3

NOUVEAU GUIDE DE
CORRESPONDANCE COMMERCIALE

MOTS CROISÉS · NIVEL 1

MON BILAN GRAMMATICAL

DICTÉES EN FRANÇAIS
· NIVELES 1-A, 1-B Y 1-C

ENTRAÎNEZ-VOUS AUX VERBES
FRANÇAIS - LIVRE DU PROFESSEUR

ENTRAÎNEZ-VOUS AUX VERBES
FRANÇAIS - ÉLÈVE

ENTRAÎNEZ-VOUS AUX VERBES
FRANÇAIS - CAHIER D'ACTIVITÉS

LECTURAS GRADUADAS EN FRANCÉS

NIVEL 0 LA FAMILLE LENOIR

"   QUI SAIT?

NIVEL 1 L'ÎLE MYSTERIEUSE

"   20.000 LIEUES SOUS LES MERS

"   LE COMTE DE MONTE-CRISTO

NIVEL 2 LES TROIS MOUSQUETAIRES

"   UN CAPITAINE DE QUINZE ANS

"   MICHEL STROGOFF

GUÍAS PARA VIAJAR

GUÍA DEL VIAJERO ESPAÑOL-INGLÉS

GUÍA DEL VIAJERO ESPAÑOL-FRANCÉS

GUÍA DEL VIAJERO ESPAÑOL-ALEMÁN

GUÍA DEL VIAJERO ESPAÑOL-ITALIANO

GUÍA DEL VIAJERO ESPAÑOL-PORTUGUÉS

GUÍA DEL VIAJERO ESPAÑOL-INGLÉS (USA)

GUÍA DE CONVERSACIÓN FRANCÉS-ESPAÑOL -L'ESPAGNE EN PARLANT

GUÍA DE CONVERSACIÓN INGLÉS-ESPAÑOL - SPANISH CONVERSATION GUIDE

GUÍA DE CONVERSACIÓN ALEMÁN-ESPAÑOL

GUÍA DE CONVERSACIÓN ITALIANO-ESPAÑOL

EDITORIAL STANLEY · Apdo. 207 · 20300 IRUN · ESPAÑA · Tel. (34) 943 64 04 12 · Fax. (34) 943 64 38 63

www.stanleyformacion.com